D1525559

THE EMPTY COUCH

The Empty Couch is an introduction to the challenges and obstacles inherent in ageing as a psychoanalyst. It addresses the previously neglected issue of ill health, as well as the significance of ageing for psychoanalysts, exploring the analyst's attitude towards getting older, transience and sense of time and space.

Covering a wide range of topics Gabriele Junkers brings together expert contributors who discuss the problems of getting physically ill and how to conduct psychoanalysis as an ill therapist. Chapters also address the effects that ageing has on professional stamina, the grief inevitably caused by the losses endured in later life and inquires into the role that institutions (the relevant psychoanalytic institutes or societies) can play in this context.

Setting out to encourage discussion on this vital topic, *The Empty Couch* brings this neglected area into sharp focus. It will be of interest to psychoanalysts, psychotherapists, counsellors, gerontologists and trainees in the psychoanalytic and psychotherapy worlds.

Gabriele Junkers, PhD, is a trained psychologist, psychoanalyst, training analyst and member of the German Psychoanalytic Association (DPV). She is a gerontologist with more than 30 years experience in treating older adults and providing institutional counselling for mature people.

Contributors: Evelyn Carlisle, Giuseppe Civitarese, Paul Denis, Cláudio Laks Eizirik, Barbara Fajardo, Antonino Ferro, Maria Teresa Savio Hooke, Audrey Kavka, Leena Klockars, Luisa Marino, Mary Kay O'Neil, Danielle Quinodoz, Martin Teising, Johan Frederik Thaulow, Tove Traesdal.

THE EMPTY COUCH

The taboo of ageing and retirement in psychoanalysis

Edited by
Gabriele Junkers

Routledge
Taylor & Francis Group

LONDON AND NEW YORK

First published 2013
by Routledge
27 Church Road, Hove, East Sussex BN3 2FA

Simultaneously published in the USA and Canada
by Routledge
711 Third Avenue, New York, NY 10017

Routledge is an imprint of the Taylor & Francis Group, an informa business

British Library Cataloguing in Publication Data
A catalogue record for this book is available from the British Library

Library of Congress Cataloging in Publication Data
    The empty couch : the taboo of ageing and retirement in psychoanalysis /
    edited by Gabriele Junkers.—Dual Edition.
    pages cm
    Includes bibliographical references.
    1. Psychoanalysts. 2. Retired scientists.
    3. Retirement—Psychological aspects.
    4. Aging—Psychological aspects. I. Junkers, Gabriele.
    BF173.E638 2013
    150.19'5--dc23
    2012040737

ISBN: 978–0–415–59861–3 (hbk)
ISBN: 978–0–415–59862–0 (pbk)
ISBN: 978–0–203–38474–9 (ebk)

Typeset in Garamond
by Swales & Willis Ltd, Exeter, Devon

Printed and bound in Great Britain by MPG Printgroup

CONTENTS

CONTENTS

CONTENTS

CONTRIBUTORS

Evelyn Carlisle: is a psychoanalyst and psychotherapist in full day practice.

Giuseppe Civitarese (Padua): is a training analyst with the Italian Psychoanalytic Association (AIPSI) and a member of the American Psychoanalytic Association (ApsA), working in private practice. He has published several papers in international psychoanalytic journals. His books include *The Intimate Room: Theory and Technique of the Analytic Field* (The New Library of Psychoanalysis, Routledge, 2010)

Paul Denis (Paris): is a supervising analyst at the Paris Psychoanalytical Society (SPP) and former director of the *Revue française de psychanalyse*.

Cláudio Laks Eizirik (Porto Allegre): is a medical doctor, psychoanalyst and training analyst with the Brazil Psychoanalytic Federation (FEBRAPSI). He is adjunct Professor, Department of Psychiatry, Federal University of Rio Grande do Sul, and former president of the International Psychoanalytic Association (IPA).

Barbara Fajardo, psychoanalyst, is deceased.

Antonino Ferro (Padua): is a medical doctor and training and supervising analyst with the Italian Psychoanalytical Society (SPI). He is former president of the Centre of Psychoanalysis in Milan and recipient of the Sigourney Award in 2007. He is presently a member of the editorial board of *Psychoanalytic Quarterly*, *Revista de Psicoanalisis (APA)*, *Monographies de Psychanalyse de la Revue française de psychanalyse*, *Revista Portuguesa de Psicanálise*, *Journal of Melanie Klein and Object Relations*, *Revista Brasileira de Psicanálise*, *Revista de Psiqiatria do Rio Grande do Sul* and *Revista de Psicanálise de SPPA*.

Maria Teresa Savio Hooke (Sydney): is a psychologist, training analyst and former president of the Australian Psychoanalytical Society. She is a member of the IPA China Committee. As Chair of Outreach and Communication she has co-organized the first IPA Centenary Conference in Beijing in 2010. She was recently awarded the Order of the Star from the Italian Government for services to psychoanalysis in Australia.

Audrey Kavka (San Francisco): is a psychiatrist, psychoanalyst and training analyst and member of the San Francisco Center for Psychoanalysis. She currently chairs the American Psychoanalytic Association's Committee on Psychoanalyst Assistance Committees. She has more than 30 years of clinical experience treating older adults and has co-authored book chapters, supervises and consults about the growing population.

Leena Klockars (Helsinki): is a psychologist, training and supervising analyst and Chair of the Psychoanalytic Training Institute of the Finnish Psychoanalytic Society. She has been President of the Finnish Psychoanalytic Society.

Luisa Marino (London): is a psychologist and psychoanalyst of the British Psychoanalytic institute, London. She was previously based in Padua, Italy for many years and was a member of the Italian Psychoanalytical Society (SPI) and former President of the International Psychoanalytical Studies Organization (IPSO).

Mary Kay O'Neil (Montreal): Is Supervising and Training Analyst of the Canadian Institute of Psychoanalysis. She works in private practice. Currently, she is Director of the Canadian Institute of Psychoanalysis (Quebec English). Her research and publications include depression and young adult development, emotional needs of sole-support mothers, post-analytic contact and psychoanalytic ethics. She has served on several IPA committees as well as on the editorial board of the *International Journal of Psychoanalysis*.

Danielle Quinodoz (Geneva): Is a psychologist and training analyst with the Swiss psychoanalytic Society (SSPsa), Geneva. She has worked at the Geneva psychiatric hospital and in private practice since 1967. She was editor of the *Bulletin de la Société Suisse de Psychanalyse* and published, among other works, *Words That Touch: A Psychoanalyst Learns to Speak* and *Growing Old: A Journey of Self-Discovery*.

Martin Teising (Berlin, Bad Hersfeld): is a psychiatrist, psychoanalyst and training analyst. He has been President of the German Psychoanalytic Association (DPV 2010–2012) and is now President of the International Psychoanalytic University Berlin.

Johan Fredrik Thaulow is deceased.

Tove Traesdal (Oslo): is a psychologist, training and supervising analyst at the Institute for Psychotherapy in Norway and works in private practice in Oslo. She worked for several years in an inpatient clinic treating young adult patients with psychosis and/or personality disorders. She also has a career as a professional classical singer and voice teacher.

FOREWORD

Antonio Ferro and Giuseppe Civitarese

Translated by Philip Slotkin

This book, conceived and edited by Gabriele Junkers, casts light on a subject that is often denied or remains in the shadows: the time of the ending of an analyst's life. Year after year the analyst lives in a kind of cyclical temporality. One analysis comes to an end and is succeeded by another; analytic children or grandchildren are joined by others, newly born or as yet unborn, on the waiting list. All of a sudden this circularity of time is shattered. A year has passed, five years, a decade, several decades, and we realise that we have more or less unaware returned to the realm of linear time. This is sometimes due to a trauma, or on other occasions may be like awakening from a dream of eternal (at least mental) youth.

What do we do when this awakening takes place? How do we react? How do we notice it? Do we just deny it again? Do we accept our transience? Does the painful awareness of the limit of existence depress us, make us fall ill, or impart a new and different fullness to our lives?

To these questions, which we have long forbidden ourselves to answer and perhaps even to ask, *The Empty Couch* seeks to give sincere and creative responses. These also include consideration of the corollary of disavowal of the limit so as to reassure ourselves about our weaknesses and the infantilisation of candidates and young analysts. It is as if the passage of time were measured by different clocks at institutes of psychoanalysis. But is it meaningful for this situation to be perpetuated? Is there any point in doing so?

When faced with an 'examination', it is as well to come prepared. Having helped so many patients to accept the temporality of life and hence the ineluctability of death – how can we not recall Searles's fine essay on the subject in his writings on schizophrenia! – we should espouse the attitude described by Wolf Erlbruch in his splendid book *Ente, Tod und Tulpe* [The Duck, Death and the Tulip]. A duck finds that Death has crept up on her from behind, telling her that he will accompany her for the rest of her days. They gradually get close to each other and an almost affectionate relationship forms between them. Then one day the duck says to Death: 'I feel cold; would you mind warming me up a bit?' Shortly afterwards the duck breathes her last. Death lays her down gently on the water, and the book ends as follows: 'He watched the duck for a long time as she floated off down the river. On losing sight of her, Death almost felt sad. But that was how life was'.

However, the contributions assembled in this volume are not devoted solely to the ageing *of the analyst* and the illnesses that might befall him or her. Its field of interest extends far beyond its declared subject matter. Problems such as the sequence of generations, old age, illness and death were key aspects of everyone's existence long before becoming important issues for the analytic profession. Most often, we approach these matters through the medium of great literature. Examples are the loneliness of Ivan Ilyich in Tolstoy's extraordinary eponymous tale, or the same author's powerful and dramatic image of Prince Andrei dreaming of Death knocking at the door – or the agonising elegy to life, which never seems more beautiful than when its end is seen to be at hand, being crafted by Philip Roth in his latest books.

The book is admittedly a meditation on life as a sequence of separations and on the transience of all things, but also one on the sense of beauty and on the beauty of analysis: as Dr Junkers reminds us, it is not a profession but a passion. Things move us because they are ephemeral. How many times have we felt sorry that not a trace remains of all the beautiful things that occur in analysis, except in the increasingly feeble form of memories?

The various chapters offer a vision of all these aspects from a number of perspectives, thus focusing on them with extreme precision. The reader observes an interweaving of private and professional life, the life of psychoanalytic institutions and of psychoanalysis as a discipline (which, if it wishes to survive, must now renew itself and accept the harsh challenge of competition).

However, illness (time fragmented) and old age (time pressing) can ultimately also be seen as a telling metaphor of temporality as an essential component of the institution of consciousness and the process of construction (and destruction) of the subject and of the mind. Every symbol, every word, is redolent of absence, mourning and separation. We should not forget Walter Benjamin's adage that it is the end that confers meaning on life. So too the biblical paradigm of the Apocalypse as final revelation. Psychoanalytic truth, whether it is called the selected fact, *Nachträglichkeit*, or καιρός, is always retrospective, backward-looking, an effect of posteriority. But every word is already a little end; meaning arises every time as the revelation of a minimal (tolerable) apocalypse.

PREFACE

Gabriele Junkers

When and how do psychoanalysts terminate their professional careers? Do we bow out gracefully while the going is good? Or do we hang on like grim death until we have no choice in the matter?

This book is about the significance of ageing for psychoanalysts. It addresses a wide range of topics such as the effects that ageing has on our professional stamina or the grief inevitably caused by the losses we have to endure in later life. It also inquires into the role that institutions (the relevant psychoanalytic institutes or societies) can play in this context.

I first talked about my plans for this book with a number of international colleagues, many of whom have since become firm friends. To my surprise, almost all of them unhesitatingly agreed to contribute to the volume. In their societies they had all experienced many instances of successful withdrawal from professional life and smooth transitions from one generation to the next. But they had also witnessed distressing situations connected with illness, old age and the death of colleagues. And they were all agreed that the desire not to hurt anyone's feelings had placed something very close to a taboo on the discussion of these matters in their own professional circles.

At this point, perhaps my readers will welcome a brief personal account of the reasons why this book was so long in the making and why the articles cover so much ground that they may initially appear to cover different points.

In the 1990s it struck me forcibly that my interest in the specific problems posed by the psychoanalytic treatment of elderly patients found little response from my European colleagues. When I proposed organising a panel on this topic at one of the EPF conferences, my proposal was rejected as irrelevant for our scientific work. Psychoanalysts such as Pearl King (1974) and Anne-Marie Sandler (1984) had already commented on this widespread refusal to engage with the elderly patients' issue, and the head-in-the-sand mentality that I came up against aroused my curiosity. The first thing I decided to do was to round up the few articles discussing this topic in the *International Journal of Psychoanalysis* and to make a reader out of them (Junkers, 2006). At the same time, I ignored the lack of overt encouragement that I had encountered and established a discussion forum at every European Federation conference, where colleagues could discuss the specific features of psychoanalytic treatment for elderly patients.

In the course of exchanges with colleagues, the 'other side' of the analytic twosome soon came into focus as well. What happens to ageing analysts arriving at a point in their lives at which inevitable losses, illness and the prospect of death can preoccupy them to such a degree as to throw them off balance? One of the major assets of the conferences of the European Psychoanalytical Federation is the opportunity they provide for participants to talk to colleagues about difficult, confidential and potentially distressing issues without risking a violation of abstinence or discretion, as might be the case 'at home'. Against the background of my long years of experience as a gerontologist and a member of our Society's ethics commission, I was surprised to learn that many colleagues were obviously at a loss about how best to address the issues of retirement for an analyst. On the other hand, this very fact confirmed me in my determination to investigate the question in greater depth. There appeared to be a general taboo on talking about the difficulties experienced by colleagues whose work was apparently no longer 'good enough' as a result of age or poor health. As if by common consent, this issue was passed over in silence. In my consternation, I sought advice from experienced older colleagues such as Betty Joseph (London), Anne-Marie Sandler (London) and Terttu Eskelinen de Folch (Barcelona). The idea they came up with struck me as a very daring one indeed. The proposal was to organise – in the framework of the EPF – a joint session of the ad hoc Group on Ageing, which I had set up in the meantime, and the Group on Ethics. I admit that I was apprehensive. It seemed only too likely that I would be pilloried for pointing the finger at my colleagues. But Betty Joseph (then 86) was adamant. 'You youngsters have to do something', she insisted (I was almost 60 at the time). Accordingly, in 2004 we organised a session on the topic of ageing and psychoanalysis, with support from Sandler and de Folch. We were completely bowled over by the huge number of participants and their willingness to talk about the subject. Many expressed their relief that a topic was to be aired that 'although it was so distressing' was completely out of bounds at the institutes they came from. They bewailed the absence of investigations on this matter, insisting that only with outside help (a lecture, an article, a book) would it be possible to get a discussion going at their respective institutes.

At one of our EPF conferences, I set out to amass more material on the subject by following up a very well-attended round table on 'The *First* Five Years as a Training Analyst' with the offer of a similar exchange of views on 'The *Last* Five Years as a Training Analyst'. Of the approximately 480 participants at the conference only one turned up.

Ultimately it was as chair of the 'IPA Committee on Ageing', established by the then president of the IPA, Claudio Eizirik, that I had the opportunity to talk to many international colleagues about ageing and its implications for patients and analysts alike.

I hope very much that my readers will regard this collection of articles as an invitation to get together with others in their societies and reflect on a subject that has widely been considered 'unthinkable' and quite definitely 'unspeakable' for so long. The next stage would then be to inquire how innovations and changes might develop from this engagement and become part and parcel of the lives of our institutes. This would benefit our generativity, improve the quality of our work and help keep psychoanalysis alive and well in a world where quick results are rapidly becoming the operative criterion for success. The book sets out to encourage group discussion, not to provide ready-made answers. But I have my own very definite views on the subject and leave my readers in no doubt about my convictions.

I should like to express my heartfelt gratitude to all those colleagues whose contributions and support have made this book a viable proposition. My very special thanks for their unflagging willingness to talk and listen go to Isolde Böhm (Cologne), Betty Joseph (London), Helmut Hinz (Tübingen), Maria Teresa Hooke (Sydney), Audrey Kavka (San Francisco), Leena Klockars (Helsinki), Richard Sherry (London) and Antje Vaihinger (Giessen).

I would also like to thank Sage Publications for their permission to reproduce the following article in this publication: Barbara Fajardo (2001) 'Life-Threatening Illness in the Analyst', *Journal of American Psychoanalytic Association* 49: 569–586.

My thanks to Lars Christian Opdal and Camilla Thaulow for their permission to reproduce the following article in this publication: Johan Fredrik Thaulow, 'Growing Older as an Analyst. Problems of Ethics and Practice Based on Personal Experience'.

References

King, P. H. (1974) 'Notes on the Psychoanalysis of Older Patients: Reappraisal of the Potentialities for Change During the Second Half of Life', *Journal of Analytic Psychology* 19: 22–37.

Sandler, A.-M. (1984) 'Problems of Development and Adaptation in an Elderly Patient', *Psychoanalytic Study of the Child* 39: 471–489.

Junkers, G. (2006) *Is It Too Late? Key Papers on Psychoanalysis and Ageing*. London: Karnac Books.

PROLOGUE

Mourning and the empty couch: A conversation between analysts

Giuseppe Civitarese and Antonio Ferro

The 'empty couch' accompanies us in our job as analysts no less than the 'occupied couch'.[1] At the beginning there is an empty corner to be filled in the room selected to host it. There isn't an analyst who wouldn't remember when he acquired his first couch.

I remember it perfectly.

I imagine that you too had to choose from different styles and wanted to satisfy different needs. It would be interesting to find out if different theoretical tendencies have as much influence as aesthetics.

Couches searching for patients

I chose mine on the base of two impulses. It was a day-couch similar to my own analyst's (who had Sicilian-Austrian origins). On top of which, it looked like the one that my Sicilian grandparents had in their bedroom. As a child I spent so many hours on it!

Where did you find it?

I bought mine through a second-hand goods magazine, 'Seconda Mano'. At the time I owned a Citroën Diane and I loaded it on the car roof to take it from Milan to Pavia. I had it restored so it acquired the look of a proper day-couch. It lay there empty for a few months until I was registered by the Board and I was able to take my first patient. I had not wanted to corrupt its status of sacred object with patients in psychotherapy. Therefore for one full year I only used it four hours a week. The hours became eight with my second patient and, once I was registered, multiplied quickly.

A couch by now fully occupied

Yes, but every now and then I had the experience of the 'empty couch' again – when a patient would skip a session and each time the 'emptiness' would be pregnant with meaning.

It would remain empty on weekends and holidays . . . But I did not take any notice. And what has changed?

Now, it's a little bit like it is with children. It's like when we start thinking that they will be leaving home. We begin to look at their rooms as something very precious that we did not notice for a long time until we discover that it's going to be over!

The famous 'empty nest' syndrome!

But let us go back to the couch. It has been empty also in the case of some seriously ill patients who couldn't agree to use it until the magic moment when they decided to 'move in'.

No, not the couch!

Of course, there are patients who aren't trusting enough to lie down. Your couch is different from mine. I have a *chaise longue*, one of those designed by Le Corbusier (but bought only because, as the patent had expired, it was dirt-cheap). It's special because it is a reclining couch. For this reason it is also suitable as a 'half-empty' couch. Year after year S, at the beginning of each session, insisted on raising the back so that her bust would be practically as straight as if she was sitting on the chair opposite her. I don't need to tell you that I tried to interpret this in a million ways. Without any success. Today, having concluded the therapy by mutual agreement, and with very mixed results, sometimes I feel that I only treated 'half' a patient.

Maybe the distance between Dr Jekyll and Mr Hyde was so great that it defeated all the effort invested in the case. Perhaps she couldn't afford to overcome a split, however deep, that provided her with a sense of security.

This is also what I tell myself. In the end, among the last things I told her, I think I said rather fondly about her having defied her father.

And what was her reply?

She smiled.

The supervisions empty couch

She had only 'half-moved' into the couch. I could even expect a 'low-intensity' transference . . .

However, on the topic of removals, my couch moved with me when I moved houses and when I opened my professional rooms in them. Altogether, three times. Throughout the years, it was always occupied many hours each day. Then, without me even taking notice, it began to be lighter. Once I became a training analyst, I very slowly began to increase the supervision hours and to decrease the hours of work behind the couch.

The emptiness again.

Not only that but the rhythm of the empty/full couch also marked the happy and sad moments of my life when I had to cancel a session because of one of the many events that can occur.

Now, as I find myself working more and more as supervisor, the couch is even emptier and lighter. At this stage I am inclined to think that, totally irresponsibly,[2] I must have used some defence mechanisms.

Or do you mean 'unconsciously'?

Ah, I would like to know that!

Anyway, as you know better than I, Ogden, our Californian friend – I don't know how but he always manages to surprise me – emphasised that, like analysis, supervision is a new and unprecedented form of relationship invented by Freud. He also added that, as when analysing a patient, it's a matter of dreaming his dream never dreamt – it is the same for the analyst's interrupted dream while supervising him.

You mean to say that ultimately it's a case of making an effort to see the couch occupied, only *apparently* empty, which means also to interpret the supervision session as a dream.

Even where you think you should be adopting only effective teaching or good 'pedagogy'.

I can see that you are starting to learn the lesson!

Where did the analyst go?

On the topic of defences sometimes it is not the couch that is empty but the analyst's chair. In fact you could see this as a particular example of the previous one, which means that in both situations what goes missing is the relationship. There are many studies on *burn out* of psychiatrists when they have to deal with serious pathologies, with chronic cases, with lack of resources or conflict with the institution in which they operate, but I believe there is not enough research on *burn out* of analysts, especially in its most insidious forms.

Of what kind?

The symptoms are lack of enthusiasm for a job that he had originally chosen with passion, the feeling of living a routine that is not gratifying, the tendency to drag along at the expense[3] of patients, an emotional withdrawal that is dangerous for him and for the others.

Would you say that another aspect of these problems is the rivalry among groups and individuals due to power issues within the institutional organs of psychoanalytic societies?

You read my mind. The status of the analyst is precarious. He feels that he has little social recognition even if he has gained a good reputation for his scientific achievements. He regrets not having followed other careers and he simply needs to be able to put a feather on his cap or to pin a medal on the lapel of his coat every now and then.

At that stage he ends up confusing a scientific society with a convent (with all its consequences: see what happens in Eco's *The Name of the Rose*) or with a political party.

I agree. An analyst's career does not offer many possibilities. It's kind of stuck. Year after year one is forced always to do the same things. And with time, a feeling of fragility takes over and the horizons of one's life begin to close. One can clearly see it in the puerile narcissism of many colleagues. Freud got that right as well: we should follow his advice more and every now and then go back to analysis.

And don't you dare to tell me now that Freud understood it all!

Why?! Isn't it true?!

The multiplication of couches

Anyway, you make me reflect . . . I realise only now that we are talking about it that the multiplication of couches is a defence mechanism that I have unconsciously put into practice. I added one at home. I justified it by telling myself that, should I become ill, I could continue to work from home without going out (*I never did it!*). I also put a second one in my rooms in Milan where I work on weekends and where I hold only supervision groups.

And there, you don't know what to do with it.

Yet, even there, where I don't need it, I convinced myself that it was necessary to have a couch. It helps to prove that I am an analyst.

After all, if I am allowed to say it, what analysts 'invest' in a piece of furniture is comic! Even more so as we said that what really matters is the internal setting of the analyst, not the material one.

To tell you the truth I believe that, both in my life at home or in the professional rooms where I meet my groups, it was a way to make it more a daily presence, not strictly connected to my job, but with a domestic usage, disconnected from the patient, as it was in my grandparents' house: the day-couch for the afternoon nap. Maybe it's a trick to prevent the grief of the empty couch by restoring its function as a piece of daily furniture.

An overcrowded couch

Of course, we should know it well, we sometimes use defences against depression that become manic. Think of when one works too much. Unfortunately this only produces one result: when one sees too many patients, the couch appears to be empty because one ends up not seeing anybody.

You mean: one really doesn't see them, even if they are there?

That is exactly what I mean. The same happens if, in between patients, one does not take a long enough pause. He loses himself maybe because he is chased by the ghosts of age and of financial crisis, by the needs of growing children, by the need to be reassured of his own worth through the dependence of his patients. Subtle forms of perversion can then creep into the relationship. It's easy to become distracted, restless, bored.

Let the one who is guiltless be the first to throw a stone . . . as the Gospel says. It must be for this reason that some time ago I happened to book two appointments at the same time, a new consultation and a catch-up session that had been decided a long time before.

It's a possibility, for sure. However, even in this case every cloud has a silver lining. The key is finding an analytical perspective to the event. Accidents of this kind, although embarrassing, push us to exercise a little auto-analysis and, if possible, to straighten the situation. Furthermore, if it is coincidental, it's also useful for analysis.

In fact, so it was. The two patients who arrived at the same time – I realised later on – from a certain point of view were the same person or, even better, carried different aspects of the same patient. As always, one must never give too much credit to the senses, and instead must rely on intuition. The famous, should I say infamous, Bion's 'Faith'!

By saying so, you make me realise that there are many ways to do that. For instance, as the couch becomes lighter the configuration of the 'chairs set in a circle' becomes more important; the chairs make the activity of supervision more relevant and at the same time they fill the room with many 'patients'. Two birds with one stone.

The supervision groups

Yes, and you shouldn't delude yourself. It's not really that the groups work so well to deny grief. I find myself playing the role of 'grandfather' and uncle to these people on supervision who come like grandchildren to fill a space.

Do you mean that it's like the feeling of rheumatic pain when the weather changes?

More or less. On the other hand, it is reasonable for the analyst gradually to lighten the couch weight. Over the years, I arrived at an extreme when I had 13 patients four times a week instead of the five sittings that I have now. I also know that in my future there are four or five new patients who are waiting for analysis but that after these I have decided to take no more.

At some stage one realises they are too old to have another child because there wouldn't be enough time to reasonably expect to bring it up to the age at which it is independent.

But since I am one of those people who think that for them to be an analyst there has to be both a '*setting*' and a patient – I ask myself *what will* I be when I do not have any more patients on my couch.

The empty chair

The problem brings another question: what will become of my analyst's chair? When, gradually, I will leave my seat vacant and I will begin the exile from my ex-kingdom, even if it is a voluntary one, what will I call myself? Ex-analyst? I could say: Member of the Psycho-Analytical Society. And I could add: with old lost functions (the couch and the chair) and with new acquired functions (groups, teaching, writing). But how will I define myself, what will I call myself? My father was a surgeon . . . Let's see . . . How did he introduce himself when he stopped operating in the theatre? Maybe 'retired doctor' . . . Maybe we, too, could call ourselves . . .

Don't say it!

I will not say it.

My father, instead, is a farmer. At 77 he does not want to hear about retiring. On the contrary, he just bought vineyards that belonged to his father, a very Freudian choice!

Turning 70

Be careful, turning 70 is a daunting finishing line!
  As you always say, a 'pivotal moment'.
  Like turning 60.
  Why not also 50?
  And 40 then?
  Don't exaggerate!
  True.
  I have a confession. When I printed the notes you sent me for this work and I saw the words '70s'[4] written on it, I actually read '170s'! Yes, a wish! When one talks about the unconscious . . .

Analysis as practice for mourning

It is something worth wishing for ourselves! The point is that, for the analyst, analysis implies a sort of 'continuous mourning', from abstinence to non-acting in the context of *setting* and time; the time of sessions, holidays, mourning for the end of analysis and for letting the patient go his own way. Then other kinds of mourning come with the end of our own analysis.
  We could also add to this list the mourning implicit in changing one's institutional status, the mourning of not understanding and the mourning related to the different stages in life that continuously end.

Who is afraid of the empty couch?

Let's go back to our story. Why do analysts find it so hard to age? In all psychoanalytical societies the powerful roles are in the hands of the most senior members, the gerontocracy, who put their brain to rest a few decades ago. Airline pilots retire and so do academics, bus drivers, surgeons, teachers, hairdressers and bank employees.
  Not the analysts.
  Not the analysts.
  Does this mean that they feel they belong to a church or a political party more than to a scientific society? Or do they nurture a subtle and very insidious lack of faith in the method? As if their role was more important than their function?
  You would need a totally secular psychoanalysis.
  Yes.
  But you well know that politics is not foreign to the struggle of ideas within the scientific community.
  It goes without saying, but isn't it possible to see the victory of a kind of politics that aims for quality of research, for originality and creativity less than for the principle of authority?

Trips

I wonder if the trips made on invitations by psychoanalytical societies might not carry the same meaning. In fact they are an instrument of politics because of the net of relationships that they allow you to establish but they also constitute a further defence mechanism. Also the famous administrative 'offices' may well have a consolatory value. Even those give you the chance to escape the claustrophobic climate that can subtly surround you when you have such a solitary job.

Interruptions

This topic brings us back to the theme of mourning. Is it the case that we have a job that from its beginning confronts us with the theme of mourning? We establish a strong bond with somebody who eventually will leave us. Obsessively, analysts refer in all they do to the mother-child relationship model or anyway to the Oedipal family model. Loewald goes to the extreme and says that curing with analysis means ending up loving a patient as you would love your own child.

But there are different types of children . . . some never want to leave home. Others go when we feel they are still too fragile to venture into the real world. Others again abandon us suddenly and these are the most painful situations. Moreover, often they were the ones whom we loved the most . . . Maybe this is exactly the reason . . .

Looking at an empty couch in the time slot of a patient who has stopped analysis is one of the hardest things to accept. We feel guilty and angry. Sometimes this all remains an unconscious feeling.

The analyst is forced to come to terms with his own limits.

Bion affirms that it is a miracle after all that a patient continues to come back day after day.

It's important for me to say this, not because it's necessarily true, but because it tears us away from the psychosis of every day banalities, when the thing has already taken its own course.

What one feels is not very different from when a romantic relationship is severed. Even the steadiness of personal professional identity starts shaking.

Sometimes our patients make us understand through the smallest clues how hard it is to deal with separation. Did it never happen to you, for example, to notice that a patient, leaving at the end of a session, left something on the couch?

Lost objects

Let me think . . . You just took a patient to the door. You go back to the room and you realise at a glance that there is something on the couch: a key, a mobile phone, a handkerchief, a few coins or a match.

That happened with A: a few days after the death of his beloved mother, when the session ends, I see on the empty couch the red and black beads of a bracelet from a not-for-profit shop that he used to wear on his wrist. The sight immediately gives me the idea of what he is going through. The thread that kept together the life of an almost home-bound person, wrapped in a very tight bond with his mother, has been cut. His emotions roll on the floor with nothing that keeps them together. But also, from a point of view closer to us, maybe a session that, because of his uncontainable pain, didn't console him at all.

This also appears to allude to the critical moment of departure.

Those beads remained for me the symbol of good and bad, black and red emotions: those emotions we can feel only if we meet somebody with whom we share an experience.

Some patients are so afraid to become alone that, in order not to be in the difficult situation of having to separate, they never come to therapy. I mean: they come, but aren't really there.

The invisible patient

What do you mean? 'Invisible' patients?!

Exactly.

Bion writes somewhere that if the analyst thinks that the patient who is coming is not married, even if he in reality is, he must take this very seriously and should not trust his senses. As you can see, it's the opposite of a medical treatment which is based on evidence. The point is that our evidence is different and is related to subjectivity, with events that one can know or grasp by intuition or feeling only, with things that one does not smell or see, even if, when one talks about them, it should be as if they were really seen, touched, smelled, suffered, tasted.

And the 'invisible patients'?

It is an example of the empty couch. The invisible patient comes regularly to sessions. He speaks. He never asks anything. He appears not to notice the presence of the analyst. Just as he came, he gets up and goes away. He is hard to see because he neither brings nor stirs emotions. What he needs instead is to transmit the sentiment that he carries inside that the world is ending. Maybe in *bonsai* scale.

I find myself pretty well in your description. I noticed E only after I upset her by cancelling a few sessions in a row at the last minute. In this way I managed to tease a lioness that was asleep in the corner. Her roars made me fear awful consequences but in the meantime her analysis became more pleasant. E came out of the cage in which she was imprisoned and in which she had unfortunately locked herself again at times and she made me see that it was possible to have lively sessions with her also.

Skipped sessions

Sometimes the patient is only temporarily invisible. Some patients need to skip many sessions. But it isn't a way *not* to be analysed. It's *their* way. They make you understand in the clearest possible way that even when they are there, it is as if they were not there or that they don't feel 'seen' by the analyst. The analyst goes through the session with the patient's phantom. It can also happen that he is the one who chases the patient away. It sometimes happened to me that I mistook the ending time of a session. By asking my too 'good' patient S to finish before time, I was making time, in her hour, even if for only a few minutes, for M, another much 'naughtier' patient. But here again, was she another patient or a hidden aspect of the first one that I unconsciously was trying to provoke?

Is Freud dead?

On the topic of phantoms, lately the 'empty couch phantom' wanders around in psychoanalytical societies. How many times have we been told that Freud is dead, that psychoanalysis is a superstition from the last century, that Wittgenstein tore it to bits and that Popper had it dead and buried! The list of writers who occasionally try to emerge from anonymity by attacking Freud's supposed misbehaviour ('He betrayed his wife to sleep with his sister in law!'), and usually in bad faith, grows continuously and gets the attention of the more superficial newspapers and audience. Cognitive sciences are aggressive (although they are themselves in a critical stage, maybe more than psychoanalysis itself), the world of academics locks itself in its caste privileges. The analyst, who already needs to deal with what is left of the ideals that led him to follow such an uncertain career (at least in regard to his conscious reasons for choosing it), endures a chronic sense of frustration. It may be not be a big worry but, in the long run, the constant dripping wears away the stone.

If this picture is also accompanied by the not-very-rosy perspective of seeing the number of patients drop, the feeling grows dramatically. The empty couch then becomes the ghost that hovers about in informal meetings, in conventions and also when he is alone with the patient. It is the usual refrain. 'Are you going through a critical stage?' is the distressed question that everybody asks you.

I would say that there is something else. It is the feeling of having devoted all your life to something that, after all, didn't deserve it and that is destined to disappear from the list of things that matter.

Maybe in this way one could explain the faith-based inflexibility and the cult of authority that underline statements such as: 'Freud said that!', with variations such as 'Freud already said that', 'Freud would have loved it', up to comical effects, when one finds, let's say, in Freud in 1908 something that anticipates Freud in 1923. Of the kind: not only that Freud said that, but also that he said it before he even said it (if you want I will send you the bibliography).

I agree, but I believe that a deeper theory of the function of the mind does not exist nor does any better cure for some disorders that most other theories would give up as untreatable. Therefore it's unlikely that psychoanalysis will die or that it's already dead without us even noticing. I would like to suggest banning certain little words that grow like weeds in our theoretical fields: 'drift', for example, or 'specificity', 'risk', 'Babel', etc. It would be nice if we were not scared to use our brain without fearing disastrous drifts at every step, losing the specificity of something or running God knows what risk. If you take notice, they are diabolical little words.

I agree. They almost always express moralistic attitudes, really anti-Freudian. The point is that this situation results in wide anxiety, due to the fear that the object (the couch) in which we have strongly invested might disappear. I repeat, the phantom of the empty couch hovers about the psychoanalytical societies.

One may think that this is a sort of trick of destiny or rather of necessity: it is as if people who, as a job, practise mourning and teach other people to practise with mourning, find it hard to identify in a discipline that requires them to stay in uncertainty and doubt.

The psychoanalyst with no couch

It appears that one of the signs of this crisis is that fewer psychiatrists apply for psychoanalytic training.

It's like this, and not only in Italy. The crisis of psychoanalysis coincides with the crisis of psychiatry inspired by Freud's thinking.

We could call it psychoanalysis (or the psychoanalyst) without a couch.

It is a species that is becoming progressively rare. Biological psychiatry dominates. The password for the National Health Service is '*manage or perish*'.

Following the same logic, cognitive therapies also become victim of this efficient mercantilism.

Or of the pharmaceutical industry.

A praise for the 'siesta'

I must tell you something. It happens occasionally, when I am too tired and a patient has cancelled a session, that I lie on the couch and have a *siesta*. I had never thought about it. But couldn't it be a good way to chase the phantom away from the empty couch? To exorcise the sudden hole? In this manner the patient becomes his own therapist's therapist, his best colleague, by inviting him, in a sort of way, to have a little extra analysis. The analyst who allows himself to have a siesta on the vacant couch, prepares concretely to dream the interrupted dream of his patient's accidental absence.

Lately, during one of these pauses, I dreamt that I was at the beach on a cliff and that I had to dive. Somebody, a friend, was loudly inviting me to do it, but I was afraid that below, in the waves, there might be a shark. But I dived . . . Mmmm . . . I am one who shakes only at the thought of swimming where there is only the reef to protect me from sharks. Even in the swimming pool I use the ladder . . . Could it be a way of telling myself that somewhere there was some aggression that it couldn't enter the room? That it was the only way to reach me? That the empty couch represents the shark that we all have to face? Could it simply represent nothing else but death? What does it all mean? *How would you interpret it?*

Empty paragraph

Notes

1 We chose not to mark the turns of speaking, even if the respective 'voices' are easy to guess. A small amount of ambiguity serves the purpose of letting us also imagine the dialogue as an interior one.
2 There is a word play here. In Italian, 'irresponsibly' is 'incoscientemente', 'unconsciously' is 'inconsciamente'.
3 In Italian: 'alle spalle', literally: 'behind his back'.
4 In Italian: 'I 70'.

References

Civitarese, G. (2008) *The Intimate Room: Theory and Technique of the Analytic Field.* London: Routledge.
Civitarese, G. (2011) *The Violence of Emotions: Bion and the Post-Bionian Psychoanalysis.* London: Routledge, in press.
Civitarese, G. (2012) *Perdere la testa. Abiezione, conflitto estetico e critica psicoanalitica.* Florence: Clinamen, in press.
Ferro, A. (1999/2006) *Psychoanalysis as Therapy and Storytelling.* London and New York: Routledge.
Ferro, A. (2002/2005) *Seeds of Illness, Seeds of Recovery: The Genesis of Suffering and the Role of Psychoanalysis.* London: Routledge.
Ferro, A. (2007/2011) *Avoiding Emotions, Living Emotions.* London: Routledge.
Ferro, A. and Civitarese, G. (2011) 'The Meaning and Use of Metaphor in Analytic Field Theory', *Psychoanalytic Inquiry*, in press.

Part I

GROWING OLDER AS PSYCHOANALYSTS

1

THE AGEING PSYCHOANALYST

Thoughts on preparing for a life without the couch

Gabriele Junkers

There is no escape. We must all face up to the ageing process and accept it for what it is. Ageing is not a psychoanalytic concept; it is a 'fact of life' (Money-Kyrle, 1971), an extremely complex process that we attempt to address with our psychoanalytic resources. Bound to the linearity of time and the irreversible effects of time's passage, it permeates all areas of our lives. Without the passage of time, our perceptions and the subjective experience of our affects and emotions would be inconceivable. Only when we begin to reflect on our own experience do we begin to develop a sense of past, present and future. Moreover, a sense of the ageing process requires an active recognition of external realities. We are inevitably and irredeemably exposed to the changes taking place in our bodies and in our social reality.

Moving forward in our life cycle we are confronted with different tasks that are essential for our development (Erikson, 1979). At mid-life stage, these tasks involve recognition and awareness of our own mortality, of death and the existence of destructive impulses within ourselves (Jaques, 1965). Successfully negotiating the many cliffs and obstacles that this stage of life holds in store for us is the prerequisite for true maturity in our later adult lives when we are called upon not only to *talk* about the inevitability of death, but to recognise and acknowledge it as something that has to do with each and every one of us, personally and individually. There are many losses clamouring to be accepted as such, most insistent of all perhaps those fantasies that have proved to be illusions and have never materialised as we had hoped. And we have to acknowledge our fear of death that Segal (1958) describes as the reason why we may run the risk of losing our psychological equilibrium as age progresses and death comes closer.

The reluctance of many psychoanalysts to engage with their own mortality and the inevitability of death is something profoundly human. Freud has taught us that evading 'work on the ageing process' is a way of fending off challenges to our omnipotent thinking and to the illusions that we need to maintain a space that can accommodate our projections into the future.

In society in general, the subject of ageing has developed real momentum in the last 50 years or so. Though years ago analysts such as Eissler (1975) and Grotjahn (1985, 1994) addressed the issue of the ageing psychoanalyst, it is true to say that the number of books and articles devoted to this topic is still very modest (e.g. Quinodoz, 1996; Horner, 2002).

Psycho-somatic individuality is never as diverse as in old age. Individuals age in their own way and in accordance with their own rhythm, which is not at all consistent. Suddenly we find ourselves in a state of upheaval; we have crossed the Rubicon and there is no return. Physical debilitation erodes the illusion that we are 'the same as ever'. Like everyone else, we psychoanalysts sustain a 'fantasy of immortality' within ourselves, which is occasionally reinforced by the covert conviction that our own analysis has made us immune to illness and ageing.

We almost invariably require some stimulus from outside that will prompt us actively to create an internal space in which to engage in an inner dialogue and to deal with our growing awareness of nothingness and death. Yet how powerful is the desire we all have to sidestep this unbearable reality! Many poets, painters and composers have succeeded in pitting their creative powers against the fear and pain caused by the confrontation with age, death and illness, and if a creative artist is forced to leave his work unfinished, he does not leave a suppurating wound, as the psychoanalyst does. André Green (1997) contends that 'for an artist the preservation of his work is more important than the preservation of his life' (p. 99). This should definitely not be the case for us psychoanalysts, because in psychoanalysis the creative process takes place between two individuals, the analysand and the psychoanalyst. It is the latter's responsibility to protect his patient against a re-traumatisation and a gaping lesion that are the consequences of an untimely termination of treatment.

Ageing forces us to realise that we can no longer reassure ourselves of our ongoing existence by projecting hopes and aspirations into the future. Also, the resources available to us in putting plans for reparation into practice are increasingly restricted. As death impinges on our field of vision, the pursuit of pleasure loses its allure and no longer contributes to the consolidation of the ego as it once did. At the same time, our imminent end urges us to relinquish the fantasy of an immortal and ideal object as an equivalent for the 'good breast'. All these hazards assail us in unison, compelling us to adopt a crucially different perspective on our earlier lives, when time did not insist so relentlessly on its finitude (Loch, 1982a, b).

Compared with other professions, the analyst's life-work cycle is out of phase. It has become increasingly normal for analysts to gain their qualifications at the mid-life stage. Accordingly, this period in their lives is outward bound, more determined by the feeling of a fresh start than by intimations of mortality. Even when our children leave home and we become grandparents, we frequently do not have the impression that we have fully scaled the career ladder. As psychoanalysts we live and work sustained by the conviction that what we do can best be done free of the restrictions imposed by clock and calendar. After all, the unconscious has no sense of time. The reality of our own limits, the definition of our lives by chronological time, flies in the face of these notions.

We should of course be glad that there is no one to tell us when our time is up, as is the case in so many other professions. But this is also the reason why relinquishing analytic work requires careful long-term preparation. When do we *actively* decide not to embark on any new analyses? Our special relationship to our work makes it particularly difficult for us to take the necessary steps. Within the 50 minutes we spend working with our analysands, time is of no concern. We may indeed be so enamoured of this very special dual relationship that we seek to evade its inevitable loss and the work of mourning bound up with it by simply letting things take their course, leaving them to their own devices. The unconscious longing for reparation rooted so deeply in all of us can be such a strong motive to go on working that we miss the 'right' moment. Another danger arises from our wish for generativity, our profoundly human desire to put as many young analysts on their professional path as we can. Others again are tormented by feelings of envy at having to leave the field to younger colleagues, resentments Leslie Sohn reminded us of in 2002, himself well over 80 at the time (personal communication). It is awfully difficult to realise that there comes a point when it is too late to father children responsibly. But who am I when I have stopped working as a psychoanalyst?

Freud himself gives us a memorable description of how significant our work can be for our psychological equilibrium. He speaks here from his own experience, having frequently judged a life without work as hardly worth living.

> No other technique for the conduct of life attaches the individual so firmly to reality as laying emphasis on work; for his work at least gives him a secure place in a portion of reality, in the human community. The possibility it offers of displacing a large amount of libidinous components, whether narcissistic, aggressive or even erotic, on to professional work and on to the human relations connected with it lends it a value by no means second to what it enjoys as something indispensable to the assertion and justification of existence in society. Professional activity is a source of special satisfaction if it is a freely chosen one – if, that is to say, by means of sublimation, it makes possible the use of existing inclinations, of persisting or constitutionally reinforced instinctual impulses.
>
> (Freud, 1930, *S.E.* 21, p. 80)

Freud's statement is a very general one. The transition to retirement is a problem in many professions, for surgeons no longer able to operate, for captains of industry who have built up an empire and have difficulty – like Ibsen's *Master Builder* – leaving their life's work for their sons to continue with. But what if there is no son interested in carrying on in his father's footsteps? With the number of potential 'heirs' dwindling rapidly, this is very definitely a problem psychoanalysts are faced with.

For this book I have chosen the couch as a symbol of our analytic work. True, as psychotherapists and supervisors we also have our place in a structured working day progressing from one hour to the next. But the intensity of communion in the analytic process with the opportunity it provides to immerse ourselves in the workings and mysteries of another person's psyche and thus feel both committed and included has a quality that we cannot experience in 'real' life outside. We can of course try to substitute the armchair for the empty couch and work with psychotherapy patients or supervisees. But it will never be the same as the couch . . .

Shakespeare's tragedy *King Lear* is incomparable in the way it describes the painful moment of withdrawal from the world of work that has been so crucial in existential terms. It is an unforgettable demonstration of how difficult it can be to relinquish accustomed roles that have taken on such immense narcissistic significance and how easily such withdrawal can turn into a disaster.

Well stricken in years, Lear has resolved to divide his kingdom among his daughters. He is convinced that their protestations of filial devotion are the right gauge by which to judge who shall be given what. It soon becomes clear that he will accord his love to the daughter who will best serve him as an object for the gratification of his own needs. He desperately yearns to be told how well loved he is so that he can protect himself against feelings of abandonment, exclusion or even annihilation. His youngest daughter Cordelia refuses to be a party to this deception and foils his bid for reassurance: 'I cannot heave my heart into my mouth: I love Your Majesty according to my bond; nor more, nor less' (Act 1, Scene 1, lines 91–92). She is disinherited and banished for her pains. Cordelia stands for the truth and the ability to mourn, but she also represents death. And this is precisely, as Freud (1913) emphasises in his interpretation of the drama, what Lear wants to banish from his environs.

The audience witnesses Lear's increasing loss of control over his mental faculties and his lack of concern for the consequences of his actions. Only hesitantly does he recognise that reality is not what he would like it to be. There is a divide between the role he would like to play and the one he has been accorded. He can no longer resort to a sense of true identity: 'Does any here know me? – Why, this is not Lear! [. . .] Who is it that can tell me who I am?' (Act 1, Scene 4, lines 226–230).

The eyes of the spectators are drawn to the roles Lear ascribes to his potential adversaries. The drama reveals starkly how he avails himself of the people in his immediate and familiar environment. He considers those to be good and affectionate towards him who collude in his illusory misconception of himself and thus reinforce him in his views. Only Cordelia has the courage to tell the truth. Though she loves him profoundly and sincerely, she is banished because she figures as the representative of the intolerable truth that Lear wishes to turn a blind eye to. He cannot bear to see her go her own way. Nothing can make him accept that the omnipotence that he thought his status as absolute ruler conferred on him has nothing to do with the way things really are. It is sheer self-deception.

The tragedy of this masterpiece is that we as the audience are fully aware of his depression and the desperate steps he is taking to ward off the recognition of pain, distress, mortality, and ultimate death, while he himself is unable to do so. We would dearly like to open his eyes to the true love of Cordelia and the cynical blandishments of his other two daughters. By identifying with the daughter who Lear banishes to spare himself the painful truth, we run the risk of being banished ourselves.

In the following chapters, five psychoanalysts focus on different aspects of this existential assignment that we call ageing. Common to all of them is the attempt to heighten our sensitivity to the tasks implicit in the ageing process, specifically for psychoanalysts.

2

DOES AN ELDERLY PSYCHO-ANALYST HAVE A ROLE TO FILL?

Danielle Quinodoz

Now that I am an elderly psychoanalyst, what can I share with my younger colleagues that can be of use to them and that is specific to their needs? At this stage in my personal evolution, what role can I fulfil in my psychoanalytic society? I ask these questions because, with the advancement of age, I have come to realise that if an individual accepts to simply be himself, if he inhabits exactly his own space, he brings to the world something original that would otherwise be lacking.

As life expectancy increases, each stage of life also increases

When considering the role that I should fulfil in the last period of my life, I conclude that my research is part of a larger issue: namely, that an increase in life expectancy demands that we redefine not only the role of the elderly in the world, but also that of other age groups as well. Indeed, the increasing number of nonagenarians in Europe has provided the illusion that the lengthening of life has only extended the segment of the population known as the 'elderly'. Yet, at present, each period of our lives is being prolonged. In particular, if one considers that old age begins at the age when a person experiences physical or psychological difficulties in pursing their professional activities, we can see that, today, old age has a tendency to begin later than before because the period when adults are active has also been extended. Today, the majority of 65-year-olds have nothing 'old' about them; they remain very active, except in physically demanding professions. We can observe the same extension of the stages of life with young people: their education continues for a longer period, many continue to live with their parents, women become mothers at a later age, and our active parental, familial and professional lives begin and end later.

Some adults in the prime of life have the tendency to accord value only to those qualities necessary for their hyperactive lives; thus, they tend to see only the failings of older people and not what they can offer. They expect that older people only renounce their previous activities, without themselves creating the necessary benevolent space where the elderly can discover their new role. The elderly can therefore feel rejected for not having any utility. Considering the role of older people in society not only allows us to recognise the activities that they can no longer accomplish, so as to help them give them up, but also to evaluate what specifically they can offer, and thereby to stimulate them to discover their new role and appreciate its value.

In Switzerland, some analysts are concerned about the ageing of our psychoanalytic society, of the advanced age of those who ask to become candidates or members, as well as the high number of 'elderly' training analysts. They have not understood that this remodelling corresponds to a large degree to society in general, and that it is a question of finding new markers to rethink the role of the individual in the light of this new situation. Such a reflection asks for all the more creativeness and freedom, as inside this general remodelling each one of us ages in his own way and at his own pace. This attitude, which I observed in Switzerland and in certain other European countries, varies around the world. For example, I have had the opportunity to see for myself the very great respect that Brazilian psychoanalysts reserve for their elderly colleagues.

What values can the elderly highlight?

In Europe, in general, adults in the prime of life are under great pressure always to produce more, and more quickly, if they want to keep their place in the economic mainstream of the consumer society. In this context, efficiency, productivity, speed, and the garnering of wealth or titles are valued attributes. These values can fall into the category of 'having'; they are valuable, provided that they are offset by the values of the category of 'being'. But, as soon as the values of 'having' are privileged, they draw us into a vortex that can cut us off from the essence of ourselves. I think that psychoanalysts do not entirely escape this risk even if, by their profession, they work principally with the values of the category of 'being'.

During our lives we are all called upon to meet a pivotal age, varying from one person to another, where we begin to feel less capable in either the physical or the psychical domain, or, indeed, in both. In addition, at this age, we are often faced with various losses such as the death of loved ones or a change in our social or professional status. A question may therefore arise: '*Am I starting to become part of the elderly?*' Thus, if we consider only the values for 'having and producing' we can grow to be afraid of becoming useless and good only for the scrap heap. Indeed, if we remain with the illusion that to feel we exist we must continue with our previous role of a capable adult, there is a risk that we could become bitter for, despite our efforts and our denial, our effectiveness is no longer the same as before. We expose ourselves therefore to being tolerated with pity by the young, or else considered as a burden or rejected. Thus, young adults arrive at almost a paradox: to celebrate the lengthening of life, while complaining of the burden constituted by the growing number of the elderly. A vicious circle of mutual aggression may develop between the rejecting young and the rejected old. As shown by Freud (1917), it is important to recognise the reality of loss to be able to work it through. This is true even with respect to losses related to old age.

Older people who approach this pivotal age with serenity are most often those who become or re-become conscious of the importance of the values related to 'being', that is to say, they possess a sense of identity and attention to the internal world. These values are part of a series of discoveries: the elderly, psychoanalysts or not, when they perceive that the end is approaching, are compelled to ask questions about their impending death, the meaning of life, the relativisation of productivity and the importance of wonder. Inevitably, these questions require a change in their scale of values: some successes seem secondary and others, seemingly mundane, become important in their eyes. Older people who are able to learn from their experiences can also attest to the complexity of each event, which can help in achieving an overview, avoiding hasty judgments and giving 'time to time'. What is more, they feel the importance of rebuilding their internal history by integrating the emotionally important moments of their lives into a coherent overall story. They perceive, therefore, that it is sometimes those events that were very simple but loaded with emotion that have, in fact, been an underground guide all their lives: that one little phrase, that particular meeting, that one seemingly innocuous act. They recognise in their lives what I have termed 'the second of eternity' (Quinodoz, 2008): those moments of intense emotion where we perceive the shock of beauty, love, certain pains, and key decisions and which seem to escape from measured chronological time, without actually denying it.

These values are constructed throughout a lifetime and are, of course, also present in younger adults, but in the latter they are often hidden because, to be perceived, they need an inner silence that is difficult to obtain whilst leading a hectic life. The elderly are better at understanding the importance of this because the end of their life is approaching; they feel it is worth stopping to savour the seconds of eternity, while those who are leading a fully active life are constantly asked to move on to something else. For an elderly person, the fact of integrating these seconds of eternity into the totality of their internal history is a way of appropriating their own life. Indeed, in order to leave a place you must already have had one, your own, and to leave life in peace it is necessary to have imbued one's life story with coherence. Each page of the book of our life counts: it gives meaning to what comes before and after, and the last sentence of the book will modify the meaning of the whole. Even if the last sentence of the book is less beautiful than we had hoped for, it still has the unique value of being ours. Stéphane Hessel, at the age of 93, wrote: 'I have the appetite for death . . . that is to say I have reached the stage where life ends . . . the closing of what was life' (2011). The death wish of which he speaks is not destructive, as it would be in a depressive person; it is a hymn to life. Older people who, like him, assume their role by trying, by their simple presence, to render the young attentive to the values of 'being' have no need to worry about being useless. I think the role of the elderly consists, justly, in imparting to the young the presence and the richness of these values in relation to being.

Most elderly people do not find their role overnight. There is often a period of adjustment, with a slow and gradual ageing process which is a first step into old age; a period that varies according to the individual. During this period, we continue to perform fairly well according to the previous criteria, but we gradually discover how to give more and more importance to the values of *being* compared with those of *having* and, thus, discover a new effectiveness. When the elderly do not benefit from this preparatory time, they run the risk of dissipating themselves by trying to prove how they are still productive in terms of having, instead of paying attention to their internal world and their sense of being. They then run the risk of being powerless when confronted with a heavier loss (physical or mental illness, serious accident, bereavement, etc.), which will quickly lead them into the second stage of old age. I have met people who have lived quite peacefully this second period of old age: they felt connected to their inner world, which was inhabited by good objects. I emphasise that, for me, good objects are not idealised objects, they are not perfect objects, because they can be criticised and the love one feels for them accepts any conflicts.

Psychoanalysis goes against the tide

The profession of psychoanalysis – as well as some other professions, such as artistic professions for example – is mostly based on the values of *being* rather than those of *having*. Psychoanalysts go against the tide in our consumer society as they emphasise in their professional practice values that may seem secondary or even unnecessary in today's society. Indeed, we live at a time when we communicate faster, farther, with more people, whilst gaining the maximum return on our time, which allows us to do even more! So how does a person take the time to lie on a couch for three quarters of an hour several times a week, drop everything, and all this only to be attentive to what is happening in regards to their psychological reality! As for the analyst, how to spend many hours a day sitting in a chair, for decades, to remain attentive to the internal world of a few patients? If efficiency is to do the maximum in the minimum amount of time, the slow pace of psychoanalysis can seem really crazy! Finally, we could say that psychoanalysis demonstrates values which, in the surrounding society, are instead demonstrated by the peacefully ageing elderly. Thus, to me, a psychoanalyst seems well prepared to continue his activity for a longer period compared with other professions. This does not mean, however, that a psychoanalyst ignores the values of *having*. For each of us, the balance between the two categories of values remains to be constructed constantly.

Moreover, I notice a big difference between an artist and an analyst; if an elderly painter is surprised by death in the full expression of his art, he leaves simply just one unfinished canvas. However, if an analyst dies or becomes disabled, he leaves behind a patient whose analysis is interrupted. The decision to undertake an analysis with a patient engages the responsibility of the analyst towards that person, because analysis requires the participation of two people in a common setting in which the process will evolve over several years. When they are old, some analysts refuse to take such a risk because of their age, even if they happen to be at the top of their form as an analyst and would like patients to benefit from their long experience, others do not take this into consideration.

A psychoanalyst has several ages at once

Awareness of his own ageing process is particular to a psychoanalyst because, by projection during the sessions, he is given the ages of the various characters of the internal world of his patient. Thus, a young analyst can be treated during the transference process as if he were the very old parent of a middle-aged patient, while an old analyst can be treated as a child. This leads the analyst to work back and forth between his objective age and his fantasy age. Indeed, a patient requires of an analyst that he takes into account his real age, the transience of life and the inevitability of his own death. But a patient also needs an analyst who takes into account his fantasy age in order to 'take away' concrete reality and listen to the psychic reality of his patient.

I think that this freedom to accept to play out a fantasy with his different ages influences the manner of ageing of a psychoanalyst. It is possible that this mobility in the way of looking at life makes him able to continue his work for longer.

When an analyst does not realise that he is no longer able to work

In this independent profession that is psychoanalysis, there are as many ways of looking at retirement as there are psychoanalysts, each dealing with retirement age under different conditions. Yet, we are all concerned when a psychoanalyst clings to his previous role and continues to receive patients or training analysts while he is no longer in full possession of his emotional or intellectual faculties, or has control over his impulses. How can we protect the patients? How can we prevent ourselves from becoming a psychoanalyst who is dangerous for our patients and embarrassing to our colleagues?

When one of our colleagues no longer appears capable of receiving patients, we hesitate to make him aware of this situation for fear of his reaction: he could experience it as a narcissistic wound, feel persecuted by those who try to talk to him and not believe them, deny his difficulties and revolt. I think, like many colleagues, that this task rests with the ethics committee of the psychoanalytic society concerned, but on the condition that it is not a way to shift on to the ethics committee the responsibility that also belongs to each of us. If we only rely on the committee it could be a way for us to avoid the issue. Indeed, some ethics committees act only on registered complaints; who then will dare to be the one to file such a complaint against a colleague or a friend? Yet, if people do not dare complain to the committee it will not be able to do its job. Other ethics committees do not need personal complaints, they also have to check the veracity of rumours criticising the behaviour of certain analysts. However, these rumours have the time to poison a society long before the committee reacts. How do we create a friendly enough atmosphere in a psychoanalytic society so that these painful tasks are accomplished in the most transparent, direct and caring way possible?

If we wait for the patients themselves to become aware of the deficiencies of their analysts and decide to leave them, it is obvious that we place them in a dramatic situation. On the one hand, the degradation in the health of their analyst is often too gradual to be easily identified by them. On the other hand, a patient is engaged in a transference relationship that makes it difficult for him to separate from his analyst if the latter's health deteriorates; he could sometimes even become the protector of his analyst and feel responsible for him. We also observe difficult situations where a candidate under supervision with an analyst sees him decline. Sometimes a candidate may ask his supervisor for the validation report required for his training, only to find that the supervisor does not understand that time is passing and that he will soon no longer be in a fit state to provide it. It can happen that candidates, after paying for years of supervision, find themselves without any official proof of the work that they have accomplished.

The sense of the ephemeral

I have had the painful experience that the inability to carry on the activity of an analyst is not necessarily related to age. I prepared the termination of my personal psychoanalysis, which lasted five and a half years, at a frequency of four times a week when, one day, arriving for my session, I found on the closed door a notice with a phone number. I learnt that my still young psychoanalyst, in his forties, had suffered a ruptured cerebral aneurysm. From one moment to the other he had become paralysed and aphasic. He never recovered. I never saw him again, except for one occasion when he did not recognise me. I recommended my analysis later on with another person, but the abrupt interruption of the first tranche of analysis made me become aware of the ephemeral, of the fragility of our state and, therefore, the importance of the present moment. When I take my leave of a patient at the end of a session I think there is a good chance for me to be present at the meeting the following day, but I know that I cannot be certain of it (Quinodoz, 1996). Far from weakening us, these insights can give us stability and an inner strength, because the present is therefore experienced with a great intensity and becomes a source of wonder constantly renewed. In addition, these insights lead us to treat our patients and ourselves with more respect and affection by trying to find the conditions of analysis that will be most comfortable, including with respect to the termination of our activity as a psychoanalyst.

Henri Danon Boileau used the term 'dying usefully' (2000). I have paraphrased this by saying that 'ageing usefully' (Quinodoz, 2008) for a psychoanalyst consists of bearing witness to his sense of the ephemeral by expressing it verbally, but also by transmitting it to his candidates under supervision through very simple acts, such as: maintaining a list of his patients in an envelope and handing it to someone trustworthy who will open it if necessary, drawing up regular interim supervision reports so that a candidate is not left without an official certificate if 'something' happens to him, providing supervision validations in good time, certificates of analysis, etc.

Tyrannical superego? Protective superego?

Some psychoanalysts have chosen to advance a deadline for the end of their psychoanalytic activity, such as Danon Boileau (2010). I do not wish to fix such a requirement because I want the cessation of my patients' analysis to be linked to the internal evolution of their analytical process, and not to some external imperative. I would fear that, if my patients were aware of this deadline from the start of their analysis, they would suffer from a sense of incompleteness. Danon Boileau suggested that to facilitate the cessation of psychoanalytic activity, it is desirable that the retirement age itself is imposed by an external rule, enacted for example by the psychoanalytic societies (op. cit.). In this case, I think the problem would remain the same for the patient who sees the end of his analysis imposed from outside and not from within. In addition, this diversion from the outside would aim to evacuate, during the transference/countertransference relationship, the aggression linked to the termination process, therefore making it difficult to analyse: the patient could not even perceive that he was angry with his analyst who gave him this date as the analyst was clearly obeying a rule to which he had himself submitted.

Personally, I envisage the termination of my professional activity differently. Freud, then Melanie Klein, described the evolution of the superego which, from being tyrannical, can become protective and enable a resolution of the Oedipus complex. If the son gives up the mother it is not only out of fear that the father carries out his threat of castration, but also because of different objectives: to conserve a loving relationship for a total non-idealised object – father and mother – without evacuating the aggression, respecting the parents' relationship with each other and to discover a new non-idealised love object of his own generation. I think that if, when thinking about retirement, the ego of a psychoanalyst listens to a protective superego he will seek solutions that will treat both the analyst and his patients with tenderness, without fleeing conflicts. That is to say, for example, he can expect that every analysis will end at the time most favourable for itself, and not all at the same time.

A retirement 'à la carte'

Personally, in the first place, I wish to withdraw from my long-term psychoanalytic activities because I recognise that the time left to me is running out. To start a training analysis now with a patient who has not already undergone a first analysis, would seem to me to run the risk of my death occurring before the end of the analysis and I would not wish a patient to be exposed to that risk. I do not take this decision with a light heart because I have a great deal of experience and it is precisely now that I feel most able to carry out analysis. Yet, I feel at peace with this decision. Even if I do not know the date of my death, and I know, of course, that death also occurs in young people, I cannot deny that the older I become, the more this deadline approaches. However, to undertake shorter forms of treatment or continue my work as a supervisor and transmitter of psychoanalysis seems less closely related to the length of life that I have left and, for these activities, I would like to retire later. I would regret not being able to share my rich psychoanalytic experience with young colleagues. At the general meeting of the Swiss Psychoanalytical Society in 2011, some colleagues proposed that all active members reaching the age of 75 automatically become honorary members. This would require training analysts (or educationalists) to withdraw at once from all their psychoanalytic activities, including that of supervisor. I am not in favour of this proposal. I prefer a personalised retirement, one that allows an analyst not to have to withdraw from all his different psychoanalytic activities at the same time.

The 'internal' couch remains occupied

As Freud (1917) demonstrated, the mourning process begins with the recognition of the reality of loss. For an elderly person, this means in particular acknowledging the reality of the somatic and psychic losses linked to one's age. This awareness is necessary, but is not sufficient by itself. It is jointly a question of working out losses and, particularly, the loss of one's occupation. For this, I find the model of grief outlined by Klein very valuable: 'every advance in the process of mourning results in a deepening in the individual's relation to his inner objects, in the happiness of regaining them after they were felt to be lost . . . in an increased trust in them and love for them' (1940, p. 359). In other words, what is lost in the external reality can be kept in the psychic reality as an internal object. For example, once an analysis is finished, I give up the almost daily links which tied me to the external reality of my patients, but I keep in me their presence as valuable internal objects with which I remain connected in my psychic reality: 'the characteristic feature of normal mourning is the individual's setting up (of) the lost loved object inside himself' (p. 361). When I finish an analysis *my couch is empty* in connection with external reality, but *it is occupied* in regard to my internal world.

In any case, I do not consider my present professional activity as an analyst as an identification with an idealised object, but with a good internal object, that is to say an object that I appreciate in its totality, enjoying some of its aspects whilst being able to criticise others. For example, I derive a great deal of pleasure working with my patients, however, I hate to be concerned sometimes with a serious crisis that one of them is going through, or be unavailable for an unexpected activity due to unforeseen demands of my work schedule. Thus, the decision to retire reflects a balance to be created between the multiple aspects of my activity as an analyst, among other things: the pleasure of working with patients, potential inconveniences associated with time constraints, respect for my health and financial necessity as an independent clinician with no institutional pension. The latter point is often underestimated by retired colleagues who have worked in institutions.

What are the steps to take for a creative retirement?

Would it be appropriate to impose from outside an age limit for the practice of psychoanalysis that would be inscribed in the statutes and guidelines of psychoanalytic societies? In my opinion, this would be to overlook the fact that the age at which a person loses the full possession of his professional abilities is highly variable. It would also deprive us of the valuable experience gained by some older psychoanalysts in order to avoid the troubles caused by the deficiencies of others. To impose the same retirement age on everyone would be to the detriment of those analysts who age 'well' and, conscious of the ageing process, know themselves when to limit their professional activity.

On the other hand, I find it a very positive development that some psychoanalytic societies arrange for their active older members (from what age? 75?) regular interviews (in what form? How often? Every three years?) with members of the teaching or ethics committees. These interviews are an opportunity for the older psychoanalysts to take stock with their colleagues, and they also help favour the possibility of a personalised retirement. However, these discussions can only be positive if they are made in a caring and free atmosphere, and I think that it is for each psychoanalytic society to oversee and try and maintain the confident climate of a protective superego and not a tyrannical superego.

To strive for a caring and free atmosphere in a psychoanalytic society

Among the areas that I find it important to work on in a psychoanalytic society to promote this atmosphere, I emphasise two:

It seems to me useful to promote a discussion among colleagues to rethink Oedipal conflicts at the group level within a psychoanalytic society. In fact, conflicts of an Oedipal nature do sometimes arise in our societies: for example, we have witnessed senior psychoanalysts unwittingly preventing the youngest ones developing so they do not seize the throne to which they cling, convinced that they alone are the only ones who should reign. We have also seen young psychoanalysts unconsciously seeking to eliminate their older colleagues, persuaded of the need to take their place to gain one themselves. Indeed, it is sometimes the same young people who, having grown older and gained responsibilities in the society, become, in their turn, the most castrating in regards to their younger colleagues, whilst continuing to reject their older ones. However, when a young psychoanalyst expresses his gratitude to an older colleague for what he has given him, or when an older psychoanalyst expresses his pleasure at the development of a younger one, we can observe the profound joy shared by both. Even in a psychoanalytic society, a father and son can sometimes rediscover that they are not two individuals competing for one place, but that each one of them has to find and create his own space because each of them has something unique to offer. Can we ever be sure of having fully developed our own Oedipal conflicts? It is a little like the search for balance: if we believe we have reached equilibrium, we have already lost it.

I also think it is important to promote reflection among colleagues so as to break the taboo of the potential loss of our professional ability or our psychic abilities, and to dare to speak without condescension of those deficiencies that can affect every one of us. This protective realism may allow us to have less fear of our own weaknesses and to dare to accept them without shame. In turn, this may cut short the rumours that haunt our corridors and that sometimes fascinate us: those rumours where we speak of each other's impairments in a veiled manner, as if the people concerned should be ashamed. If we have our eyes fixed on the deficiencies of those who age, is it because we fear to see those same deficiencies develop in ourselves and then be ashamed of them in our turn? Thus we sometimes remain fixed in front of a 'veteran' analyst whose endless speeches we dare not stop, while we listen stunned. We therefore no longer perceive the wealth that persists in each of us, despite our deficiencies. It is clear that, like everyone else, I also risk mental deterioration or any other impairment. I therefore asked two colleagues to warn me if they noticed any deficiencies which I could not be aware of and which would interfere with my psychoanalytical activities. Of course, I will still need to be able to understand and believe them when the time comes! To be receptive to their efforts, I need to be prepared by a caring attitude among colleagues which helps me to look reality squarely in the face, to accept it in advance and to dare to speak about it now as a possibility.

The measures taken by a psychoanalytic society to protect patients and analysts will never be perfect, but if these measures are carried out in a caring and free atmosphere they will be accepted more positively and help each of us to prepare as serenely as possible, not just for the end of our psychoanalytic practice, but its termination.

3

LATER, PERHAPS . . .

Transience and its significance for the psychoanalyst

Gabriele Junkers

> To the ego, therefore, living means the same as being loved.
> (Freud, 1923, p. 58)

We analysts consider reflection on limitation, temporality, finitude, transience and mortality to be essential to the phase of termination of an analytic treatment and a sign that infantile fantasies of omnipotence have been relinquished (Loewald, 1988). But what of our capacity to anticipate the empty couch as a symbol of the finitude and transience of our professional activity and to mourn and plan for it accordingly?

In this essay I shall venture an examination of selected aspects of transience in its significance for us as analysts. My starting point is the assumption that there exist in psychoanalysts specific conditions that make it particularly difficult for them to undertake the necessary task of analysing their wishes and anxieties in relation to their own transience. I shall show that, towards the end of one's professional career, a subjectively threatening psychological situation may develop that places at risk the secure foundation of the analytic capacity to mediate between inside and outside and between limited time and infinite time. Inherent in a situation of this kind is the danger that the fact of 'being a psychoanalyst' might be misused in order to deaden one's anxieties by a misunderstanding of what it means to be a psychoanalyst.

The wish, later perhaps, to become a psychoanalyst

The wish to become a psychoanalyst has a long history for every one of us. When I begin to translate my decision into reality, I do not yet know what is in store for me. In my innermost being, however, a blueprint for my professional future already exists, for I am imbued with fantasies, both conscious and unconscious, about what it means to *me* to 'be a psychoanalyst'. Within these fantasies there lie concealed anticipated wish fulfilments by projection in the form of hopes that seem to me impossible to achieve except by 'becoming an analyst'. These wishes have developed on the basis of my early personal history with its both good and painful experiences.

As his creative life was drawing to a close, Freud was able to write: 'It cannot be disputed that analysts in their own personalities have not invariably come up to the standard of psychical normality to which they wish to educate their patients' (1937, p. 247). Personal discussions with colleagues have persuaded me that our choice of profession is influenced by early mental suffering that disrupts our 'continuity of being' (Winnicott, 1960, p. 591) and calls into question our ability to say 'I am' (cf. Loch, 1982a, p. 148).

We consider ourselves fortunate to have known that we needed an analysis; we hoped that our training analysis would provide us with a 'remodelling of the ego' (Freud, 1937, p. 249); and we hoped to find our way to satisfying object relationships and to be in a position to examine and accept external and internal realities and to mourn for what could not be changed. This process of working through was supposed to give us the tools to distinguish between our own issues and the problems brought to us, and transferred on to us, by our patients.

Ferro (2003, p. 137) sees the mental wounds we carry with us as a *sine qua non*. He is convinced that, without having experienced mental pain, we cannot understand and empathise with our patients.[1] According to this author, it is only on the basis of a certain 'painful sensibility' and of having adequately worked through his own wounds in the training analysis that an analyst can develop his 'tool', thus enabling him 'to be in harmony with what has hurt the patient'. In the most favourable case, our training analysis should enable us to undertake ongoing self-analysis – that is, attentive and critical reflection on our own experience, thinking and action – throughout our lives.

Yet we also know that changes in our life situation can reopen old wounds that we had assumed to have healed, thus potentially impeding the necessary work of mastering them. I agree with Loch (1982a, p. 139, translated) that one can 'successfully master life crises only if we have been able to overcome the earlier crises at least "reasonably well"'. There is always the risk that we might 'learn to make use of defensive mechanisms which allow [us] to divert the implications and demands of analysis from [ourselves] (probably by directing them on to other people), so that [we ourselves] remain as [we] are' (Freud, 1937, p. 249).

When we eventually embark on our analytic work, we are usually surprised to find how different the practice of this longed-for profession can be from what we expected, and hence how difficult it is, how great are the demands on our entire person, and how often we are exposed in the course of our daily work to affects that we experience as compelling and peremptory. During our training, we as yet had no idea that we would experience relationships involving 'overflowing, tempestuous, hot feelings of love, hate, wanting to know and not wanting to know that had already overwhelmed the capacity for containment of *one* consciousness' (Gutwinski-Jeggle, 2001, translated). Nor did we suspect how far this dynamic in our patients would confront us with our own unconscious wishes and stir up our own anxieties. We had no conception of the degree of vigilance, discipline and self-control we would have to bring to bear in order to be able to accept and at the same time to analyse and 'detoxify' the manifold entanglements at issue, thus rendering our patients capable of enduring and understanding what is experienced as unendurable. We were equally unaware that life in an analytic practice could be very lonely; that by virtue of the particularity of this 'work *à deux* alone' we would have to forgo many of the helpful corrective influences available in other social environments, both professional and private; that we could expect to be transformed by projections into a wicked, frustrating, malicious or triumphant object utterly at variance with our internal wishful self-image; and in particular we did not know how tempting it could be at such times to evade such undesired ascriptions. We could not yet imagine that even experienced analysts must disappointedly confess to themselves that they and their patient or candidate can no longer work on the destructive impulses that arise, whether because of a limit set by external factors or by the patient or candidate or owing to the specific 'fit', the analyst's incapacity or indeed the painful realisation that the method one has learnt – this special method which I as a beginner perhaps thought 'could do absolutely anything' – has its limitations (cf., for instance, Klein, 1950, p. 79).

Our analytic career is not unaffected by the fact that, as Sandler (1983) observes, many of us are constantly assailed by gnawing self-doubt and the conviction that as analysts we are not 'doing a good job'. The feeling of not working analytically enough is simply lying in wait for an opportunity to be projected on to one or other of our colleagues.

All the feelings that are mobilised in us as psychoanalysts in the course of analytic work, whether by our patients or by our own strict superego – these difficult feelings that extend across the entire spectrum from disappointment via self-doubt to (almost) hatred of an occupation that is so infinitely hard to endure – may in certain circumstances impair our capacity to tolerate the wishes, anxieties and tensions aroused in us and to keep intact the barrier that protects us from excessively close entanglements. In such a situation we are at risk of succumbing to feelings that we are no longer able to perceive, reflect upon and name, and of instead discharging them in concrete action. I imagine that all of us have experienced something of the kind. It is then helpful if we can activate an internalised *analytic attitude, a professional 'psychic home'* (Kennedy, 2012) – not least on the basis of the example set, if all went well, by our training analyst. Notwithstanding an enactment, a stable internalised setting then enables us to keep at the ready an inner self-critically observing agency that will help us to regain our capacity to think.

When dedication becomes a passion . . .

'Being a psychoanalyst is not a profession; it's a passion!' I have repeatedly heard this pronouncement, accompanied by an arch smile, from colleagues jokingly wishing to excuse their self-imposed volume of work. It bears out my assumption that a 'powerful emotional factor' (Freud, 1916, p. 306) underlies our choice of profession as analysts. There is virtually no other occupation that calls for such a combination of theoretical understanding and practical learning with the involvement of one's individual personality. This means that, when we experience disappointment or offence, we find it particularly hard to see it as not directed at us personally and to keep it at bay.

When in the grip of passion, one is driven by powerful, intense affects stemming partly from love *for* the object and partly from one's own narcissism. In a state of mind dominated by passion, idealisation and ideas of omnipotence may keep our doubts and ignorance to a tolerable level (Bion, 1963; Green, 1980; Potamianou, 2010). An inner state of this kind is at the same time apt to eliminate feelings of loss and separation and to defend against the onslaughts of transience, so that we can feel protected, supported and strong. A presumed sacrifice on behalf of the passionately loved object may be an extremely subtle way of concealing the subject's aspiration to banish separation by availability. As a result, the passionately desired object is almost always perceived as substantially isolated from the rest of the world (Racamier, 1980, p. 237). Should anything oppose the connection with the object, the powerful force of passion may turn instead to destructiveness.

I therefore pondered how the relationship between psychoanalysis, dedication and passion should be understood. In *favourable* cases, we develop a living dedication both to the theoretical and intellectual edifice of analysis and to its application in the work with our patients. Satisfaction may legitimately accrue, and strength be derived, from such dedication, in which omnipotent needs can withstand reality testing and love can be integrated with hate, thus overcoming the risk of a forced one-sidedness.

When the situation is *less favourable*, perception may be narrowed to such an extent that all fields of life have to be subordinated to psychoanalysis and one's view of the world bears the stamp of a manically idealising exclusiveness and one-sidedness. The danger then is that no room will be left either for doubt about the theory and one's own activity or for the perception of quite different realities of life. A passionate psychoanalyst of this kind risks living out what he calls 'psychoanalysis' on the basis of idealisation and omnipotence, perhaps in order to defend against the frustrations of external reality by idealising the analytic situation so that he can feel elevated above any doubts of his own. If nothing but psychoanalysis, as the object of dedication, love and passion, is allowed to exist, it may be feared that the passion for psychoanalysis is being used as a defence against relating to real people and is therefore overlain by excessive expectations of satisfaction. This presents the threat of a misuse of psychoanalysis culminating, say, in the following conviction: 'I live for psychoanalysis, which means everything to me, and because it is everything for me it makes me unassailable!' In such an internal world, there is no place either for recognition of the limitations of one's own understanding or for self-analysis of one's transience; instead, the idea holds sway that things will continue as they are for ever, and one at most accepts a vague sense of 'well, later, perhaps . . .'

However, tolerance of separation anxiety is not merely the essential mark of mental health, but constitutes the very foundation of an analyst's approach to gaining knowledge. In our work from session to session, we must cut ourselves loose from all certainties of memory, desire and belief and endure this uncomfortable state without any 'irritable reaching after facts and reason' (Bion, 1970, p. 124) until we discover a pattern, a Gestalt, that we can subsume in an interpretation.

Given the limitation of the session, the issue repeatedly arises anew of the inner forces that may be activated in the patient and ourselves by separation, transience and finitude. As the end of an analysis approaches, early experiences of separation and hence intense early painful feelings are newly aroused. Only if persecutory and depressive anxieties, and loving and hate-filled tendencies, have been adequately worked through in both the positive and the negative transference will the patient be able, by virtue of the resulting capacity for integration, to continue his self-analysis after termination (Klein, 1950, p. 80).

For us as psychoanalysts, every confrontation with the termination of an analysis activates our own separation anxieties, so that we must renounce the wish not to end the analysis until we think it complete. We must live with the wound inflicted by the realisation that apprehension of the ultimate reality of an object in Kant's sense will remain but a pipedream and that we can never have the feeling that 'it is accomplished'. However, if the quest for an 'ultimate reality' was an important reason for my choice of profession, this aspiration will inevitably be disappointed again and again. After all, we cannot apprehend the materials with which an analyst works – love, hate and anxiety – with our sense organs, but can merely discern verbal or bodily transformations. In the end there is imperfection, along the lines of Freud's regretful comment about the analysis of a dream (1900, p. 525) that we arrive at the dream's *navel*, the spot that must remain obscure, which we cannot unravel. The same applies to a patient's analysis, which can be terminable but not complete, as well as to the knowledge of psychoanalysis as an entire theoretical edifice – we do our best to penetrate into it as deeply as possible and from all directions, but the fact is that we can never wholly or completely 'own' it.

If *my* relationship with psychoanalysis is to possess some of the qualities of a Bionian *K* object, I must be prepared to expose myself repeatedly to disappointment, frustration and pain, but without lapsing into a masochistic attitude (Thorner, 1988, p. 593). This capacity to obtain true knowledge of myself by introspection was attributed by Freud (1900, p. 574) to consciousness as the 'sense organ for the apprehension of psychical qualities'. Hence this faculty, which is so fundamentally bound up with the knowledge of psychic reality, can develop in me only if I am prepared to tolerate uncertainty, doubt and ignorance. For the quest for truth in our work will become a constant source of pain – we were not aware of this when we began our training – and the same pain, like that of growth and development, will also, as a rule unexpectedly, accompany us as we grow older.

The foregoing considerations are intended to show that without dedication we cannot practise this 'impossible' profession, the learning and exercise of which call for so much renunciation. But if *passionate* dedication is misused to ward off separation anxiety and transience, and psychoanalysis is elevated into a certainty that is the fount of security, then psychoanalysis is being misused for the purpose of disavowing the facts of life. The above mental vulnerabilities may mate in us with an uncertainly developed sense of temporality in such a way that, by virtue of particular life circumstances, there arises an internal situation that can no longer be withstood or endured, thus causing old wounds to reopen and mobilising massive defences against unendurable feelings.

Ageing: Transience as an attack on the analyst's life and work

Nearly everyone aspires to a long life, but hardly anyone is happy to grow old. To avoid the perception that our time is limited and will inevitably end in death, we often behave as if we had an infinite life ahead of us (Freud, 1916). Our reluctance to concern ourselves with the end, with our own transience and finitude, is something profoundly human. For if the illusory future that we need for a living existence and survival is taken from us, and with it all intentionality too, then we are compelled to relinquish the idea of an 'immortal' object and death becomes our 'object' (Loch, 1982b, p. 270).

We know from the termination phases of our analyses how infinitely difficult and painful it is to contemplate the end. Precisely because this end is in view, old problems are often reactivated with sometimes unsuspected intensity and a sense of impending catastrophe. Psychoanalysts such as Winnicott (1963), Klein and others have assigned annihilation anxiety an important role in early mental life. For Klein (1946), the fear of personal extinction, fragmentation or disintegration is the earliest anxiety of all, experienced as a catastrophic threat emanating from internal objects. Hanna Segal (1958) holds the reactivation of precisely these early annihilation anxieties responsible for breakdowns in old age.

Growing old is a highly individual, gradual, sometimes imperceptible process which is a matter of intermittent experience and to which both positive and negative attributes are ascribed. It is only when we are confronted with changed external and in particular also internal realities that our own ageing becomes an undeniable fact of life (Money-Kyrle, 1971) that can not only arouse affects such as pleasure, pain and hate but also give rise to feelings of satisfaction, inner tranquillity and increased self-confidence. If we have succeeded in developing a 'psychic home' (Kennedy, 2012, p. 4), a sense of personal identity, a 'locus of belonging' (Hinshelwood, 1997, p. 195), from the vantage point of which we can realistically say 'I am' and 'I can', then we can not only endure, but also actively shape, the withdrawal that is demanded by and commences with the ageing process. If we can concentrate more on 'being' (Quinodoz, p. 8 in this book), we shall find it easier to distinguish between our professional and personal identities. In this way, analytic identity, bound up with the couch and the consulting room, need not necessarily serve as a prop in the theatre of a fragile personal identity.

As a rule it is external factors – unwanted realities such as, in particular, painful losses or disease of one kind or another – that set limits to our wishes and desires and cause ageing to appear to us as a misfortune. More than two millennia ago, Cicero identified four reasons for this: ageing disqualifies us for the enjoyment of the sensual gratifications; it incapacitates us for acting in the affairs of the world; it produces great infirmities of the body; and it confronts us with death as a fact of life. Three forms of such experiences of loss are, in my opinion, typical examples of the onslaughts to which our inner mental equilibrium may be exposed as we grow older – onslaughts to which we may sometimes react by reinforcing our individual defences, so that certain character traits are accentuated to a more or less extreme degree. They are the loss of other human beings, of ideals and life plans, and of physical integrity. The more persons I lose whom I have come to love, the less often I shall be able in future to make 'appointments in memory' (Bovenschen, 2006, translated) and thereby to be held by virtue of thus being known and recognised. The impending and eventually real external losses give rise at the same time to crucial changes in our internal world. We must now come to terms in an entirely new way with the capacity to be alone. The threat of being lost and isolated in the world revives feelings of exclusion, and hence the anxieties associated with our Oedipal problems, with new and unprecedented intensity. It is therefore unsurprising that all psychoanalytic contributions on the subject of 'loneliness' have been composed by psychoanalysts over the age of 60 (Winnicott, 1958; Fromm-Reichmann, 1959; Klein, 1963; Erlich, 1998; Kennedy, 2011).

The limitation of my life span compels me to recognise the boundaries of my creativity and to renounce the future possibility of feeling better by constantly repeated reparation. Increasingly tight limits are set to what I can *still* achieve; indeed, the word 'still' becomes ever more significant. We must acknowledge that our need to be liked, loved and consulted is likely to remain unsatisfied more and more frequently. Depending on my personality I may wish to impose myself so that I am still after all seen, or to withdraw so as not to expose myself to new wounds. I should like to cling to what offers me continuity and hence security, and to banish the new, the alien and the uncertain from myself. We must now therefore review our hopes, ideals and plans, as Freud stresses in his letter to Abraham of 25 August 1914, written just before the publication of his essay 'On Transience'.

Our bodies impress the fact of transience on us with particular force. At first the signs may be only external, such as grey hair, sagging skin and failing potency, but soon the ageing process takes hold of our entire condition: our stamina and vitality decline, our overall state becomes more unpredictable and we are increasingly threatened by diseases so that we can enjoy only 'relative health'. We become forgetful and hope that no one will notice; we try to disguise the gaps in our memory and may suffer because we no longer feel really well in consequence. On the other hand, we may tell ourselves, perhaps with a modicum of defiance: 'Well, what can happen to me now, at my age?'

Physical health is an important foundation of our intellectual performance and mental health. Although we all know that in ageing, as Eissler (1975, p. 317) points out, a biological factor progressively takes over the control of our intellectual performance and mental health, we have, I believe, given little thought to the resulting possible changes in our capacity to analyse.

As we grow older we are called upon to review our hitherto familiar ways of coping with disappointments and losses, to redefine our internal position and to establish a new balance between our working and social lives and our inner private space. I have called this work of mental reconstruction, which is necessary if we are to adapt constructively to changing conditions, 'work on the ageing process', by analogy with the working through of the depressive position (Junkers, 2001).[2]

By this I mean the entire mental work that we must accomplish, along similar lines to the working through of the depressive position (Klein, 1946, p. 99), if we are not simply to give up when faced with the demands of change. If I can summon the courage to confront my own ageing creatively and actively, I shall be able to acknowledge, with regret but not in desperation, that there are limits to putting matters off for the future, to the idea of 'later, perhaps', and that I am called upon to concentrate all my strength on the here and now and on what is still possible.

23

To enable us to live with the knowledge of our own finitude, we need defence and acknowledgement in *equal* measure. After all, I cannot be constantly thinking of the end, but must continue to plunge into the river of life, while *also* contemplating the end. Just as we cannot attain the depressive position once and for all, so it is with this 'work on the ageing process': I cannot finish it off and file it away, but must now allow it to become my constant companion, fight with it and accept the challenge of adapting again and again to new conditions – both internal and external – thus repeatedly taking my leave anew. If one can fully engage in this process of mourning for what is transient and successfully give priority to the 'values related to "being"' (Quinodoz, p. 8 in this book), this phase of life can be an extraordinarily enriching and fulfilling experience, to be enjoyed in contentment: one can feel calmer, cease to take things excessively seriously, take pleasure in watching one's children and grandchildren grow up and candidates become colleagues. Success in seeing the 'approach to the end' as a kind of new beginning that we can shape consciously and actively could no doubt be deemed tantamount to wisdom.

It is my impression that, owing to a variety of internal and external conditions, we psychoanalysts find this necessary *'work on the ageing process'* difficult. The problems that flare up in our patients as the end of their treatment draws near must be thoroughly worked through if the self-analytic capacity they have acquired is to be stably integrated. It is equally important for aspiring analysts to work through the termination of their own training analysis, even if, unlike our patients, we know in advance that we shall presumably continue to meet and speak to our training analyst in a different context. In other words, we can 'cheat' on the process of taking our leave. However, the finitude of our lives permits no cheating. The relentlessness of ageing may stir up old wounds in the psychoanalyst, so that we run the risk of not being able to cope appropriately with reactivated primitive extinction anxieties, the fear of loneliness, of physical disintegration and, in particular, of increasing dependence.

The external situation concerns life and work in a specific temporality. When we embark on an analysis, we at first envisage a seemingly 'infinite duration'. In the state of evenly suspended attention, we immerse ourselves in our analysands' unconscious and hence timeless world, in order to devote ourselves in this 'state of discovery' (Grinberg *et al.*, 1975, p. 67) to the 'psychoanalytic object' – namely, the internal world of the other. A part of the personality that occupies a reflective third position in thought is then paralleled by another in which linear time is suspended and someone else's mental life can become our own mental life. This experience is the source of the temptation to succumb to an attitude of having unlimited time at our disposal. We are particularly at risk of falling victim to this temptation at times when the pressure of 'emotional storms and turbulence' becomes too great and arouses the unconscious wish in us to evade something enormously threatening. Just when I passively allow 'it' – that is, precisely this moment – to pass because I am not equal to the task incumbent on me of emotionally withstanding the pull of affective entanglement and of maintaining the capacity for separate experiencing, I have entered into a state in which I have lost sight of reality and hence of time. Now we know that we must first allow ourselves to become involved and entangled; but the acceptance of turbulence is also necessary for subsequently distancing ourselves from the entanglement – and that occasionally appears simply too difficult. If we notice this and in fact cling to our profession with great dedication, we may well at the same time begin to hate that profession.

In addition, I believe too that the regular repetition of the situation in our practice – the coming and going of patients, the beginning and end of sessions, the extended perspectives of analyses that need abundant time – particularly predisposes us to contemplate an end to our own work only on the theoretical level as something for 'later, perhaps', but not to be able to anticipate it as 'my end'. According to Bleger (1967, p. 511), the analytic frame is in effect an institution: 'A relationship which lasts for years, in which a set of norms and attitudes is kept up, is nothing less than a true definition of institution.' He reminds us that institutions to which we belong become a part of our identity and thus lend themselves to serving as a target for the projection of our unresolved primitive symbiotic fantasies. So it is surely understandable that the institution of the 'couch', together with our consulting room and the coming and going of analysands from session to session, can be unconsciously experienced as the unlimited availability of a vital elixir (the good maternal breast).

The final 'no', or the fear of the empty couch

In a discussion of 'psychoanalytic identity' a colleague exclaimed vehemently: 'After all, we remain analysts and training analysts as long as we live!' In his application interview a candidate enthused: 'I'd really like to die behind the couch!' These spontaneous utterances seemingly leave no place for the preparatory experience and acceptance of one's transience and hence ultimately also for the exercise of the analytic function.

For us as psychoanalysts, work on the ageing process includes long-term planning about when to respond to a request by a potential patient or training analysand with a clear 'no' – that is, when to refuse. I must then combine my anticipation of the phase of life represented by old age with vigilant heedfulness and active self-monitoring. How will I feel in three years' time, or seven? Am I confident that I shall retain the capacity to observe and monitor myself in the way that I expect from myself, or know that I can, today? How afraid am I of this final 'no'? How steadfast do I think I shall be if the younger generation do not want to let me go or if a candidate flatters me by saying: 'It was because of you that I came to psychoanalysis in the first place. My fondest wish is to have my training analysis with you too!'? What will a life feel like without the hourly rhythm, without the experience of having my finger on the pulse of life outside, without the vivacity contributed by my young patients and analysands?

This necessity of planning unavoidably confronts us with a balancing inner contemplation of ourselves as whole persons: instead of talking intellectually about the 'interesting subject of transience', how can I apply my analytic capacity to myself and to *my own, my very own, utterly concrete transience*? For a panel discussion at an EPF conference, I asked the then 83-year-old Scandinavian training analyst Frederik Thaulow (Chapter 5 in this book) to speak about his experience of retirement from his profession. He found the decision concerning the final 'no' to be the most difficult of all aspects of ageing and explained: 'It is as if the place behind the couch exerted a kind of pull that is almost impossible to withstand'. It is a pull that promises continuity and is thus in the service of the inner need for 'it' to carry on. Unconscious fantasies of helplessness and immobilisation (Jaques, 1965, p. 507) can be deadened by 'going on' unthinkingly.

If the final 'no' has been successfully pronounced, everything grows still and the couch stays empty. I must now ask myself: who am I when faced with my empty couch? The psychoanalysts mentioned earlier who have written about loneliness regard a sense of one's own identity as the principal form of protection from the inner threat of feelings of loneliness: who am I given the constant dialectic of the constancy of my mental structure and its lifelong transformation? In his definition, Erikson (1951) particularly emphasises the interaction between the subjective perception of one's identity and its perception by others. My own question in this context, however, is: have I succeeded in developing not only a psychoanalytic attitude and identity but also a sense of personal identity that is vital and stable enough for me to be able, when the time comes, to dispense with the transient professional identity that only remains at my disposal, in the form of a surrogate identity, through the active exercise of my profession? And is this the case even if I know perfectly well that our internalised analytic posture has become a part of our personality that will continue to enrich our creativity, albeit not in the consulting room? Do we possess an 'internal couch' that will make it easier for us to relinquish the real couch?

The transience of the analytic toolkit: Attacks on the analyst's feeling and thinking

Our analytic toolkit consists of the unique interaction of our thinking and feeling as an expression of our personality as it develops throughout our lives and absorbs and processes experiences that can be implicitly or explicitly accessed and relived and on which self-critical reflection is up to a point possible. However, if the 'software' of our personality is to be able to unfold and to operate efficiently, the bodily functions that in effect constitute our brain's power supply or 'hardware' must be intact.

We psychoanalysts are accustomed to accommodate mental particularities in the mental domain. We are acquainted with the expression of mental conflicts in the body as psychosomatic manifestations. We are less familiar with the modification of mental processes that may be prompted by physical agencies.

I should now like to draw attention to two difficulties that may arise in the course of ageing, when our bodies undergo gradual and indeed insidious and imperceptible changes that attack our analytic toolkit and may alter our capacity for thinking and reflection on the level of the secondary process and cause it to shift in the direction of primary-process mental functioning. Age-related changes of this kind impair our ability to tolerate emotional turbulences triggered in ourselves, to respond to them with sustained affective resonance and at the same time attentively to observe our own thoughts and feelings. In these circumstances, we risk lapsing into over-hasty action on the level of the primary process without any internal emotional moorings. Modifications of the setting, as well as over-hasty interpretations intended to reas-

26

sure the analyst, or indeed stereotyped interventions neither based on the analyst's thinking and feeling nor related to the patient's actual affect, may cause the analysis to degenerate into an 'as if' or pseudo-analysis. Continuing to go through the motions of analysis in this way has the aim of maintaining a situation that is of vital psychological importance to the analyst because it preserves his internal equilibrium and gives him the illusion of being able to go on working as an analyst.

I shall illustrate this situation with two examples. The first shows how a serious, *life-threatening physical illness* may have the consequence that the perceived inner threat facilitates the illusory non-recognition of our situation with concomitant disavowal of reality; while the second demonstrates the kind of attacks on our thinking, feeling and remembering that may be presented by *dementia-related alterations*.

A colleague from an international society reports the following situation:

> Dr A, a highly esteemed analyst, has reached the age of 69 and is totally involved in his institute and in other professional activities. He is extremely well respected in his society. In this situation he is diagnosed with cancer and undergoes surgery followed by many months of treatment. He does not know what is in store for him; he tells his patients and candidates that he will be away for a while and will show up again eventually. When he resumes work several months later, his colleagues notice drastic psychological changes in him: he seems unable to concentrate, is inclined to lose his temper, cannot accept any opinion other than his own and forgets appointments; sessions arranged with patients and candidates sometimes take place, but then he cancels them again. Despite his wretched appearance, he continues to attend all meetings. In his presence his colleagues have a sense of paralysis that makes it hard for them to contradict his views; at the same time they are unable to say to his face that they are worried about him and his patients and candidates. Nor do they feel capable of approaching the candidates in training analysis with him. After the next extended interruption, which he again introduces by saying that he will show up again eventually, his patient happens to see his obituary in a newspaper.

After the death of her analyst, this patient had asked my colleague for help in coming to terms with the sudden breaking off of her analysis. The patient's memory is of an analyst to whom she had to keep going as if under a compulsion: 'I thought he could not stand a separation and that I would kill him if I were to leave him in this situation'. She recalls her sense of rejection whenever he forgot sessions, opened the door to her unshaven and in his bathrobe, and arranged a new appointment with her. At the same time she was full of rage: 'He'd been marked by death for a long time, so why couldn't he face up to his situation? After all, he knew about the separation traumas that brought me into analysis in the first place, so why did he have to do that to me? The same thing all over again, only this time much worse!'

This example is intended to indicate how infinitely difficult we find it to cope with the irrefutable reality of a serious or indeed life-threatening disease. On the one hand we should like to observe the rule of abstinence and give away as little as possible of our personal situation, while on the other the pressure of the illness may have the effect that the analytic capacity that we always knew to be at our disposal in the past is now so badly affected that our critical self-reflection and containment fail us. Dr A seems to have been assailed by such overwhelming anxiety that the only recourse open to him was absolute disavowal. He reassured *himself* by justifying his continuing to work on the grounds that he could not abandon his patients, but was incapable of seeing that he was misusing his patients in order to go on basking behind the couch in the comforting illusion of a future without end. The patient mentioned above found herself in a situation in which the increasing neediness of her analyst resulted in a reversal of the 'caring function': the analyst uses (or misuses) his patients for the purposes of mental survival, while the patient is trapped in what is now an exclusive relationship with a needy parent. Dr A's colleagues colluded with his disavowal. His defence was seemingly so powerful that it paralysed their critical self-analytic faculties too. Years later the colleague who had taken on the abandoned patient revealed to me that psychoanalysis had been Dr A's great passion in life. He had devoted himself to it body and soul and it subsequently emerged that he had had hardly any friends apart from his professional colleagues. He must have died a very lonely man.

Many analysts who have overcome a serious illness attempt to describe the resulting subjective experiences and problems of treatment technique in publications. Without exception they report an intense sense of shame that prevented them from talking about their condition to colleagues (e.g. Abend, 1982, 1986; Eissler, 1975; Halpert, 1982; Lasky, 1992). They mostly adduce the conscious concern that no more patients would be referred to them, but I see this rather as a projective defence against the great anxiety that would be aroused by allowing the theoretically familiar concept of transience to be transformed into recognition of *their own* finitude – that is, against tolerating the pain of being separated from the ideal good object (the 'good breast') and excluded from the parental relationship in the Oedipal situation. I have often heard colleagues ask rhetorically – as it were, with a hand in front of their mouth – whether the illness might not in fact be a token of an inadequate analysis. I see this as confirming my presumption that we analysts can readily succumb to the temptation to elevate 'our' psychoanalysis to the status of an omnipotent object that can make us immune to the onslaughts of life's realities.

All the authors who have reported on their illnesses experienced these caesuras as seismic shocks to their previously familiar inner equilibrium, felt subjectively to be an attack on their mental and intellectual constitution, emotional stability and capacity to think, clothed in fantasies of earlier experiences and suffering. We combat these threats with the forms of defence that belong to our individual character. Precisely because somatic disorders, even before they are diagnosed, are often expressed unconsciously in the mental sphere – by an intensification of familiar character traits – we are misled into disregarding the possibility of a physical illness and into concentrating exclusively on the psychological situation. However, in so doing we ignore the likelihood of a transfer to the mental level in the form of a projection of the body into consciousness (Freud, 1923, p. 25). Acknowledgement of the bodily source of the disturbance is essential if we are to plan ahead as necessary.

The second threat to our ability to work as good-enough analysts is in my view the onset of *dementing processes*. As everyone knows, dementia is an irreversible degeneration of the mental and intellectual faculties. The first symptoms often overlap with the normal changes inherent in ageing, so that differential diagnosis in the case of forgetfulness, lack of concentration, declining stamina and emotional instability may be difficult. Such losses, perceived from within, have 'character-syntonic' mental effects in the form of a reinforcement of proven defensive measures. The manifest, unequivocal onset of symptoms of dementia is frequently preceded by depressive mood swings extending over a number of years. I have described the possible accompanying subtle emotional changes in my contribution on the psychoanalytic diagnosis of incipient dementia via the countertransference (Junkers, 2007b). The attempt to preserve the formal aspects becomes paramount, while the capacity for emotional reception and also expression grows increasingly shallow. Affected individuals who sense that they are becoming forgetful do not want anyone to notice that something is amiss. Anxiety and shame, as well as disappointment and anger, in the face of this situation may lead to the development of an 'as if' façade of mental life intended to conceal how we really feel. Bayley (1999) and Suter (2003) have given impressive descriptions of such a process. Here is a further example, supplied by a colleague from another international society:

> A candidate is in the second half of her training when her highly valued training analyst gradually exhibits significant changes. She experiences him as mentally absent, he forgets things she has previously reported, he falls asleep more and more often in her sessions, and occasionally he reacts with seemingly inappropriate vehemence. Under intense inner pressure she turns to experienced colleagues for advice, but they refer her back to her training analyst: she should discuss the problem with him. However, she now knows that that is impossible, but cannot make anyone understand her distress. A year later her training analyst has a stroke, which leaves him unable to speak. After one more year she completes her training analysis in the old people's home to which her training analyst has moved; he has recovered his faculty of speech to a limited extent only.

In each of these selected cases, our sick colleague was convinced that he was doing the right thing. The onslaughts of the ageing process on the bodily basis of our capacity to work have the effect of impairing understanding and memory, the *sine qua non* of our profession, and cause our faculty of critical self-reflection to fail. As colleagues of the affected person we as a rule accept the collusive role in which we are cast and espouse his subjective vision, which admits of no dissent. By usually remaining passive and silent, we become accessories to something we know to be harmful. We know that our primary responsibility is to our patients and training candidates. So why do we not act accordingly, but instead put our generativity at risk?

In our psychoanalytic societies we live within a network of projections, unresolved transferences, friendships and also hostile relationships. If our training analyst has remained active after the completion of our training, we shall never have had to separate from him or her fully. Old wounds that we carry with us are often associated with ambivalence towards our parents. We would rather let our valued colleague destroy his laboriously acquired reputation by the current changed behaviour due to his illness than summon up the courage to oppose his powerful illusion of 'acting for the best'.

I have found in exchanges with European colleagues that perplexity is everywhere the rule the more it becomes clear that a colleague is no longer working as a good-enough analyst. We should all prefer to tolerate the situation, to keep silent and to wait, so as to protect our colleague whose actions no longer conform to reality by not disturbing with our criticism his conviction that he is doing good work. Because we believe that this colleague will be unable to stand the truth and will turn away from us, we abandon him to a situation in which he is damaging himself, his life's work and in particular his patients and candidates, whom he may even be retraumatising. We are especially paralysed if the individual concerned is one of the senior figures in our society or institute.

Transience and the analytic institution

We are bound to recognise today that the previously familiar balance of our institution, which comes alive only through its members, is at risk of attack by transience. Fewer and fewer young academics are interested in our psychoanalytic training, while statutory and professional requirements place us under enormous pressure to adapt. Lastly, the conditions of our work within our institutions have been modified by demographic change, with an increasing number of older members, more and more of whom are living to a very advanced age, as against fewer and fewer young colleagues: we are an ageing trade. Klockars (Chapter 12 in this book) gives a full account of the results of the survey conducted at my instigation within the European Psychoanalytical Federation (EPF).

Why have we dispensed with parting rituals in the evolution of our institutions notwithstanding a wide variety of restructuring operations? It is in my view because we as a group, as if under the sway of a taboo, are unable to share with each other an internal representation of the significance for us of old age and the end of our professional and biological lives. This is I believe borne out by a survey of European training analysts' assessment of their training activity in relation to the personal course of their lives: not one of the respondents touched on or mentioned the subjects of ageing, retirement or death. This scotomisation of a fact of life helps us to understand why, on the one hand, we have problems with bidding farewell to working behind the couch and, on the other, why we have been unable to address this changed life situation institutionally. It also explains why we have been unable to muster the courage, in terms of professional ethics, to protect the patients of our older, sick colleagues, as well as the colleagues themselves, from the harmful consequences of their illness.

Hardly any European society recommends an age limit for retirement from analytic practice; the German limit of 68 years on practising under the statutory health insurance scheme has now been dropped by the association of statutory health insurance fund practitioners. Although many societies would like to set age limits for the acceptance of training analyses (the recommendations range between 65 and 75 years), there are no fixed rules. Where recommendations exist, they are often not observed; in particular, colleagues are reluctant to remind highly respected psychoanalysts of the relevant limit. We have not so far formulated any structural provisions for a 'fair' division of labour between the generations in our societies; we have not to date developed a shared vision of how to make the older members' enormous reservoir of knowledge and experience available for use by the entire group, and in particular its younger members. In my view, we lack guidelines concerning responsibility for our patients and especially our training candidates in terms of the possible age-related limitation of the capacity to conduct analyses, so as to avoid harming the transmission of psychoanalysis and hence psychoanalysis itself.

After all, let me categorically stress that it is not analysts' age that constitutes a problem, but instead the possible, but not inevitable, repercussions of physical restrictions on analytic work. In my experience it is not enough for me to say to my colleagues and friends: 'Tell me when it is time for me to go'. I have now come to the conclusion that it is the responsibility of the institution to help contain problems that may not be amenable to individual solution. We must open up spaces within our institution to enable us to mourn together for the things to which we must bid farewell for the sake of our analytic survival, so that we can make way creatively for the new. Whenever I have communicated these concerns of mine to colleagues, the result has been an embarrassed silence, or else they have remarked: 'Yes, later perhaps; you need to be very careful with such things'. Why?

I have shown that ensuring the observance of clear boundaries in our treatments involves repeated hard work within ourselves; similarly hard work on the part of our psychoanalytic organisation is entailed by, on the one hand, the *need* to scotomise transience in order to be able to transmit that which has evolved and is valued and, on the other, the need to guarantee generativity. We today are called upon to confer new forms and structures on the coexistence of the different generations so as to protect our posterity, our candidates and patients and to spare our older colleagues damage to their hard-earned reputations.

Only in this way can we permit old and new, young and old, to come into contact with each other within secure boundaries. By means of these considerations I should like to initiate a debate on these issues, so that they are not relegated to the uncertain realm of a possible future enshrined in the phrase 'later, perhaps . . .'

Notes

1 Alexander Mitscherlich, for instance, writes about his 'quite unhappy childhood', in which he experienced his father as 'brutal and humiliating [. . .] the biggest source of anxiety in my childhood' (in: *Ein Leben für die Psychoanalyse*. 1983, Frankfurt: Suhrkamp [translated]). Other examples can be found in Herrmanns (1992) *Psychoanalyse in Selbstdarstellungen*.

2 Danielle Quinodoz and I, each in our respective language area, were engaging in similar reflections at about the same time and reached similar conclusions: she uses the phrase 'the work of growing old', whereas my own term is 'work on the ageing process'.

4

PSYCHOANALYST

A profession for an immortal?

Paul Denis

> And all the days of Methuselah were nine hundred sixty and nine years:
> and he died.
>
> [. . .]
>
> And it came to pass, when men began to multiply on the face of the
> earth, and daughters were born unto them, that the sons of God saw
> the daughters of men that they were fair; and they took them wives of
> all which they chose. And the LORD said, My Spirit shall not always
> strive with man, for that he also is flesh: yet his days shall be a hundred
> and twenty years.
>
> (Genesis 5:27; 6:1–3)

To his colleagues who were concerned about the increasing age of candidates for psychoanalytic training, an experienced psychoanalyst gladly told them: 'Psychoanalysis is a profession for the old'. Indeed, it has probably always been – in the sense that one speaks of 'my elders' when speaking of one's parents – and it is unlikely that one can become a psychoanalyst at 20 years of age. That said, Loewenstein was not yet 30 years old when he settled in Paris to help found the Paris Psychoanalytic Society, and many of its members have had institutional training responsibilities at around 35 years of age; their dynamism has been considerable and their output remarkable. It should also be borne in mind that Maurice Bouvet was not even 49 years old when he died. So, is psychoanalysis a profession for the young or a profession for the old? Clinical experience and the simple experience of the difficulties of life itself can only favour the practice of psychoanalysis, but does the youth of an analyst not have some advantages, and can one remain a psychoanalyst indefinitely regardless of the circumstances?

Clinical memories come back to me, too many. First, that of a patient whose psychoanalyst had become insane due to senility. He experienced many nightmarish months before understanding what was happening, and before really becoming conscious of the state that his analyst was in; a state that he no more wished to see than the entourage of the analyst himself, an entourage that eventually finished, however, by putting a stop to the activity of the practitioner who had become incapable. And another example, almost the inverse, as it concerned a young analyst without any apparent intellectual impediment whose patient, during sessions, reported experiencing pain located where the scars of a serious intervention marked the face of the analyst: 'The left of my head . . .' the patient exclaimed; something that the analyst could not relate to as he had, in his heroism of resisting a mortal illness, thought that the makeup to cover the scars of his surgery was imperceptible.

Another example: the case that one of our colleagues remembers as a trauma that she struggled to overcome, the saga of the haemoptysis that her analyst, John Leuba, stricken with pulmonary cancer, gave her when she visited to find out how he was.

Caught in another form of medical misfortune, slowly evolving but fatal, a highly regarded analyst, knowing that he only had a few years left, tried to hasten the termination of his patients' analyses, inducing some of them to seek psychoanalytic training with, no doubt, the fantasy of living on through his analytic descendants. I may die, but my way of analysis will not disappear if my patients become psychoanalysts after me; thus, a part of me at least will escape death. The unconscious fantasy driving such behaviour could well be: my immortal psychoanalytic soul will be carried onwards by my former patients who have become psychoanalysts. The fantasy of 'analytic affiliations' is a powerful one, and certainly a behavioural motor.

Whether it relates to great old age, to too great an age or illness, the question is obviously that of the relationship with death; the rapport of a psychoanalyst to the event, that is to say, the denied certainty of his own death.

It is not clear why psychoanalysts should be any different from other individuals whom Freud has shown us inasmuch as their unconscious ignores their mortal character: 'our unconscious, then, does not believe in its own death; it behaves as if it were immortal . . . This may be the secret of heroism' (1915). The heroism of the psychoanalyst who knows that he is suffering a mortal disease in the relatively short-term and who continues to receive his patients? In any case, it is too obvious that the examples mentioned above, and indeed many others, oblige us to understand that many psychoanalysts at the end of their lives behave as if they were immortal.

The unconscious idea that psychoanalysis confers a kind of immortality is actually quite common; Paul A. Dewald (1982) puts it, not without humour: 'I would guess that many analysts harbor a fantasy that their own personal analysis has "immunized" them against some of the diseases that afflict others . . . experience demonstrates that analysts can and do have serious and life-threatening illnesses'. This fantasy of being protected from disease by psychoanalysis is sometimes underpinned by a conscious consideration stemming from the experience of psychosomaticiens: because it develops the psychic elaboration of the analysand-analyst and promotes psychosomatic homeostasis, psychoanalysis protects against somatisation and somatosis and provides a form of psychosomatic immunity, a 'psycho-immunity' that renders us invulnerable. A serious illness of the analyst, therefore, inflicts simultaneously two narcissistic wounds: one results in a banal impairment of his physical integrity, and the other affects his illusions concerning the protective value of his analysis in psychosomatic terms.

The paucity of articles relating directly or indirectly to the possible, imminent or actual death of an analyst is striking. One must essentially refer to an ancient article by Gregory Zilboorg (1938), which deals with the fantasy of immortality in a way that accords well with the question of the drives in the middle (or end . . .) of life, and a paper by K. R. Eissler of 1975: 'Possible Effects of Aging on the Practice of Psychoanalysis', which is the only one of its kind on this topic. (This is discussed by Balter, 1977, at a meeting of the New York Psychoanalytic Society.)

The ageing of the analyst

Let us first dwell on the contents of the article by K. R. Eissler. For him, ageing causes an increase in narcissistic investment. He distinguishes schematically three possible situations: if the narcissism of the analyst is based on his superego, the analyst becomes more rigid, more obsessive, and more intolerant in his practice (this is a scenario that it is possible to observe quite often). If this increase of narcissism is focused on the ego, the analyst will expect admiration, reverence and respect from the patient. Obviously, these attitudes have an influence – negative, although the author does not say it – on the analytical work of the patient and the analysability of his transference. But a note of optimism is expressed in a scenario that would be better: if the increase in narcissism is in fact so evenly distributed (which would help reduce the pressure of the id and hence the conflict) the superego and the id would be more harmonious. This would result in a greater tolerance of the analyst to the illness of the patient, a reduction in therapeutic ambition, and a greater acceptance of the ordinary human character of the patient. This would therefore be a privilege of age. Additionally, due to the decrease in activity which tends to accompany ageing and the greater interest in knowledge and insight that increases with age, a better attitude towards the resistances of the patient would develop. Ageing also increases interest in childhood memories, and the ageing analyst may have a greater empathy in relation to the child that the patient has been when it reappears during analysis. So far, in summary, the advantages and disadvantages offset one another; a form of wisdom provided by age can improve analytical functioning. But for Eissler, beyond a certain time, the ageing process means that death becomes an issue that affects life, with all its attendant consequences. However, for him, if the analyst has integrated that death is a necessity, he will be able to deal with the inevitable as a factor of the life of the patient, and also be better able to help analyse his fears and death wishes. Yet, not without wisdom, he advises us that *we must remain appearing heroic in the eyes of the patient*. For a patient to think that he has a heroic analyst is likely to reduce the esteem that he has for himself and arouse in him reactions of guilt. Women analysts would be more successful at this because of their better integration of passivity.

In addition to the reduction of memory that can be only very imperfectly compensated by taking notes, another disturbing factor – emotional this time – for the analyst who is ageing is that he starts to witness his contemporaries dying, which leads him to a greater investment in his patients, an over-investment that can have either a positive or negative effect on the quality of their analysis.

Overall, Eissler believes that ageing decreases the therapeutic power of the analyst, while analysts, as a group, prefer to consider that this power is better for the lack of being bigger. For him, the essential is that two inevitable consequences follow from the ageing of the analyst, each posing their own specific technical problems: First, the probability that the analyst dies unexpectedly during the analyses of his patients increases with age, which, in this case, leads to a series of practical implications: what to do with the dead analyst's patients, etc. The other consequence that he sees – which is no doubt ultimately more difficult to deal with – is that the analyst dies slowly during his patients' analyses. In this circumstance, a heroic stance by the analyst is not beneficial for the patient. He recommends addressing the issue with the patient, continuing the analysis for some time so that the patient can express his feelings and fantasies in relation to what is happening, and then sending the patient to a colleague. According to his experience, it is very important that the patient continues his treatment with this new analyst whilst the first is still alive. The validity of this provision, which poses a sort of last desire of the analyst for his patient, was discussed by some authors who believe that it cannot be of general value and that a policy involving a break, leaving a place for grieving and a possible future recovery of the analysis, has its value. A wise counsel, and on which a consensus is forming, in any case emerges: the need to establish an early termination. Rachelle Dattner (1989), in the journal she devoted to the death of the analyst, cites an article by Kaplan and Rothman (1986) based on the clinical notes of the dead therapist, and also on interviews conducted one and a half years after the death of Rothman, an article that Kaplan concludes: 'despite all good intentions, the communication of a terminal illness becomes obscure unless a planned termination of treatment takes place. Otherwise, the therapist is denying his or her own illness and the patient cannot accept the reality either'.

Despite the interest of its wise position, Eissler's article remains limited in its considerations, in particular because it does not evoke the fantasy world of the analyst and its implications in the treatment of the situation.

Serious illness of the analyst and countertransference

What appears in the analyst obliged to stop his activity because of serious illness can be illuminated by analogy with certain psychic impulses susceptible to appear in an analyst faced with the possibility of his death due to age. An experience like this has been reported in two separate articles by two psychoanalysts in 1982, Paul A. Dewald and Sander M. Abend. Both of them were struck by serious illness, they noted their countertransference reactions and established their difficulties in handling the reality of the situation of the interruption of their patients' analyses.

Abend writes, for example: 'we would not intentionally ask our patients to be caring, sympathetic, and concerned about us, but telling them of our troubles may be a subtle way of doing just that. The regressive impact of pain, illness, injury, and danger can influence us unconsciously to invite such responses'.

Dewald describes, thus, one aspect of the consequences of the information transmitted to his patients about the reality of his situation:

as the patients found out about the severity of my illness and where I was hospitalized, some of them sent cards, flowers, or other signs of interest, concern, and sympathy. One patient, for example, wrote several lengthy letters offering suggestions and advice in regard to the medical treatment of infectious disease. Several others came to my hospital room in an effort to see me, and others asked questions of my friends and colleagues regarding my condition. The countertransference issues stimulated by these behaviors revolved around the question of the reversal of roles.

Note here the issue of role reversal caused by illness. Excessive age of the analyst can induce the same movement.

Even though he had taken the decision not to give his patients any element of reality justifying his absence, Abend found that he was not able to maintain his policy and that he felt countertransferentially pushed to break the rule he had imposed:

as I regained a more usual state of mind, I was profoundly impressed by the fact that it had proven impossible to do as I had intended with the majority of my analytic patients. In fact, I had ended by doing exactly as Dewald and many other colleagues had done, that is, I had attempted to assess each patient's needs on an individual basis. In retrospect, however, I believe that my assessments were neither accurate nor objective. I can only reach the conclusion that my own countertransferences, rather than a correct appraisal of what was best for each patient's analysis, decided me to provide factual information.

The testimonies of Abend and Dewald confirm what less strictly observed examples suggest: the situation is impossible. The analyst is confronted, despite himself, with a double bind as, on the one hand, he wants to 'remain an analyst' but is unable to do so precisely because he is injured in his operational capacities, and because he introduces, despite himself, a foreign body – psychoanalytically foreign – into the mind of the patient simply because of the sudden interruption, whether it is accompanied by factual information or not. As regards the patient, he is also subject to a double bind situation because his fantasies meet a reality that deprives him of the situation in which they could be developed.

Abend emphasised very well the contradictory nature of the explanations given in the name of reality:

it is artificial to attempt to separate analysands' "realistic" perceptions, thoughts, worries, and judgments about the analyst and the analytic situation from unconsciously determined transference reactions. This is not to deny that there are real events which have an impact on the analytic situation, or that analysands, as well as analysts, possess the capacity to perceive and think about things realistically. I mean merely to emphasize that what is "real" for every patient is what that patient observes, feels, thinks, wishes, fears, wonders about, and decides by means of the operations of a mental apparatus of which the unconscious component is invariably a significant part, just as is true for every analyst.

What the analyst transmits of 'reality' is tainted by his own personal fantasies and anxieties but also regressive unconscious needs: 'at times it may actually be easier on the analyst to make patients privy to his or her personal plight than it would be to deal with patients' fully expressed fantasies and feelings'. This remark seems essential; the analyst wounded in his being and in his psychic functioning – and particularly in his countertransference – may prefer to try to channel the expression of the emotions and ideas of his patient by giving him factual information to avoid the emotional backlash, on himself, of this expression.

As Dewald wrote: 'the therapeutic problem lies in the need adequately to explore the full gamut of patients' responses, affects, and associations to the illness, and to do this in the face of countertransference temptations either defensively to promote premature closure and evasion of more threatening affects, or to use the experience for exhibitionistic, masochistic, narcissistic or other neurotic satisfactions'. Could we not also talk about the sadism that can exist in presenting oneself almost dying in front of a patient? And in the exhibitionism of dying in public, as with the case of Molière on stage?

The unconscious research for compensations for serious illness or old age inevitably occurs in significant fashion as soon as the analyst has become aware of his condition, and the pitfalls of the analytic situation are therefore numerous. I shall quote Abend here again:

> It seems advisable to consider the potential countertransference motives for modifying the principle of abstinence in such situations . . . What is the beneficial effect of revealing anything more informative than the fact of interruption and the scheduling of the resumption of sessions? What is the basis for deciding that specific information relieves unbearable anxiety? . . . The transmission of factual information about the analyst's illness subserves unconscious needs in the analyst which may not always be recognized and acknowledged. This is so even when the analyst is convinced it is technically correct to provide such information.

What Abend is speaking about is a *modification of the principle of abstinence*, a term that should be strongly emphasised. Without directly employing the term, Abend in fact defines as seduction the rupture of analytical reserve that should leave the patient the freedom of his imagination. Dewald's patients, with their flowers and letters, had also interpreted as seduction what was given to them as information; they not only felt authorised but encouraged to come forward.

Role reversal and rupture of the rule of abstinence, that is to say seduction, are the risks that are posed to his patients by the analyst who becomes ill, or by the analyst whose clearly excessive age is information, if not a secret, only to himself.

And what about the paralysis of all the different forms of sadism imposed on the patient by his perception of the analyst's state? If one does not kick a man when he is down one does not kick an injured doctor either.

The fantasy of immortality

The courage of Freud in facing illness, pain and death has given an example to each of us which is hard to elaborate. He lived and worked for 17 years with his tumour of the jaw; almost to the end. But did he not at the end of the road take, him the first, his patients as a support, in addition to Anna? Was the development of the 'death drive' when he had his own daughter on the sofa not one of the reaction formations necessary for rejecting the incestuous fantasies that could assail him? Does the place, less and less hypothetical and more and more important, assigned to the death drive in his writings as his health declined, not testify to an effort against the reinforcement of his incestuous fantasies compared with the love he bore his patients? Have the reversal of the therapeutic relationship and the rupture of the rule of abstinence due to the illness of the analyst in the examples cited not also had their equivalent in the case of the father of psychoanalysis?

The obscure perception of the risks run by the analyst and the patient when the analyst approaches a too possible death, a perception that would be the effect of the principle of reality, should lead practitioners of psychoanalysis to stop 'early enough'; some do succeed in doing this. For others, a form of denial becomes established that installs in them the psychic status of immortals.

'I know very well that I am too old, or at risk of dying unexpectedly – or being stricken by an illness that could kill me within a few months – but I still keep receiving my patients as before'. 'I know very well, but nevertheless . . .' The division installed in this way aims to avoid 'self-mourning', to use the term of Christian David (1996). A loss of identity, self-mourning would trigger in the psychoanalyst the renunciation of his activities and the investment in his patients. But it also means the loss of the challenge to elaborate what imposes on him the stimulation of the sessions, to the loss of pleasure in the analytic functioning.

In the story entitled 'The Immortal', Borges (1949) describes the strange fate of a man who has become immortal by contagion after he has reached the land of the immortals: 'the story I told seems unreal because in it are mixed the events of two different men'. Here, the two different men are the psychoanalyst in good health and the psychoanalyst transformed by illness or old age. The division is established between the psychoanalyst, a timeless man and therefore immortal – psychoanalysis, like germ cells, can be immortal as long as it is transmitted – and man, mortal and perishable, that serves as the support. There comes a day when one does not want to recognise the other. It would ideally be the role for a 'Wild Bunch' group of psychoanalysts to intervene, but how? To close in the immortal this division that carries the risk of damaging his patients. But assuming that the ageing of analysts is such that the number of 'immortals' becomes the majority, would we not enter into a strangely divided world in which the idea of immortality is implicitly accepted? 'Taught by centuries of living, the republic of immortal men had achieved a perfection of tolerance, almost of disdain. They knew that over an infinitely long span of time, all things happen to all men', wrote Borges. If 'to infinite waiting, here below, all may come', each delay is acceptable and any reprieve favourable.

But this idea of 'self-mourning', could it not be too general? What fantasy world created by the risk of death must be suppressed or repressed by its negation? The attack on the body through illness, by pain, by the excess of ageing, induces revolt, counter-attack, the temptation of submission and its refusal. Maintaining this movement within the limits of the ego risks leading to a form of melancholy: self-denial and deflection of the exterior on others is a possible solution. Patients can only become the target of raised sadomasochistic impulses, or counter-investments established to preserve them.

Zilboorg (1938), in his study of the fantasies of immortality, notes that 'all the pre-genital cathexes, particularly the sadistic ones, which are taken over by the superego to use as munitions against man's instinctual freedom are refunded to him, since he agrees to accept immortality in exchange for his total genitality'. It would be fascinating to work on the comparison of the ideal without immortal life, which dominates the mystical conversion of the individual and the ideas developed in different social Utopias, or the ideals born of social demands. The link between 'immortality' and revival of pregenital and sadistic impulses is thus emphasised.

Another way of considering the fantasy of immortality from the instinctual aspect, which combines a necrophilic impulse with 'an obscure but persistent preoccupation with immortality', is given by Tauber (1982). For him, the term necrophilic covers a preferential investment in inanimate objects, a hostility to change which aims to suspend time. The analogy with the idea of Bertram Lewin, following which the ideal patient for a doctor is the one on which he has complete power similar to the cadaver that he dissects, suggests an association between power and immortality certainly, but also the fact that the sadomasochistic regression induced by illness or old age reinforces such fantasies of which the outcome during countertransference is subject to an activity of repression or intense repression. Behind necrophilia, incest . . . a form of vampirism, develops: an over-investment in patients, necessary for remaining psychically alive despite the threat of death, is analogous to a depressive over-investment of the shadow of the object that we have lost; the patients that we can no longer follow are patients that we will lose as love objects. The dying analyst clings all the more to them as a source of life to draw upon. The psychic resources of the patients deplete and their analyst becomes for them a vampirising object similar to those described by Perel Wilgowicz. The analyst, in fact, under the veil of a good professional conscience, searches for an expression of emotion or pain from his patients; a proof of love and a rejuvenation cure. The anguish of the patients then takes the place of 'those baths of blood that come to us from Rome and which the powerful bring to mind in their final days' (Baudelaire, 2006).

The denial of feelings of hatred towards patients who are going to survive us is a requirement to continue to receive them without them fleeing. The latent content, 'they will continue to live; they discard me when I need them to deny that I am dying, to confirm myself as immortal', reverses itself thus: 'I am not going to let them drop whilst they still need me'. Repressed sadism is expressed in the exhibitionist act of illness or excessive old age. Chronos devours his children; in fact, to avoid being devoured by time and to deny fate, one must be nourished by one's patients and identify with time itself, identify with the aggressor Chronos, immortal by nature.

Could we not consider, in the analyst who will die, a psychoanalytic form of a 'work of demise' as described by Michel de M'Uzan (1977)? The libidinous urge that accompanies it would lead the dying analyst to a behaviour that takes possession of his patients by the exhibition of his death, an enactment of a sexual seduction finally permitted by the fate that embraces him, an ultimate incest under the mantle of the approaching night . . .

5

GROWING OLDER AS AN ANALYST

Problems of ethics and practice based on personal experience[1]

Johan Fredrik Thaulow

'To be or not to be, that is the question.' To an octogenarian analyst and psychotherapist the problem inherent in this centuries-old question becomes increasingly acute. What is gained and what is lost in becoming old? Am I a help or a burden? Is my mind sufficiently perceptive to continue practising as a therapist?

Reason and experience tell me that I still ought to undergo supervision or 'sidevision'. But, when glancing around at my colleagues in my own country I must ask myself in whom I confide? Who would tell me, and make me accept that 'enough is enough'; that it is time to let go of my identity as a therapist, and that I should settle into my new existence?

I have sought in vain for guidance in old articles, in Freud's *Analysis Terminable and Interminable*, for instance. Finally, it was the advice I sought for this chapter from one younger therapist and another of my own generation which was to prove helpful. Both are colleagues in whom I have confidence, and who are aware of my strengths and weaknesses. Aside from these last, I must confess to a sense of loneliness as an old psychotherapist. On the whole, the few patients and candidates I have maintained for supervision are impressed about my age and the 'breadth' of my experience. This may all seem very flattering, but such remarks remain empty unless examined more closely. Bearing this in mind, and in the hope that it may serve both as a corrective and secure point of departure for our discussion, I have decided to make a note of my reflections here.

Drawing on my own experiences, the present chapter focuses on two types of problem that seem pertinent to this discussion. The first is what we might call *the therapist's outer limitations*, as imposed on us by society and institutions, while the second relates to *our inner limitations*, and our own, not to be overlooked, potential.

I would first like to point out just a few of the limitations regarding the first of these problem types, leaving the rest to later discussion.

I find it right and proper that when the day comes the authorities should inform me when 'enough is enough', though, naturally, I hope to be the first to recognize the signs.

Noticing changes or conditions in a colleague we deem professionally untenable or damaging to our patients is an especially sensitive affair. Occasionally, we may observe how the capacity for self-criticism has been slowly, almost imperceptibly, diminished in a colleague or friend who has otherwise enjoyed considerable respect. I once enquired of a dear friend and colleague as to how I should convey to my colleague that he is no longer capable of continuing work as a therapist. Her answer was brief and concise, 'tell him!' It was easy for her, whose authority is based on real empathy and care for others. We might argue that if this abrupt 'tell him!' comes from the heart as well as from the head, then the chances of forming an alliance are good, as they are in so many other impersonal relations. Of course, this is not easy in a serious situation.

Another outer constraint is the automatic loss of authorization to practise as a medical doctor in Norway beyond the age of 75. One is entitled to apply for an extension, which may be granted for a period of up to one year at a time. All applications for an extension of the right to practise are submitted to a central office in the Ministry of Health – in short, a bureaucracy far removed from practice. This bureaucratic model allows little scope for the care and kindness to which the person excluded also has a right, particularly within a field professing to acknowledge the supreme importance of human qualities. In my view, the associations connected with various professions ought to be involved in such evaluations, thereby guaranteeing a more individualized assessment of the applicant. Over the many years as a medical expert at the Ministry of Health, I have noticed the extent to which the evaluation is susceptible to subjective 'interpretations' and prejudices. This is particularly true in cases of sexual abuse by a professional, where reactions from the Ministry of Health may be subjective and dangerously at variance with one another.

Now let us turn to the second problem area, which we might refer to as *our inner problems*, such as those of an elderly therapist and his problems with regard to initiating and concluding different work-related tasks? It is tempting, indeed, to begin new projects, and flattering still to be asked. However, caressing the narcissist within may lead to a somewhat superficial diagnostic assessment. It is doubtless of major importance for us to be capable of acknowledging our limitations, above all, by not accepting tasks beyond our powers. Becoming older, however, may have different implications for an analyst than it does for other psychotherapists. Those whose approach tends to be more eclectic may easily be carried away by non-critical, personal experiences of life. A taste of omnipotence begins to set in consequently making it increasingly difficult to maintain analytical neutrality. The eclectic approach in psychotherapy is becoming increasingly widespread. The psychoanalyst, however, finds it easier to follow 'the written word', to stay close to the book, as it were, while others may prefer their own writing, which may involve greater risks and lead us astray.

Terminating a course of therapy naturally creates problems; for the elderly therapist, however, it is more important to master the art of understanding and of knowing when and when *not* to begin a new therapy. Tempting challenges may evolve into a battle between narcissism and realism, where realism is not always the victor. We no longer tackle challenges the way we used to. This is in part due to altered intellectual capacity, and partly owing to sheer lack of time. Work can no longer be conducted safely according to the *perspective of eternity*, and I have always insisted that therapy takes the time it needs.

I have always made this clear to my patients from the outset. Working according to what I have dubbed 'calendar' termination, i.e. stopping at a given date or season of the year, has proved utterly incompatible with psychodynamic thinking. Termination in so-called short-term therapies, where one works towards the clearly defined goal of symptom relief, may be acceptable. My basic principle has been that the chief responsibility for the therapy rests with the patient – much like the captain of a ship, where the pilot functions as a responsible supervisor.

I also have compared psychodynamic psychotherapy with child rearing, where the parents' greatest challenge is to teach the child to take responsibility for its own life. The real foundations of successful therapy lie in the effort to make the patient gradually assume control over his/her own life – a process that may demand considerable discipline from an ambitious therapist. As an octogenarian it has proved easier to allow therapies the time they need, to some extent because the number of patients waiting to begin treatment has diminished. But it must be made clear from the outset that time is no longer an unlimited therapeutic asset. The perspective of eternity has lost its validity. To have enough time has become a limited asset. By contrast, as far as I am concerned, with a relatively limited practice, terminating therapies has come naturally; in other words, allowing my analysands enough time for recognition, recollection and working through.

In this respect, I have been lucky. I also believe that the art of therapy in our age lies less in handling termination than it does in avoiding taking on too much work. New patient challenges are tempting for a person who has been doing psychotherapy all his/her life. By and large, termination has been natural, as it were. Perhaps, one reason is that the patient has been playing first violin in our complex interpersonal orchestra – especially in the last movement.

But there have been surprises.

A gifted artist came for therapy, lay down on the couch and talked incessantly for eight or ten sessions. She then rose, happy and contented, before thanking me for my assistance and leaving. Doubtless, she let quite a few sleeping dogs lie.

A young man who came to me complaining of potency problems and a very strict father broke off after three sessions, claiming that he saw little point in talking to someone who was much older than him, namely me. Not without severe misgivings, I then called him about a year later and asked him how he was. He said that he was much better, but that he could hardly remember who I was. Was it important and appropriate to permit these two patients to finish therapy without so much as posing a question or raising an objection? I think it was.

Whenever a patient has asked me about the right time to stop therapy, I have almost always answered that we shall both know when the time is right. I think that such a reply underlines my confidence in the patient's ability to govern his own life – an answer that has become easier to give as time passes! I sometimes believe that I have been lucky, but I do think that the most important factor has been a tacit insistence on patient responsibility, his/her life and destiny; not mine. I have sometimes employed a useful metaphor: therapy is like two planets moving in opposite directions and different orbits. At a given moment they enter into each other's gravitational field. After a period of reciprocal influence, they then alter course before once again sallying forth into their respective orbits.

I always ask new patients who have come to me more recently whether they are aware of my age. The common response is, 'but you have so much experience!' Indeed, a seductive response for an old and experienced therapist, and one that easily brings us 'from know-how to nowhere', as a philosopher friend once put it.

One of the other benefits of increasing age is that transference/countertransference themes are less persistent and risky, at least as far as erotic transference is concerned. It loses some if its power and intensity as therapeutic material. This is, perhaps, wishful thinking. But I have experienced that the patient somehow seems to finish it early in therapy, and that I myself am no longer so eager to get hold of it. Other, more insistent existential problems seem more relevant. Perhaps we sail into more tranquil waters the older we become. Or is this the self-deception of my old age?

Yet another benefit of advanced age is the greater tranquillity for both patient and therapist. It is more important to be wise than clever. It gives more space for what I think is fundamental to all therapies, namely, to create suitable conditions for the patient to become slowly reconciled to his/her old and fairly useless introjects before establishing new, more appropriate ones with the support of the therapist. Perhaps, this is all theoretical oversimplification, and simply my wish to find unambiguous and universal explanations. This, I think, is where the question as to duration of a course of therapy again assumes relevancy as a problem.

Terminating *supervision* involves other questions. Formerly, when age was not an important factor, I used to stick to the principle that it was the other person who played first violin. Only once in the last few years have I had a candidate in obligatory supervision who requested his certificate before completing the required number of sessions. The reason given was that I might disappear due to illness, or worse. I accepted without further comment. Was this right? One thing, however, has changed, namely, the fact that it would be clearly unethical to hand over to the candidate the responsibility for assessing my intellectual capacity which is, of course, mine. This is not easy when candidates wish to continue, and where I have the feeling that my intellectual capacities are no longer up to par. As flattering as it may be to one's self-esteem when a candidate does not wish to quit, continuing under such conditions may easily lead to both moral and therapeutic exploitation on my part. Thus, *I* decide when to stop, and I am prepared to accept the discomfort that may arise for both parties.

I found it a helpful experience when, one summer's day some years ago, a training analyst declared 'from this autumn you can no longer count on me!' She was a very old lady at the time, and did not give one word of explanation as to why she wanted to cease. This incident revealed two things within me: fantasies that were therapeutically useful, and intensive efforts on my part to find a new analyst – which I needed at that time.

It is important for me that someone still asks for me and needs my help. I find it curious to note that, even if I may feel both tired and despondent, the fatigue disappears as soon as the patient or supervisory candidate enters my office. This happens repeatedly and, of course, touches on countertransference reactions of various kinds.

It is important to be sought after, for it strengthens one's self-esteem. While I do find it gratifying to be asked to present a paper here in Helsinki, a colleague of mine, of more or less my generation, does not think it particularly important to be asked for. Hence, though equal, we are different.

The points I have outlined in the foregoing are obviously only fragments of a vast and complex professional and ethical field. Nevertheless, I would like to contribute a few things that I find important.

The first is the importance of learning and maintaining *the analytical basic rules that are and should be the foundation of all responsible therapy*, as well as being present in all meetings between patient and therapist. These are best taught in psychoanalytic training: like music, the more we master the finger exercises, the more harmonious and vivid is our performance of the masterpiece!

Another point concerns *truth and theory*. The prevailing mindset in psychoanalytic and psychotherapeutic practice in former years took its cue from methods derived from natural scientific research, such as the connection between cause and effect, the clarification of force and counter-force. For a medical professional such as me this contained a number of truths and absolutes that left little scope for further doubts and wondering. Doubtless this provided secure foundations. Age and experience have subsequently engendered a certain inherent scepticism towards most things. Here, I refer to the earlier 'truths' pertaining to cause and effect that have since undergone such radical transformation. The causes of autism and the belief in lobotomy are among many such grotesque examples.

A Norwegian philosopher, Arne Naess, once claimed that, 'the most important thing about science is not that it presents one, objectively true point of view, but rather systematic wonder, the temporality of all knowledge, and its ability to be corrected through argued debate.'

This has been my professional creed, which I believe to be of great practical, therapeutic, and theoretical value.

Note

1 The present text is a slightly amended version of a paper held at the EPF Conference Helsinki, 2004.

6

NARCISSISTIC CHALLENGES FOR AGEING ANALYSTS

Martin Teising

Time, timelessness and transience

A conception of time and transience is made possible by the presence of another: their disappearance, their reappearance and their final disappearance. The experience of time is a prerequisite for the perception of constancy, and change and development in subject and object. It is only with this perception that an idea of age in time can be formed. We are aware of our own mortality and the transience of real objects, and we also have the wonderful ability mentally to represent objects that are not present. The intrapsychic representations exist independently of time. With this ability, and perhaps only with it, we can live with the knowledge of transience. Physical change and the processes of decay confront us with our own transience and mortality and, denying reality, are repelled time and again: a fact that can be observed even in psychoanalysts' dealings with their own ageing process.

'We have learnt', wrote Freud, 'that unconscious mental processes are in themselves "timeless". This means in the first place that they are not ordered temporally, that time does not change them in any way and that the idea of time cannot be applied to them' (1920, p. 31). Ego functions underlie the perception of time and transience, and of our dependence on time, interacting with 'timeless' unconscious processes. However, even the unconscious is not completely timeless, as Thomä has recently shown (2011). He interprets Freud's acceptance of the timelessness of the unconscious as a narcissistic phenomenon: 'It is probably our fantasy of immortality that recurs in the supposed timelessness of the unconscious and in the Nirvana principle' (p. 306).

Everyone knows their ultimate dependency, their own mortality, and yet they also unconsciously accept the contrary. In one patient, who had witnessed the fatal accident of his partner, it appeared in the analysis that the terrible experience had unconsciously confirmed to him that others die, but he himself escapes death. Freud recalls, 'the remark attributed to the husband: "If one of us dies I shall move to Paris". Such cynical jokes would not be possible if they did not have an unavowed truth to reveal which we cannot admit when it is baldly and seriously stated. It is well known that one may even speak the truth in jest' (1915): namely, that we cannot rightly imagine our own mortality. The dependence on the unconscious, which keeps us from being aware of our mortality, is probably an essential condition of human existence. We need psychological ways of operating that have the quality of denial, of narcissism, if we are to be able to live with the knowledge of our own mortality. 'In narcissism we protect ourselves from the painful experience of dependence' (Altmeyer, 2000).

The narcissistic defensive position is marked by a search for a quality of experience with which the feelings of helplessness and despair caused by separation or injury can be overridden. Narcissistic fantasies make it possible to regain control over a situation that threatens to spiral out of control.

Consciousness of time, on the other hand, requires giving up omnipotent thinking; requires recognising the historical dimension of one's life. To develop the sense of time, it is necessary to integrate past, present and future. The consciousness of temporality, defended against in so many ways, penetrates into consciousness more and more with age. An expression of this is the sense of time passing more quickly. Age confronts us with the fact that postponement into the future is only realistic to an increasingly limited extent. The reality of old age compels us, according to Roy Schafer (1968), to give up the fantasies of immortal objects and the hunt for an ideal object. Manic and narcissistic defence mechanisms, through which dependence and neediness are so controlled and prevented that human objects become unimportant, lose strength in more mature adults and are replaced in successful ageing by a growing acceptance. As an 85-year-old patient put it: It is necessary to develop a second submission, by which he meant submission to the authority of the body. Submission is accompanied by the recognition of generational differences, of loss and death.

Freud's work 'On transience' (1916) begins with the description of 'a summer walk through a smiling countryside in the company of a young but already famous poet' (p. 305). It is here that the conversation about transience takes place, not in a barren winter landscape. The work, written during the First World War, ends with the phrase: 'We shall build up again all that war has destroyed, and perhaps on firmer ground and more lastingly than before' (p. 303).

Freud presented his reflections on transience with this seemingly almost defiant conclusion against the background of his sons being soldiers in the war. He also saw his own work in this period seriously threatened by its renunciation by the younger generation including C.G. Jung. Freud's central idea in this short work is that it is transience that gives value to what exists. Transience demands a grieving recognition of what is lost, of what is transitory, and without transience what is precious would often not be worth anything. Every analytical session is influenced by this. We invite patients to regress; we provide a therapeutic space in which the most boundless phantasies can unfold, which we then terminate, in accordance with the reality principle, after 50 minutes. One of my older patients regularly feels this occurrence as if he were being driven out of the immortality of Paradise, into which he had entered with infinite hopes, with expectations that are raised at the start of every session and followed by disillusion at every session's end. For psychoanalysts, confronting their own limitations and phantasies of immortality has an importance that should not be underestimated. Narcissistic, timeless phantasies can be the basis of an inability to terminate the treatment of younger patients, whose mental life the analyst wants to participate in. Such participation can take on a seemingly vampire-like quality.

Generational conflicts

The relationship between younger analysts and significantly older patients contains a characteristic constellation that corresponds to the Laius-Oedipus complex. Laius does not want his son Oedipus, who will one day replace him, to live – in the prophecy it says 'kill' – and he sets out with the intent of murdering him so that he himself can rule for ever. Ultimately, however, he becomes the victim of his attack on the life of the next generation. Laius and Oedipus have apparently lived independently of each other until they meet, but because they are existentially dependent on each other, though they are not aware of this, their encounter has a fatal outcome. In our profession, the Laius-Oedipus problem becomes concrete, for example, in the design of examination and admission regulations, and in the handing over of practices. On the one hand, we want to encourage our young colleagues, allowing them a reliable income and thereby also contributing to the survival of psychoanalysis. On the other hand, we keep raising the bar to qualification to a seemingly higher level of quality, so that completion of training and appointment as a training analyst happen at an ever-older age. In addition, we want every practice transfer to generate the highest possible cash return. So the young colleagues' hands are tied, even if not, as with Oedipus, their feet.

With older people, personal skills and important functions that nourish the sense of self-esteem are devalued by renewable generations with accelerating speed in a rapidly moving world. A normally developed narcissism, with adequately internalised object representations and appropriately formed object relations, can forego constantly new narcissistic confirmation and usually allows the signs of ageing and its losses to be experienced and sufficiently mourned without excessive denial, and without a sense of devastating anxiety. The elderly can then identify with the younger ones who have their future ahead of them, with their greater capacities and their development. However, if the ageing person remains entirely dependent on ever-new external recognition, which internally leaves few traces, strong feelings of envy and jealousy towards the younger generation can be activated when the external recognition fails to materialise. The developmental challenge for ageing people, based on the work of mourning, to make way for the younger generation (or the failure of this challenge) is a theme in different tales, perhaps the most well-known being Snow White, who is envied by her step-mother for her youthful beauty and pursued with deadly hatred.

On the significance of the body and its changes

Consciously experienced dependence and independence in old age depends primarily on the condition of the body, and in particular on whether bodily functions continue to be controlled. The ability to think is also based on bodily functions remaining intact. In age the body becomes the organiser of the psyche, as Heuft *et al.* (2000) write, following René Spitz. The body defines well-being, and by often requiring care shapes the new interpersonal relationships that have to be formed. In these, qualities of experience in early childhood caring relationships can be reactivated if help from other people becomes necessary for food intake, locomotion, bodily excretions or hygiene; for thinking and the orientation that depends on this; and for communication.

The self proves to be relatively resistant to ageing processes. It is stubborn and for a long time refuses to integrate physical changes into the body self. A commonly used strategy for dealing with the ageing body consists in splitting the ageing or ill body from the self. 'Why can I not send my eyes, my knees and my heart to the doctor and stay quietly at home, without pain, and enjoy the remainder of life?' wondered an older patient.

Severe narcissistic conflicts can arise when the discrepancies between body self and real body can no longer be denied. The loss of physical or mental abilities, such as hearing loss or restrictions in movement, can be seen as a grave humiliation. It has effects on interactions with the environment and often forces withdrawal from interpersonal relationships.

We know that serious physical illnesses cause narcissistic crises and increase the risk of suicide, and so they can be of special importance in old age (Teising, 2007). Suicidal behaviour is in most cases the expression of a regressive attempt at conflict resolution. An end to pain, freedom from stress or peaceful rest are sought in death: the expression of a primary narcissistic wish. However, only very few patients suffering from a hopeless physical illness take their own life in the terminal phase of their illness. More frequent are suicide attempts in the early stages of a fatal illness, especially following the diagnosis (McKenzie and Popkin, 1990). It is the phantasies of the feared consequences of the disease, the fears and the despair, which govern the inner life and lead to suicidal behaviour. With increasing age, depressive content becomes more frequently expressed through physical symptoms and hypochondriacal fears (Bron, 1991).

The body becomes a site of perception, of projection and expression, as well as a medium of interaction with the doctor. In 1926, shortly before his 70th birthday, Freud, at the time having already been ill with cancer for three years, wrote to Eitingon: 'The only real dread I have is of a long invalidism with no possibility of working: to put it more plainly, with no possibility of earning' (Jones, 1957, p. 128). The inability to work, which Freud perceived as threatening, can be understood as a fear of being unable to deal actively with the environment, of having to endure it only passively. No longer being able to work means becoming dependent on the care of others. The fear of infirmity drives us today perhaps more than ever. It seems so unbearable that the flight from nursing care is actively thought about in terms of euthanasia, which is practised in some countries with a troublingly increasing frequency.

Characteristic illnesses in the ageing process

Many people are able narcissistically to deny dependency on and separateness from the needed object for a long time, as well as denying changes in the self and the objects. External and internal changes associated with the biological, social and psychological ageing process increasingly soften these negating and denying defence mechanisms in old age. The awareness of an often long-denied dependence on the body and on other people, now maybe even on one's own children, partners, friends, nurses or social welfare institutions, is often felt as an intolerable dependence, as an unbearable surrender, the more so if the person affected has lived with the 'illusion of self-determination and independence' (cf. Mieth, 2008). Psychoanalysts belong to the privileged professional group of those whose quality of work remains relatively independent of physical abilities, as long as the brain is not affected. The increasingly frequent experiences of loss, sometimes only mentally anticipated and often tied to the body and its associated potential humiliations, also have to be managed in the course of ageing.

The loss of objects that have been chosen on a narcissistic basis is experienced as mortification (cf. Henseler, 1991). Typical humiliations in the ageing process include, for example, those of the psychosexual self-image as a man or woman. Restrictions on power and influence, such as those related to leaving working life and being overtaken by younger people, are experiences that are hard to cope with. Beyond the 75th year, restrictions on basic life activities such as locomotion, food intake and excretory functions have increasingly to be psychologically integrated.

Dependence on care is the most feared potential characteristic of older age, as if one never again wanted to be dependent on another person for personal care; as if one held terrible memories of this constellation from early childhood. Being dependent on care means depending on the actual presence of another who can determine their own presence and absence, to be reliant on them and to have to recognise their importance. 'It is not the latest slight – which, in itself, is minimal . . . but the small slight of the present moment has aroused and set working the memories of very many, more intense, earlier slights, behind all of which there lies in addition the memory of a serious slight in childhood which has never been overcome' (Freud, 1896, p. 217) and 31 years later, when 71 years old and already having been ill with cancer for years, Freud put this in concrete terms:

> There are diseases, which we have only recently recognised as attacks by other organisms; and finally there is the painful riddle of death, against which no medicine has yet been found, nor probably will be. With these forces nature rises up against us, majestic, cruel and inexorable; she brings to our mind once more our weakness and helplessness, which we thought to escape through the work of civilisation . . . One might suppose that this condition of things would result in a permanent state of anxious expectation in him and a severe injury to his natural narcissism . . . For this situation is nothing new. It has an infantile prototype, of which it is in fact only the continuation. For once before one has found oneself in a similar state of helplessness: as a small child, in relation to one's parents. One had reason to fear them.
>
> (Freud, 1927, p. 16)

The struggle for recognition

In his concept of the recognition of the facts of life, Money-Kyrle (1971) described metaphors for psychological realities, which he derived from biological conditions, that are of great importance for understanding what we are exploring here. They should now be put into the context of the ageing process. It has to do, metaphorically speaking, first, with the recognition of the breast as a good and indispensable object, as it were a milk – or money – dispenser. This means the recognition of dependency as a basic existential condition. Second, it has to do with the recognition of parental sexual intercourse as a creative act; that is, with the experience of being excluded. And third, it has to do with the recognition of the inevitability of time and, eventually, of death.

The recognition of the good breast requires havinge to humbly acknowledge that it is only possible to exist with dependency on others. The fact has to be recognised that the mother, and by extension the environment, cannot always satisfy every request or desire immediately, and even more bitterly, does not always want to fulfil every wish; that she is her own separate self with her own independent interests.

A 70-year-old patient wrestles with the recognition of his dependence on another. 'You know in the Western movies', he says, 'where a cowboy falls in love with a woman. Usually, the affair ends with his leaving her the next morning and riding off into the wide, open prairie. But in some films he turns around and stays with her. I can't really believe that.'

Behind the idea of independence can hide illusory images of grandiosity, which came to light with another 75-year-old patient when he said: 'What do I need medication for? I am God'. It is known from psychoanalytic treatments that this size of fantasy of grandiosity in men often functions as a defence against the deeply humiliating dependence, which is experienced as a threat, on a woman: ultimately on the mother, and even on mother nature.

The more securely experiences with a good maternal object have been internalised and the stronger the sense of basic trust, the more the dependence on another can be acknowledged and the easier it will be possible to recognise the second fact of life: namely, the fact that two people are doing something together and one is excluded, with limited or even no way of influencing what is happening. We encounter the second fact of life in the course of life in various forms and it affects old people with particular force. It begins when the parents have not asked us whether we want to be put into this world. The infant learns this fact, for example, if a younger sibling is born and it feels excluded from the intimate relationship of the new baby with the mother. The young person must deal with his raging jealousy; the pensioner is excluded from the decisions of younger colleagues at work; the patient often has little say in matters of his institutionalisation and related financial issues. The psychoanalyst Martin Grotjahn, when over 80, writes: 'I cannot accept the idea that my friends will greet the sun tomorrow (and enjoy their breakfast) and I will not be able to do the same' (Grotjahn, 1994, p. 122).

Equipped with sufficiently good internal objects, older people can share the happiness of their children, need to feel less excluded and can react less jealously, enviously and resentfully.

Most people oscillate throughout their lives between recognition and denial of the third fact of life: namely, the limitation of one's own life and one's own mortality.

If psychoanalysts, as indicated above, need patients in the sense of external objects, it will be difficult to say goodbye to them. This can manifest itself in the individual treatments themselves as well as in the issue of restricting one's own practice in old age. The claim can be heard from various colleagues that they recognise the biological limits and the associated higher risk of dying and (soon) will take on no more long-term therapy. However, it can then just as often be heard that they are actually still at the height of their psychoanalytic skills and are carrying on practising psychoanalysis in short-term therapy, supervision, teaching and other tasks. Certainly, this self-perception can often correspond to external reality, but it can also at the same time strengthen a phantasy of unlimited timelessness in psychoanalytic practice. Does this phantasy have to be maintained, or can what is given up in the outer reality be preserved in the inner reality, as Danielle Quinodoz describes in this volume (*cf.* p. 14). The Laius-Oedipus problem referred to above becomes concrete when handing over the couch to younger colleagues. Would we manage better as Snow White's stepmother? Doesn't what was once our own couch remain empty if we no longer sit behind it? If this narcissistic problem in the generational context is not adequately worked through, the generativity of psychoanalysis is threatened with destruction.

BIBLIOGRAPHY FOR PART I

Abend, S. M. (1982) 'Serious Illness in the Analyst: Countertransference Considerations', *Journal of the American Psychoanalytic Association* 30: 365–379.

Abend, S. M. (1986) 'Countertransference, Empathy and the Analytic Ideal: The Impact of Life Stresses and Analytic Capability', *Psychoanalytic Quarterly* 55: 563–575.

Altmeyer, M. (2000) *Narzißmus und Objekt*. Göttingen: Vandenhoeck und Ruprecht.

Balter, L. (1977) 'On the Possible Effects of Aging on the Practice of Psychoanalysis, by K. R. Eissler', *Psychoanalytic Quarterly* 46: 182–183.

Baudelaire, C. (2006) *The Flowers of Evil*. Keith Waldrop (tr.) Middletown, CT: Wesleyan University Press.

Bayley, J. (1999) *Elegy for Iris*. New York: St. Martin's Press.

Bion, W. R. (1963) *Elements of Psychoanalysis*. London: Heineman.

Bion, W. R. (1970) *Attention and Interpretation*. London: Tavistock Publications.

Bleger, J. (1967) 'Psycho-Analysis of the Psycho-Analytic Frame', *International Journal of Psychoanalysis* 48: 511–519.

Bolgar, H. (2002) 'When the Glass Is Full', *Psychoanalytic Inquiry* 22: 640–651.

Borges, J.-L. (1949) *The Aleph and Other Stories*. London: Penguin Books, 2000.

Bovenschen, S. (2006) *Älter Werden*. Frankfurt a. M.: S. Fischer Verlag; Büchergilde Gutenberg.

Bron, B. (1991) 'Alterstypische psychopathologische Besonderheiten bei endogenen und neurotisch-reaktiven Depressionen im höheren Lebensalter', *Nervenarzt* 61: 170–175.

Casement, P. (2006) *Learning from Life. Becoming a Psychoanalyst*. London: Routledge.

Danon Boileau, H. (2000) *De la vieillesse à la mort. Point de vue d'un usager*. Paris: Calmann-Lévy Hachette.

Danon Boileau, H. (2010) 'Analyste terminé, analyste interminable?' *Revue Française de Psychanalyse* 74: 771–784.

Dattner, R. (1989) 'On the Death of the Analyst: A Review', *Contemporary Psychoanalysis* 25: 419–426.

David, C. (1996) 'Le deuil de soi-même', *Revue française de psychanalyse* 60: 419–426.

De M'Uzan, M. (1977) 'Le travail du trépas' in *De l'art à la mort*. Paris: Gallimard, pp. 182–189.

Denis, P. (1997) *Emprise et satisfaction, les deux formants de la pulsion*. Paris: Le fil rouge, PUF.

Dewald, P. A. (1982) 'Serious Illness in the Analyst: Transference, Countertransference, and Reality Responses', *Journal of the American Psychoanalytic Association* 30: 347–363.

Eissler, K. (1955) *The Psychiatrist and the Dying Patient*. New York: International Universities Press.

Eissler, K. R. (1975) 'On the Possible Effects of Aging on the Practice of Psychoanalysis: An Essay', *Journal of the Philadelphia Association of Psychoanalysts* 11: 138–152. Reprinted: (1993) *Psychoanalytic Inquiry* 13: 316–332.

Erikson, E. (1951) *Childhood and Society.* New York: Norton.

Erikson, E. (1959/80) *Identity and the Life Cycle.* New York: W. W. Norton & Company Ltd.

Erikson, E. (1979/2006) 'On the Generational Cycle: An Address', presented at the 31st International Psychoanalytical Congress, New York, 1979. Reprint in G. Junkers (ed.), *Is It Too Late? Key Papers on Ageing.* London: Karnac, 2006.

Erlbruch, W. (2008) *Duck, Death and the Tulip.* Wellington, NZ: Gecko Press.

Erlich, S. (1998). 'On Loneliness, Narcissism and Intimacy', *American Journal of Psychoanalysis* 58: 135–162.

Erlich, S. (2003) 'Über Einsamkeit, Narzissmus und Intimität', *Forum der Psychoanalyse* 19: 5–17.

Ferro, A. (2003) 'The Analyst as an Individual, His Self-Analysis and Gradients of Functioning', *EPF Bulletin* 57: 134–141.

Freud, S. (1896) 'The Aetiology of Hysteria', *S. E.* 3.

Freud, S. (1900) *The Interpretation of Dreams. S. E.* 4.

Freud, S. (1913) 'The Theme of the Three Caskets', *S. E.* 12.

Freud, S. (1914) 'Letter to Abraham of 25.8.1914', in M. Schur, *Sigmund Freud: Living and Dying.* London: Hogarth Press, 1972.

Freud, S. (1915) 'Thoughts for the Times on War and Death', *S. E.* 14.

Freud, S. (1916) 'On Transience', *S. E.* 14.

Freud, S. (1917) 'Mourning and Melancholia', *S. E.* 14.

Freud, S. (1920) *Beyond the Pleasure Principle. S. E.* 18.

Freud, S. (1923) *The Ego and the Id. S. E.* 19.

Freud, S. (1927) *The Future of an Illusion. S. E.* 21.

Freud, S. (1930) *Civilization and Its Discontents, S. E.* 21.

Freud, S. (1937) 'Analysis Terminable and Interminable', *S. E.* 23.

Freud, S. (1991) 'Wir und der Tod', *Psyche* 45(2): 97–131.

Fromm-Reichmann, F. (1959) 'Loneliness', *Psychiatry* 22: 1–15. Reprint: *Contemporary Psychoanalysis* 26: 305–329, 1990.

Green, A. (1980) 'Passion et destin des passions', *Nouvelle revue de psychanalyse* 21: 5–49.

Green, A. (1997) 'Interview', in L. W. Raymond and S. Rosbrow-Reich, *The Inward Eye.* London: The Analytic Press.

Grinberg, L., Sor, D. and Tabak de Bianchedi, E. (1975/1985) *Introduction to the Work of Bion.* London: Karnac.

Grotjahn, M. (1940) 'Psychoanalytic Investigation of a 71-Year-Old Man with Senile Dementia', *Psychoanalytic Quarterly* 9(2): 80–97.

Grotjahn, M. (1951) 'Some Analytic Observations about the Process of Growing Old', *Psychoanalysis and the Social Sciences* 3: 301–312.

Grotjahn, M. (1985) 'Being Sick and Facing Eighty: Observations on an Ageing Therapist', in R. A. Nemiroff and C. A. Colarusso (eds), *The Race against Time: Psychotherapy and Psychoanalysis in the Second Half of Life.* New York: Plenum Press, pp. 293–302.

Grotjahn, M. (1994) 'A Psychoanalyst's Thoughts on the Start of His 86th Year of Life', in G. H. Pollock (ed.), *How Psychiatrists Look at Aging. Vol. 2.* Madison, CT: International Universities Press, pp. 121–127.

Gutwinski-Jeggle, J. (2001) Wie arbeitet ein Psychoanalytiker? Unpublished lecture.

Halpert, E. (1982) 'When the Analyst Is Chronically Ill or Dying', *Psychoanalytic Quarterly* 51: 372–389.

Henseler, H. (1991) 'Narcissism as a Form of Relationship', in J. Sandler, E. S. Person and P. Fonagy (eds), *Freud's 'On Narcissism': An Introduction*. New Haven, CT: Yale University Press, pp. 195–215.

Hermanns, L. (1992) *Psychoanalyse in Selbstdarstellungen*. Tübingen: edition diskord.

Hessel, S. (2011) Interview, in Colette Mesnage, *Eloge d'une vieillesse heureuse*. Gordes: Les éditions Le Relié, p. 96.

Heuft, G., Kruse, A. and Radebold, H. (2000) *Lehrbuch der Gerontopsychosomatik und Alterspsychotherapie*. München: Ernst Reinhardt Verlag.

Hinshelwood, R. (1997) *Therapy Or Coercion: Does Psychoanalysis Differ from Brainwashing?* London: Karnac.

Horner, A. J. (2002) 'Frontline: Is There Life after Psychoanalysis? On Retirement from Clinical Practice', *Journal of the American Academy of Psychoanalysis* 30: 325–328.

Jaques, E. (1965/2006) 'Death and the Mid-Life Crisis', *International Journal of Psychoanalysis* 46: 502–514. Reprint in G. Junkers (ed.), *Is It Too Late?* London: Karnac, 2006.

Jaques, E. (1981) 'The Mid-Life Crisis', in S. I. Greenspan and G. H. Pollock (eds.), *Adulthood and the Ageing Process, Vol. III: The Course of Life*. Washington, DC: US Department of Health, pp. 1–24.

Jones, E. (1957) *Sigmund Freud Life and Work, Volume Three: The Last Phase 1919–1939*. London: The Hogarth Press.

Junkers, G. (1994) 'Psychotherapie mit älteren Menschen', Psychiatrisches Kolloquium 16.3.1994. Unpublished lecture.

Junkers, G. (2001) 'Psychoanalysis Beyond the Age of 50?' Paper presented at the Conference of the International Psychoanalytical Association (IPA), 23 July 2001, Nice.

Junkers, G. (2006) *Is It Too Late? Key Papers on Ageing*. London: Karnac.

Junkers, G. (2007a) 'Der Abschied vom Leben als Psychoanalytiker', in S. Zwettler-Otte, *Entgleisungen in der Psychoanalyse*. Göttingen: Vandenhoeck & Ruprecht.

Junkers, G. (2007b) 'The Risk of Dementalisation: A Psychodynamic Approach to Mental Decline Caused by the Onset of Dementing Processes'. Presentation at the IPA Conference, Berlin. Published in German in K. Röckerath, V. Strauss and M. Leuzinger-Bohleber (2009), *Verletztes Gehirn – Verletztes Ich. Treffpunkt zwischen Psychoanalyse und Neurowissenschaften*. Göttingen: Vandenhoeck & Ruprecht.

Kaplan, A. H. and Rothman, D. (1986) 'The Dying Psychotherapist', *American Journal of Psychiatry* 143: 561–572.

Kennedy, R. (2011) 'The Loneliness of the Psychoanalyst', *The Bulletin of the British Psychoanalytical Society* 47: 12–22.

Kennedy, R. (2012) *Having a Psychic Home: Aspects of Identity*. Free Association Press, in print.

King, P. (1974) 'Notes on the Psychoanalysis of Older Patients', *Journal of Analytic Psychology* 19: 22–37.

King, P. (1980) 'The Life Cycle as Indicated by the Nature of the Transference in the Psychoanalysis of the Middle-Aged and Elderly', *International Journal of Psychoanalysis* 61: 153–160.

Klein, M. (1940) 'Mourning and Its Relation to Manic Depressive States', in *The Writings of Melanie Klein, Vol. 1*. London: Hogarth Press, 1975.

Klein, M. (1946) 'Notes on Some Schizoid Mechanisms', *International Journal of Psychoanalysis* 27: 99–127.

Klein, M. (1950/2000) 'On the Criteria for the Termination of a Psychoanalysis', *International Journal of Psychoanalysis* 31: 78–80.

Klein, M. (1963/1975) 'On the Sense of Loneliness', in *Envy and Gratitude*. London: Hogarth Press.

Lasky, R. (1990) 'Catastrophic Illness in the Analyst and the Analysand's Emotional Reaction to It', *International Journal of Psychoanalysis* 71: 455–473.

Lasky, R. (1992) 'Some Superego Conflicts in the Analyst Who Has Suffered a Catastrophic Illness', *International Journal of Psychoanalysis* 73: 127–136.

Loch, W. (1981/82) Comments on Dr. Normans Cohen's paper 'On Loneliness and the Ageing Process'. Paper presented at the 32nd International Psychoanalytical Congress, Helsinki. Published in *International Journal of Psychoanalysis* 63: 267–273, 1982. Reprint in G. Junkers (ed.), *Is It Too Late? Key Papers on Ageing*. London: Karnac, 2006.

Loch, W. (1982) 'Psychoanalytische Bemerkungen zur Krise in der mittleren Lebensphase', *Jahrbuch der Psychoanalyse* 14: 137–157.

Loewald, H. W. (1988) 'Termination analyzable and unanalyzable', *Psychoanalytic Study of the Child* 43: 155–166.

McKenzie, T. and Popkin, M. K. (1990) 'Medical Illness and Suicide', in M. Blumenthal and D. Kupfer (eds), *Suicide Over the Life-Cycle*. Washington, DC: American Psychiatric Press, pp. 205–332.

Mannoni, O. (1982) *Ca n'empeche pas d'exister*. Paris: Seuil.

Mieth, D. (2008) *Grenzenlose Selbstbestimmung*. Düsseldorf: Pathmos.

Money-Kyrle, R. (1971) 'The Aim of Psychoanalysis', *International Journal of Psychoanalysis* 52: 103–106.

Morrison, A. (1990) Doing psychotherapy while living with a life-threatening illness, in H. Schwartz and A.-L. Silver (eds) *Illness in the Analyst: Implications for the Treatment Relationship*. New York: International Universities Press, pp. 227–253.

Ogden, T. (1994) 'The Analytic Third: Working with Intersubjective Clinical Facts', *International Journal of Psychoanalysis* 75, 3–19.

Pizer, B. (1997) 'When the Analyst Is Ill: Dimensions of Self-Disclosure', *Psychoanalytic Quarterly* 66, 450–469.

Pollock, G. H. (1975) 'On Mourning, Immortality, and Utopia', *Journal of the American Psychoanalytic Association* 23: 334–362.

Ponsi, M. (2000) 'Therapeutic Alliance and Collaborative Interactions'. *International Journal of Psychoanalysis* 81, 687–704.

Potamianou, A. (2010) 'At the Crossroads of Passion and Omnipotence'. Unpublished paper given at the EPF Conference, London.

Quinodoz, D. (1996) 'Etre psychanalyste et vieillir', *Revue française de psychanalyse* 60: 113–122.

Quinodoz, D. (2008) *Vieillir: une découverte*. Paris: PUF (*Growing Old: A Journey of Self Discovery*, Routledge, 2010).

Racamier, P. (1980) 'De l'objet non-objet. Entre folie, psychose et passion', *Nouvelle revue de psychanalyse* 21: 235–241.

Raymond, L. W. and Rosbrow-Reich, S. (1997) *The Inward Eye. Psychoanalysts Reflect on Their Lives and Work*. London: The Analytic Press.

Sandler, J. (1983) 'Reflections on Psychoanalytic Concepts and Psychoanalytic Practice', *International Journal of Psychoanalysis* 64: 35–46.

Sandler, A. (1984) 'Problems of Development and Adaption in an Elderly Patient', *Psychoanalytic Study of the Child* 39: 471–489.

Sandler, J., Spector Person, E. and Fonagy, P. (eds) (2012) *Freud's 'On Narcissism: An Introduction'* for the International Psychoanalytical Association. New Haven & London: Yale University Press, pp. 195–215.

Segal, H. (1958) 'Fear of Death: Notes on the Analysis of an Old Man', *International Journal of Psychoanalysis* 39: 178–181. Reprint in G. Junkers (ed.), *Is It Too Late? Key Papers on Ageing*. London: Karnac, 2006.

Schafer, R. (1968) *Aspects of Internalization*. New York: International Universities Press.

Schur, M. (1972) *Freud. Living and Dying*. London: The Hogarth Press.

Schwaber, E.A. (1998) 'Traveling Affectively Alone', *Journal of the American Psychoanalytic Association* 46, 1004–1065.

Schwartz, H. (1987) 'Illness in the Doctor: Implications for Analytic Process', *Journal of the American Psychoanalytic Association* 35, 657–692.

Schwartz, H. and Silver, A.-L. (eds) (1990) *Illness in the Analyst: Implications for the Treatment Relationship*. New York: International Universities Press.

Shakespeare, W. (MDCCCXCVI) *King Lear*. In *Shakespeare's Works, Vol. X,* London: Kegan Paul, Trench. Trübner & Co.

Silver, A.-L. (1990) 'Resuming the Work with a Life-Threatening Illness: And Further Reflections', *Contemporary Psychoanalysis* 18, 314–326.

Suter, M. (2003) *Small World*. London: Random House.

Tauber, E. S. (1982) 'Preoccupation with Immortality Expressive of a Negation of Life', *Contemporary Psychoanalysis* 18: 119–132.

Teising, M. (2007) 'Narcissistic Mortification of Ageing Men', *International Journal of Psychoanalysis* 88: 1329–1344.

Thomä, H. (2011) 'Zeitlosigkeit und Vergänglichkeit (in) der Psychoanalyse', *Forum der Psychoanalyse* 27: 299–308.

Thorner, H. A. (1988) 'Notes on the Desire for Knowledge', in J. S. Grotstein (ed.), *Do I Dare Disturb the Universe?* London: Karnac, Maresfield Library.

Winnicott, D. W. (1960) 'The Theory of the Parent-Infant Relationship', *International Journal of Psychoanalysis* 41: 585–595.

Winnicott, D. W. (1958/1965) 'The Capacity to Be Alone', in *The Maturational Processes and the Facilitating Environment*. London: Hogarth Press and the Institute of Psycho-Analysis.

Winnicott, D. W. (1963/1965) 'Dependence in Infant-Care, in Child-Care, and the Psycho-Analytic Setting', in *The Maturational Processes and the Facilitating Environment*. London: Hogarth Press and the Institute of Psycho-Analysis.

Zilboorg, G. (1938) 'The Sense of Immortality', *Psychoanalytic Quarterly* 7: 171–199.

Part II

ILLNESS AND ENDING

7

WHEN THE BODY SPEAKS AND THE PSYCHOANALYST FALLS ILL

Gabriele Junkers

For much of our lives, we think of good health in the sense of physical and mental well-being as the norm. We are used to experiencing our bodies as kind of mute companions and take it for granted that they will 'function' as they should. They only draw attention to themselves – sometimes in no uncertain terms – when we fall ill. Of course illness can afflict us at any time in our lives. But the likelihood of falling ill and above all the probability of contracting a chronic and ultimately life-threatening ailment markedly increase with age.[1]

In terms of average age, practising psychoanalysts are a particularly old group of professionals. Accordingly, our risk of falling ill is heightened and we are more likely to be impaired in our professional vitality by serious illnesses or even death. This makes it all the more remarkable that many of our colleagues display an unexpected reluctance to engage with the transient nature of their own actual physical existence. We tend to experience age-related changes, illnesses and impairments as an unexpected incursion into what Eissler (1976) and Kaplan (1994) have described as a stage in our lives where we tacitly consider ourselves 'ageless'. Experience of such an incursion can give rise to powerful fantasies of deformation, retribution and abandonment (Schwartz, 1990). Various factors threaten to make us relatively oblivious to the signals emanating from our bodies. These include our own psychological dynamics, the experiences gleaned over the entire course of our lives and an attitude that is first and foremost focussed on largely timeless psychological processes.

Freud grappled with severe cancer for 17 years. He worked with his patients until shortly before his death. He saw illness and the ageing process as an unbearable assault on his stamina and his capacity for work. But he has left us no testimony as to how he felt about the situation and how this condition affected his work (Schur, 1972). This is perhaps no surprise. We are often reluctant to admit to ourselves how profoundly fatigue, physical frailty and acute and chronic pain can interfere with our ability to respond to what our patients bring with them to the sessions. For example, physical pain and a poor state of health can prompt us to tone down the patients' frequently explosive affects, their attacks on the object that they make us into and their massive defence mechanisms. In this way, we will not be so deeply moved or stirred up by them. But it also means that we will be unable to adequately acknowledge our patient's dramatic psychological dynamics in our interpretations. Underlying this is a defence protecting the analyst's own self and it frequently asserts itself more strongly in direct contact with the patients than in the less immediate situation of a supervision.

That sick analysts have often felt duty bound to emulate Freud in this stoic ideal has inflicted many a painful experience on candidates and patients, who are convinced that they should unwaveringly stay with their sick therapist. Although he is no longer able to function as a 'good enough' analyst, they do not leave him for fear that he might die. And then, suddenly and unexpectedly, the positions are reversed and they feel abandoned by him. Members from a whole range of international psychoanalytic societies have told me that the inability to realistically assess one's own situation inflicts major psychological distress and severe injuries on the patients and poses ethical problems that are hardly ever discussed, not even between colleagues. In the face of illness and imminent death, analysts tend to lapse into silence and frequently distressing emotional isolation, while their patients and candidates run the risk of re-traumatisation.

But the demands made on psychoanalysts are addressed to them as whole persons, not just as professional specialists. The physical changes and the distress that a severe illness involves will set in train psychological processes that can impair an analyst's attitude, his perception of his countertransference and his ability to formulate interpretations. In short, the tools of his trade will no longer be fully at his disposal. Above all, we tend to forget that the incursions caused by illness can vitiate or sometimes even totally stultify access to the pretend or metaphorical level and the elucidation of fantasies. So when has the right moment come to take the consequences resulting from illness? On the one hand, no analyst will want to jeopardise the analytic situation by interrupting therapy and informing his patients about his illness. But as a person responsible for training candidates and treating patients, he has no right to simply handle that illness as a private matter.

In retrospect we see that articles about the analyst's physical/mental state and the way analysts experience illness date no farther back than the 1980s, when the analyst as a person started being introduced into the clinical debate. (Before that, only Little, 1967 and Eissler, 1976 immersed themselves in these issues). Although many authors routinely begin with complaints about how few and far between publications on this topic are, a glance at the bibliography at the end of this section will suffice to show that in fact we are now in possession of an almost overwhelmingly large number of testimonies in which psychoanalysts report on the illnesses they have been through, the technical problems those illnesses pose in their dealings with patients and the sometimes extremely confusing feelings bound up with these situations. With some dismay, Schwartz (1990) notes that in their own days many of these authors had had very similar experiences with their own training analysts.

The pioneering thoughts advanced by Dewald and Abend at the conference of the American Psychoanalytic Association (APsA) in December 1980[2] triggered an extremely lively debate about the meaning of severe and potentially fatal illnesses for analysts. This debate continued in the various groupings of the APsA in the years to follow. In working groups, psychoanalysts exchanged views on their anxieties and feelings of isolation, shame and guilt caused by their illnesses, as well as anxieties about a premature return to clinical practice. They also gave expression to their doubts about their own lives, their treatments and their professional future. They were particularly apprehensive about the way they would be regarded by their colleagues, doubting that these would ever refer patients to them again and thus implicitly expressing their fear of an uncertain economic future. It is striking to see how strongly their thinking about their colleagues is marked by anxiety, shame and suspicion. We are obviously completely obsessed by the need to ensure that no one, neither patients, nor colleagues, should notice 'it', perhaps because we ourselves hope that if we close our eyes, 'it' may quite simply go away.

Assailed by the confusing array of feelings triggered by such discussions and the powerful fantasies they activate, Feinsilver (1998) admits that the new situation brought about by his illness caused him to experience feelings he would never have anticipated in a state of good health. In the last days of his professional life, he too entertained fantasies of total dereliction and penury.

The impressive collection of articles edited by Schwartz and Silver *Illness in the Analyst: Implications for the Treatment Relationship* (1990) documents many of the findings the American discussion groups arrived at. Most of these reports are very personal. As analysts relinquished their silence about their illnesses, the opportunity also presented itself to talk about how stout our defences are against addressing topics indissolubly bound up with severe illness, topics centring on frailty, helplessness or imminent death. Arlow (in Schwartz and Silver, 1992, p. 19) was surprised to realise how great his need was to deny the severity of his illness and the way in which his ability to assume the 'analytic' attitude of a detached observer supported that tendency. 'To be calm and self-possessed in the face of grave illness may . . . serve to reassure the patient. However adopting such a brave stance may . . . enlist the patient as a witness to the analyst's omnipotence' (Schwartz and Silver, p. 22).

Dewald (in Schwartz and Silver, 1990) emphasises the increasing preoccupation with oneself that every seriously ill person goes through. He describes how he went so far as to have his patients notified by his secretary about the repeated postponements and the uncertain commencement of their treatment. 'This procedure had been rationalized by me as *protecting the patient* (his italics) from undue anxiety associated with learning I was seriously ill'. 'As my illness deepened, my previous sense of responsibility and concern for the welfare of my patients . . . how they would manage this interruption . . . began to fade' (p. 77).

Linna (2002) describes the severe difficulties she had maintaining the internal structure of the analytic setting: 'Struggling with crutches I felt that the role of the analyst to act as container, prepared to face such powerful feelings as fear, fury, envy and hatred felt to be a parody of an ideal although I strived hard to achieve the ideal. My own situation made me both physically and mentally weak. It was difficult to move as all routine functions were an effort and mentally because I was struggling with my feelings'. Lasky (1992) also admits to the distressing superego conflicts he felt exposed to as an analyst with a potentially fatal illness. Gurtmann (1990, p. 612) is convinced that in the face of death analysts are most likely to run the risk of 'abusing' their patients and trainees by 'acting out'. Only too frequently, he contends, denial is confused with hope.

The death of an analyst is invariably a disaster that Freedman and Firestein (1990, p. 334) look at in terms of a disruption of treatment caused by the analyst. These authors are convinced that treatment has been finished as soon as a patient learns that his/her analyst is ill.

Cohen (2002) inquires whether the widespread denial of the 'reality' of the analytic relationship reinforces our tendency to deny the analyst's mortality.

Like Freedman and Firestein (1990), many authors looking after patients and candidates after the death of their original analyst conclude from their experiences that it is absolutely essential to 'devise a more effective way of planning termination when the analyst has a fatal illness and to care for the patient following the death of his therapist' (p. 301). But there is no mistaking just how difficult it is to put this demand into practice. However, what the chapters in this volume also demonstrate is that it can be helpful and supportive for the sick analyst to accept support, both in the form of psychoanalytic supervision and of personal psychological help. Some find it helpful to turn to colleagues of long standing who have become friends. Others, by contrast, experience this very intimacy as a breach of professional discretion and use their fears on this point as a rationale for refusing the help of colleagues from the same institute or society. In so doing, they manoeuvre themselves into a form of emotional isolation that encourages denial and puts them at risk of 'abusing' their patients for the sake of their own stabilisation. Here it makes a major difference whether the ageing and ailing psychoanalyst lives alone and has no children or is part of a familial care network.

How exactly does illness influence the ability to practise one's profession? Are there signs that make it possible to divine that an analyst will soon die? How is a foreseeable end best dealt with? How do patients find out that their analyst has died? How can 'abandoned' patients be helped?

The debate on these technical problems is frequently very heated, due to the very different personal and/or theoretical persuasions underlying our analytic work. The articles by Dewald and Abend represent opposing attitudes towards the question of whether or not one should reveal one's personal situation.

Abend is in favour of abstention, recommending the adoption of the role of the 'white sheet'. Like him, many analysts are convinced that the maintenance of abstinence is an essential factor in enabling patients to unfold their fantasies. He found it liberating not to inform his patients of his illness, being convinced that more information invites the patient to behave in a caring and compassionate way towards the analyst. Accordingly, he fears that patients may have difficulty expressing their anger, while the sickly or convalescent analyst may have trouble in tolerating and containing such rage.

By contrast, Dewald feels that one should inform one's patients about the reality of an illness. He is convinced that in some way his patients will sense 'it' and thus, like many of his colleagues (Feinsilver, 1988, etc.), prefers to tell them about the state of affairs. Barbara Pizer (1997) is another analyst who sees this information as an 'inescapable disclosure' and accordingly prefers to 'take up the elephant in the room', as it addresses fundamental human concerns: 'Life and death, change, loss and grief are at the centre of human experience and growth' (p. 456). Other authors advocating self-revelation as well are convinced that in this way reality-based parameters can be drawn upon to restrict threatening fantasies effectively enough to prevent them from overwhelming the patients.

The number of articles in which analysts report on their illnesses far exceeds those in which analysts inquire how patients actually cope with their analyst's infirmity. This may be due to the fact that it is so cripplingly difficult to take the necessary measures. In the last resort, after all, anticipating the time when 'I am no longer' is something we cannot think about. It appears that here the prime concern is not so much to submit this difficult situation to scientific analysis but rather the need to make a traumatic situation easier to face up to by telling others about it. Though there has recently been an increase in the number of publications in which patients or candidates report on how they experienced the death of their analyst, we may still speculate on the number of instances in which a veil of silence has been drawn over such losses (Galatzer-Levy, 2004).

Some of the chapters in Part III of the book are devoted to the difficult role of psychoanalysts outside the dyad who keep silence and find it beyond their powers to stand by a sick colleague and/or patients or candidates in distress.

The inclusion of the following three chapters is designed to draw attention to the potential sufferings of analysts and patients alike.

In a highly detailed and sensitive way, Barbara Fajardo investigates the articles published so far by psychoanalysts reporting on their illness, proceeding from there to give a very personal account of her own experience of severe sickness. She tells of the way she found to talk to her patients about her illness (or not) and how arduous her struggle was with her own anxiety and hopelessness, plus the temptations of denial. She also indicates why she urgently advises all those in similar situations to seek professional psychological assistance. Here she concurs with Dewald and Clark (2001, p. 7). Professional help can make it easier for sick analysts not only to make ethically conscionable decisions but also to cope with this personal crisis in their lives. In her chapter, Fajardo reports an improvement in her condition, but ultimately the cancer she was suffering from led to her death.

Evelyn Carlisle confronts us with a situation in which an analyst's old age and illness create a situation that ultimately leaves behind a severely injured, damaged and solitary candidate whose distress will inevitably become a constant companion of his own professional activity unless he can find someone to help him among the colleagues of his training analyst. She describes her memories of her training analyst as someone who was mentally no longer present, increasingly unsubstantial, uncontained, unreliable and unable to control his affects. To read this account is to experience an analyst who was no longer able to work as a 'good enough' analyst. Can we as observers privy to developments like these give them our ethical approval?

Tove Traesdal indicates the re-traumatisation and renewed suffering that a sick analyst can cause. For some colleagues it may come as a surprise that she was able to discuss with her analyst prior to her own analysis (he was in his late sixties) the fact that 'something might happen'. How fortunate that both of them found the courage to do so, thus helping the unexpectedly abandoned analysand to summon up her memories of the indications provided by an analyst who was no longer there 'in the flesh'. She vividly conveys to us how helpful a personal and sincere letter of farewell from the analyst can be. In addition, all the more distressing was that her second analysis was disrupted again by the sudden death of her new analyst. The author heightens our awareness of how important it is for us as analysts to analyse thoroughly our fears of death and dying in order to be able to come to terms with them realistically in our dealings with our patients. The point is that in the context of a potentially fatal illness the dividing line between realistic hope and optimistic denial is very thin indeed.

Thus, we see that analysts confronted by such difficult situations are frequently unable to deal with them 'appropriately' on their own. Accordingly, in the third part of this book we shall attempt to cast light on the role of the institution, be it a psychoanalytic association, group or society.

Notes

1 As we grow older, research confronts us with an increasing number of diagnoses (multimorbidity) and an increasing number of disorders qualifying as illnesses (polypathy). Every sixth individual over 75 suffers from minor cognitive deficiencies. The risk of dementia is 5 per cent up to the age of 75 and 10 per cent up to 80. Mental morbidity in people over 70 is approximately 10 per cent (Weyerer and Bickel, 2007).
2 They have not been included in this volume because most of the articles assembled here make reference to them.

8

LIFE-THREATENING ILLNESS IN THE ANALYST

Barbara Fajardo

Life-threatening illness in the analyst has a major impact on the treatment and its setting, which presumes unending availability of the analyst, both as to physical presence and emotional responsiveness. The abrupt confrontation with the prospect of the analyst's illness and possible death stimulates, in both partners of the analytic dyad, powerful reactions and fantasies that threaten to throw the process into chaos.

I will begin with a brief review of the growing literature on life-threatening illness in the analyst. I will highlight major themes, with particular focus on the significant disagreement over the analyst's self-disclosure of information about the illness and his or her internal states regarding it. I will then recount my own experiences and observations as an analyst living through and continuing to face such an illness with my patients, and present my own view of its impact. Finally, I will make recommendations for working in such distracting and disruptive circumstances.

The effects of a life-threatening illness can be seen in the discrete arenas of two interacting aspects of the analytic work: the patient's symbolic and semantic discourse about unconscious transference fantasies concerning the analyst, and the experienced working relationship between analyst and patient. The relational part of the analytic relationship includes the therapeutic alliance, well-described by Ponsi (2000); she describes analysis as comprising both experience and knowing, as a process based on the activity of analyst and patient in a relatedness that makes possible their working together at times to use the analytic tool of interpretation.

Ponsi finds Ogden's concept of the 'analytic third' (1994) helpful in describing an essentially analytic product of the dyadic relationship: a unique type of object generated by this dialectical working together of the analyst's and the patient's separate subjectivities in the analytic setting. For the patient, the 'object' for the therapeutic alliance relationship is both the analyst and the analytic treatment, as experienced through the patient's subjectivity. When the analyst's state changes, as it must during serious illness, so must the intersubjective third and the closely related therapeutic alliance. As Ponsi argues, all analyses work in both the interpretive and the relational arenas, but with differences in the degree that one or the other is at the forefront of consideration. Some patients require little attention to the development and maintenance of the analytic third and the therapeutic alliance, and allow most of the work to be devoted to the search for meaning through interpretation; others require that more time be given to a relational focus on the moment-to-moment, action-based collaborative relationship, with interpretive work placed in the background for intermittent or at times extended periods. The understanding of analytic work as necessarily occurring in both of these arenas, in varying degree, will be useful in understanding the basis for differences among the authors addressing the topic of the analyst's illness.

Literature review

With a few exceptions, the best of this literature has been collected in a volume edited by Schwartz and Silver and published in 1990. Since then at least three more notable papers have appeared (Feinsilver, 1998; Pizer, 1997; Schwaber, 1998). While there are striking differences among these authors, who come from varied analytic perspectives, all agree on the problematic technical questions: how and when to reveal the illness to the patient, what and how much to reveal about it, and how to work with the patient during the illness or, if it has been temporarily discontinued, once it is resumed. Another question is how the work can continue if the analyst believes he or she is dying. There will certainly be significant impact on the therapeutic alliance and on collaboration in the analytic dyad. An influence on the nature of transference fantasies would also be expected; however, in the clinical work described in these papers, there is less effect on core transference fantasies themselves and more on changes in the resistances to their being observed.

The various perspectives represented in the literature can perhaps best be understood as evolving from two camps: the 'one-body' and the 'two-body'. The one-body view focuses on the patient's transference fantasies and interpretive work about them; in the two-body view, the subjectivities of both patient and analyst form the basis of the relational aspect of the analysis, including the therapeutic alliance, which is the basis both for the analytic action and for discourse about that action. Dewald (1982), Abend (1982), and Schwartz (1987), in papers later collected in the Schwartz and Silver compilation, share the belief that the primary analytic tool is the interpretation of the patient's transference as determined by his or her unconscious interests, the analyst's task being to maintain neutrality in listening and in the analytic setting. Clark (1995) agrees, while underscoring the importance of the ill analyst's having help as a patient from another analyst to repair the psychic injury associated with being ill. All in this camp believe it best to say little or nothing about the facts of the illness or even its existence except in special circumstances (e.g. with patients who are more regressed and therefore need some disclosure). Information about the analyst, these authors maintain, will distract from the analytic task of interpreting the patient's unconscious fantasies. By contrast, the two-body group, which includes Silver (1990), Morrison (1990), and Pizer (1997), define transference as a process evolving out of the conscious and unconscious interaction of both partners in the analytic dyad, and so give greater emphasis to a relational focus. Schwaber (1998) vacillates between the two positions, coming down on the two-body side in her conclusion that the ill analyst must in some circumstances, in the service of the process, take care of his or her own needs by a disclosure to the patient.

Subscribers to the one-body view believe the analyst should make every effort to keep from the patient any factual information pertaining to the illness. Even direct inquiries, they hold, should be deflected in favour of exploring transference implications of the patient's fantasies. For Dewald, however, outright refusal to answer an insistent inquiry should usually be avoided, lest the therapeutic situation be harmed by evasion and secrecy; he recommends greater flexibility regarding disclosure, particularly for patients in supportive psychotherapy or at the beginning of analysis. With this concern, he shows more interest in the relational and therapeutic alliance aspects than do others in the one-body group. By contrast, Abend is most outspoken about his worry that the ill analyst will find countertransference needs so pressing and distracting as to contaminate judgments about disclosure; he recommends that nothing at all be said. Schwartz believes one's judgment is restored only after recovery from the illness, and that no disclosure of factual information should occur until then, unless further serious medical problems are expected, in which case the analytic frame is not dependable and the patient should be told as much. Schwartz's recommendations for continuing treatment are not clear, but the implication is that the analyst should suspend practice until recovery is assured. The analyst is expected to have great difficulty seeing the illness as but a metaphor in the analytic 'as if,' a basis for the patient's transference experiences.

For the one-body group, for whom interpretation of the patient's transference is the specifically analytic tool, the observing of that transference is understood to be possible only through the neutral eyes of the analyst and, eventually, through the observing ego of the patient. Continuing to work with a life-threatening illness is problematic, as the analyst risks being caught on the horns of a dilemma, denial on the one side and need-driven disruptive self-disclosure on the other. With this in mind, Clark is emphatic in her recommendation that the ill analyst must be in psychoanalytic treatment; because the self is used as part of the analysing instrument, it is essential to repair it as much as possible in order to recover the capacity for neutrality.

Analysts taking the two-body approach believe that their illness does not have to disrupt or prevent the analytic work; in their broader view of transference as relational, it must always be shaped by input from the analyst. Analysts, when ill, can continue as usual with this kind of transference-focused work, as long as they can maintain their emotional steadiness in the face of an uncertain prognosis. There is a danger, of course, that analysts in this situation will disavow possible death, or use the patient to gratify their own narcissistic needs. Unlike the one-body group, however, analysts holding the two-body view believe these dangers can be averted with support from colleagues, friends, family, medical doctors, and analytic consultants, often including one's own analyst. Sometimes this can come from patients as well, though certainly this cannot be the main source of support. Schwaber's paper highlights her struggle to accept the need for such support, an antidote to the frightening and debilitating emotional isolation often accompanying serious illness when the analyst attempts to be self-contained; some form of disclosure is obviously necessary, both with colleagues and with those patients who allow it. The analyst has legitimate needs that can be fulfilled without distorting the transference focus, although their disclosure and fulfilment in the treatment situation will change the process. As always, the process should be explored and interpreted as transference expression.

Silver is specially attuned to unconscious communication between patient and analyst, having learned this from the many borderline and psychotic patients in her practice. She believes that many patients, regardless of diagnostic category, perceive subtle changes in the analyst's bodily and emotional states, including those associated with serious, even life-threatening illness. She recommends that the analyst should stay alert to themes in the material that suggest the patient's awareness of the illness, and should respond openly with appropriate factual information and exploration of transference wishes and fears. She accepts the resultant changes in the process as inevitable, and as grist for the mill of interpretation, as are changes resulting from other aspects of the analyst's emotional states in healthier times. Pizer is in agreement on this point, believing that factual disclosure to patients is desirable, and can be used in the service of the analytic process. She draws some useful distinctions among types of disclosure. An inescapable disclosure as dictated not by intrinsic clinical process but by obtrusive circumstances such as illness, which usually imply a threat of disruption but allow the analyst time to decide what must be said. In contrast, a deliberate self-disclosure is dictated by the process, expressed for instance in a dream with obvious referents to the illness that indicate a readiness to receive information. Inadvertent self-disclosure is a spontaneous explicit communication by the analyst of a subjective response to the patient, in unconscious enactment or in old-fashioned slips of the tongue and other parapraxes.

Morrison is more cautious about what to disclose and to whom; she recommends deliberate disclosure, after careful consideration of what is gained or lost, in the service of facilitating and developing the transference relationship. She suggests that there are no rules for the disclosure and management of the patient's response to the analyst's illness. Instead she advocates disclosure in response to the intrinsic process; for instance, where there is evidence of the patient's unconscious awareness of the illness, the analyst should not initiate disclosure without waiting for a signal of the patient's readiness to receive the information. She emphasizes the necessity of support for the analyst, who needs help to recognize and respond appropriately to the patient without interference from the press of personal needs. She agrees with Schwaber that the silence of the disease is deafening (for both analysts, the illness was a cancer not readily evident); feeling emotionally isolated, with no explicit and shared consciousness of the illness, interfered with their capacity to listen and be with their patients. Upon entering remission, Morrison initially informed prospective new patients of her history of cancer. After being in remission for some time, no longer plagued with fearful thoughts of her own death and in spite of a likelihood of the cancer's recurrence, Morrison reports that she stopped telling new patients of her illness.[1]

An important problem, one noted by many authors, is the analyst's need to be hopeful about prognosis, as balanced against a tendency to deny the prospect of one's death. The authors differ as to how analytic work can continue, or indeed if it can, when analysts believe they are dying, and the possibility is that they will become preoccupied with intense fears of separation and loss. There is a polarization between authors who recommend ending practice when faced with the likelihood of death, and others who believe analytic work can continue under these circumstances. Analysts who believe that hopefulness is compatible with a realistic acceptance and discussion of their likely impending death are convinced they can continue practice as long as they feel physically healthy. These same analysts emphasize the collaborative relational aspects of treatment, in which the analyst is experienced as a new object, with interpretation to follow; these analysts also describe patients who have trouble maintaining a steady therapeutic alliance and a collaborative relationship.

Analysts who believe that interpretation, verbally expressed knowledge, and ego observation are the mainstays of analytic work, who regard the experiencing of the relationship and the therapeutic alliance as necessary but peripheral, are inclined to the opinion that the analytic work cannot proceed when the analyst's neutrality is disturbed by a frightening illness, and recommend that practice cease in such instances. Of course this puts pressure on any analyst sharing this opinion who falls ill but wants to continue work. A strong tendency sets in to disavow the mortal consequences of the illness and not talk about it to patients. This creates an impasse in the treatment: the patient will eventually guess the analyst's condition but cannot talk about it. Unfortunate situations of this sort are described by Freedman and Firestein (1990), who spoke to a number of patients whose analyst's death occurred before the topic of the analyst's illness and impending death had ever been discussed.

Finding one's path through these contradictory recommendations in the literature is helped by the notion that all good analyses will include both interpretive work and varying degrees of attention to the relational aspect and ongoing shifts in the therapeutic alliance. Analyst and patient must be capable of both types of work, though there may be periods of time, perhaps briefly during the analyst's illness, when one or the other is not possible, whether because of the patient's or the analyst's temporary limitations. Examples of such situations are to be found in the cases cited in this literature, as well as in my own practice during my illness.

Phases of the illness: The analyst's capacity to listen and work

In my practice I see a range of patients in psychoanalysis and psychoanalytic psychotherapy, some requiring more attention to the therapeutic alliance and relational actions and others being more able to focus on the transference more narrowly defined as evolving from the one-body model. With most patients, I can see that my illness and at times altered emotional state require disclosure in response to its having already been perceived by the patient through subtle changes in my demeanour. Other patients continue working without discernible reaction to my at times altered state.

I have learned that there are several phases of an illness, not necessarily chronologically sequential, each eliciting different emotional states in the analyst, and therefore affecting the analysis most immediately in its relational aspect – in Ogden's terms, where the altered subjective state of the analyst will change the shape of the analytic third. The patient will experience the analyst's subjective relatedness differently during the illness, and the analyst's state will consequently be altered. When the illness is first known, or later, when changes in the analyst's physical condition occur, the fact and experience of the illness intrudes as a reality, initially precluding the possibility of the analyst's regarding it as a metaphor with transference references to areas of the patient's life experience. Patient and analyst *experience* the metaphor together, not yet *knowing* its meaning, altering the relationship and often the nature of the therapeutic alliance. When one feels the crushing terror of inevitable death brought on by the illness, it is unlikely that death can seem anything other than starkly real; hence one's ability to consider it as metaphor with transference meaning is compromised. If you believe you are dying, and the patient talks about it, it is initially difficult to see this as an 'as if' moment, a transference, which of course it often is.

Each of the analysts who have written papers about their experience working during a life-threatening illness has had an illness with a unique course, no two being the same; the fear of death surfaced differently and in varying degree. For some, there were long periods of time when anxiety and fear were absent.

First phase: Fear of death

For me, fears of death came with great frequency and intensity for the several discouraging weeks after my diagnosis and before I had found a physician I trusted. In those weeks I had been told by one well-regarded oncologist that I would die; two others allowed some hope but had little confidence and expected the treatment to have acute, lasting, and debilitating side-effects. Based on the treatment protocol they proposed, I was expecting to have extensive surgery very soon, followed by chemotherapy, and to be away from work for a number of weeks. I felt terrified. Although I had not yet chosen a physician, I assumed this would be the protocol in any case, and informed my patients over these weeks that I would be away for surgery in the near future.

I will describe the response of two patients to my announcement of my cancer diagnosis, which I chose to make immediately because I expected to be away from my work soon, and because I thought my anxiety was palpable to them. Each of these patients reacted differently on the continuum from experiencing (relatedness) to self-observing, hence making my analytic task different for each.

An 18-year-old diagnosed with schizo-affective disorder, Lisa had been in four-days-a-week psychotherapy for six months. Of all my patients, she required the most attention to the relational issues in treatment. One of her symptoms had been self-cutting, but this had stopped two months earlier. Her appearance was distinguished by bright orange and sometimes pink hair. She was recovering from a psychosis and was working well with me on the underlying affect dissociation and fantasies about needing and having to comply with an authoritarian 'guru' who simultaneously gave her activities meaning and robbed her of her sense of self. We had just had our first separation, when she was away for a two-week vacation with her family. This separation was the occasion of her realization that I was really important to her, since she had been aware of missing me and of feeling sad and lethargic. Several sessions after her return, I told her of my diagnosis, the upcoming surgery and chemotherapy, and of my being away for several weeks. As I gave her this news, her face flushed and tears welled up in her eyes. When I was finished, she said 'Oh,' with little affect. I told her I could see she was upset, and that this was understandable, especially now that she was just finding out how important I am to her. That was the end of the hour. The next day she returned and reported that she had cut herself again. After some inquiry, it emerged that she had felt worthless, like she used to feel a lot, and this was a feeling associated with cutting herself. I asked if she might have had any more feelings about the news I had given her, and this led to our connecting the meaning of her cutting with a drop in self-esteem as she reacted to the news of my absence and the frightening implications of death that came with a cancer diagnosis. She responded, saying she was glad I was talking about this with her. Over the next week she talked about feeling lifeless, without a guru, and she was missing her old boyfriend, who once served that function for her. She asked how I would feel when I lost my hair from the chemotherapy. I replied that I would hate it, and would have to wear a wig that might alter my appearance. The next session she arrived with a big grin, wearing a startling electric-blue wig. I laughed and asked what her ideas were about this; she said it was about being sympathetic with me. We agreed after some discussion that it was a way of reconnecting with me after feeling separated and lost.

Mrs A was a 35-year-old health care professional in analysis for four years. Her treatment had focused recently on the fantasy of being neglected and dismissed by people she needed and admired. She felt depressed and unworthy when she thought this happened, and masochistically surrendered to these people, taking care of their needs instead of her own; they then were ungrateful and treated her even worse. After I knew my diagnosis but before I told her, Mrs A began to be preoccupied with a fear that I was ill and she would lose me, hence becoming lost herself. She had extensive associations to her father's lengthy and eventually fatal illness in her late childhood, the seriousness of which he had disavowed; she had felt it was her job to take care of him. I had cancelled one of her sessions without telling her it was for one of my medical appointments, and raised the possibility that she had some fantasies about that missed session, which she denied. She continued with her fearful preoccupations, adding an apprehension that her neediness and sadness might be toxic to me and cause me to turn away.

I believed the experience with her father's being ill and disavowing it was being enacted with me. I thought she had a sense that I was ill and frightened, and was afraid that talking about it would be overwhelming to me. The next hour I told her of my diagnosis and treatment plan, trying to be matter-of-fact about it but actually feeling anxious. She was glad I had brought up the topic of my illness and was talking about it now, because she was very worried about my health and wanted to help me find the best doctors. She continued to be afraid of losing me; her own problems seemed diminished in contrast to mine. I responded by suggesting she felt she had to repeat what had happened in childhood with her father when he was ill, where her own needs were neglected and she had to serve his needs. She felt relieved. However, several sessions later she had the fantasy that this would be our last session, and this theme was unabated until my anxiety diminished two weeks later, when I found Dr E, whom I trusted and who was more optimistic about the prognosis.

I now understand Mrs A's continuing fantasies of losing me, even after the explicit discussion of my illness, as her response to her awareness of my fear and anxiety about my possible death, and my disavowal of that possibility, by not discussing or acknowledging it. The treatment got back on track and our search for transference meanings resumed once I calmed down upon beginning the treatment directed by Dr E. It was the beginning of the next month, and Mrs A had not paid her last month's bill; when I brought this up with her for discussion, she became openly angry, complaining I was 'hooking her to a plough'. My needs and hers could not coexist; for instance, one or the other of us would get the money owed; one or the other of us would be ill and therefore get her needs met by the other. We could now explore her previously disavowed anger as a transference.

One of the important differences in the treatments of these two patients is that for Lisa the resolution of her response to my illness was solely in the arena of our relatedness and actions in the relationship (in this case, my action in telling her about the illness and her action of wearing the blue wig to join me). Interpretation followed, but seemed less significant than the action in restoring the treatment momentum. Mrs A's treatment, like Lisa's, was detoured by both of our responses to my altered and anxious state, and the recovery of its momentum required action (my telling her of my illness). In contrast to Lisa's, however, Mrs A's treatment required interpretation (my challenging her about the unpaid bill and its transference meaning, which was also an action that showed her I was back on my feet) to get back on track. Returning to the interpretive mode was possible for me only with the shift in my inner state; when my anxiety lessened, I could see beyond my concerns and those of Mrs A about continuing of life and the treatment relationship.

Second phase: Uncertain optimism

The initial phase of terror and despair ended when I began treatment for my cancer with Dr E, who had recommended a different protocol, one that reduced the dangers of surgery, which was postponed until several months after chemotherapy. I felt much better emotionally and resolved to fight the disease and survive. Aware of the danger of denial, of holding false hope, I had been deliberate in choosing a doctor, not committing myself until I thoroughly understood how his treatment protocol was different and why his prognosis was so optimistic. Dr E was open, direct, and truthful, and while in my vulnerability I experienced him as a powerful figure, he was not a grandiose character. Clearly pleased with his professional stature and success, he had not lost modesty and respect for others. I felt in good hands.

In this second phase of illness, my work with patients quickly returned to a more typical mode. I informed them of the revised surgery schedule, saying that my absence would not be immediate and would extend for a few weeks rather than the several months originally projected. My listening capacity was restored, though with occasional lapses, along with some return of my stability and confidence in the face of an uncertain future. My listening was compromised at times by my need to feel strong and to take an aggressive posture towards the cancer, which made it hard to hear my patients' anxious worries about losing me. Over the next six months my cancer treatments, though arduous, had good results, as hoped, and interruptions in my analytic schedule were usually expected and planned. During this period I felt almost my usual self at work, as I had not during the initial phase. I could usually hear my patients' fantasies, inquiries, and other comments about my death and illness as metaphor.

Clinical examples of patients' comments and my responses will illustrate the contrast in process characteristic of each phase. Shortly after I had disclosed my illness to Mr J, a patient in analysis for some time, he told me a detailed story about a relative who had my kind of cancer and who ultimately died. He thought her physician had been overconfident and had not treated her with all the chemotherapy available. This extra treatment, Mr J thought, might have stopped the disease; doctors, he said, cannot be trusted to do the right thing. I said nothing to this comment, instead sitting silently with an anxious internal uproar stimulated by his tale. Could I trust my doctors? Might this happen to me? Was it already too late? I was not immediately able to hear the transference meaning of his remarks and to explore it with him as I usually would. Nor could I respond to the relational question implicit in the session: Would I survive my illness and be there for him?

I had a quite different response to a similar story told several months later by a patient who was a nurse. She was caring for a cancer patient who did not yet feel very sick, but she thought he was terminal; his oncologist had not told him the truth about his prognosis, and he and his family were planning their lives as if there would be no end. I asked her if she was worried about me. She agreed that she was, but couldn't say why it would be coming up now. I asked her to tell me more about her experience with this patient, and she added that it was very difficult to take care of this man when she thought she knew something important about him that he didn't know. She felt angry with his doctor for not taking the responsibility of informing him of the prognosis. She wondered if she should bring it up to the patient but was scared and overwhelmed by having to take on that task. This led to further material about her disappointment and anger at having to do difficult jobs for people who were actually better able to take care of these things than she. This was how she had felt as a child when her parents did not take their responsibility for her younger siblings, leaving her to take care of their problems. I suggested she might feel responsible for me now with my illness, maybe angry, aware of her own inadequate resources to take proper care of me.

Third phase: Remission or recovery

The third phase of working with a life-threatening illness is the recovery period, which for most cancer patients will last for several years or more before remission is considered a cure. As the analyst continues to feel healthy, with medical check-ups spaced increasingly further apart, the illness usually becomes a distant presence for both partners in the treatment process. From time to time, the illness intrudes, as at times of separation, such as vacations and other times when the schedule is inter-rupted by the analyst for the occasions of an ordinary life. It also is raised in some patients' fantasies on the anniversaries of significant times in the analyst's medical treatment (for instance, the one-year anniversary of my surgery). Sometimes fantasies and memories about the analyst's illness and absence are stimulated not by an event but by the patient's wishes and fears in the transference (for instance, one patient felt especially needy and then had the thought I might get sick again and be unavailable).

For the analyst, being reminded of the illness can precipitate a change from calm to an anxious inner state. Medical appointments for tests and follow-up can cause the analyst to become preoccupied. For me, a typical error in this phase has been to respond to the patient's allusion to my illness with matter-of-fact reassurances that I am fine; this denial of my anxiety leads to a shutting off of feelings in the patient that ought to be explored. In analysis for many years, Ms P is uncannily attuned to my inner states. Raised in a family in which disavowal is the typical reaction to any emo-tional state, she has struggled long in her treatment to integrate her own disavowed painful states. She gets distraught whenever I disavow my anxiety, which is easily apparent to her; she feels I am pushing her away by reassuring her I am healthy when I am not. She believes my giving her no information but only reassurance is hiding an awful truth, which is actually my own anxiety about my health but to her seems a reality about my illness. Interpretation of this need for concrete information gets nowhere, except to increase her anxiety about what she is sure I must be hiding since I am not addressing it. It seems she is unable to inquire with me into the transfer-ence meaning of her need for information unless I grant her a concrete response in the context of our relatedness. We have understood that the urgent requirement for my concrete response is caused by threats of disorganization kindled by a re-enact-ment of the psychic trauma she experienced in childhood when her inquiries and conclusions about her parents' inner states and motives were repeatedly dismissed and negated. This traumatic experience occurred particularly with her mother, who seems to have been a borderline personality with depressed and dissociated states that were quite frightening to the patient as a child.

Whom to tell what?

The questions of what, how, and to whom to disclose are always answered in the con-text of the particular treatment with each patient. Except on the occasions when I was distracted by my own anxiety, notably in the first phase of the illness, I listened and learned what my patients needed and wanted to know, and indeed what they might already have guessed, as evidenced in dreams, fantasies, interactions, and questions. My decisions about deliberate disclosure were directed by the same considerations I gave to talking to my patients about my pregnancies years ago. My work with child patients then had been particularly instructive in this regard, since issues of develop-mental level and capacity to absorb factual information are at the forefront of any deliberation about self-disclosure. Regarding my illness, I was direct and open with all my patients, and told most of them soon after the diagnosis. My anxiety was palpable and disruptive, at least to me, and probably for each of them. I knew our schedules would have to be interrupted in the near future and later on at various times, so I judged disclosure to be inescapable.

I did not tell patients whom I was seeing only briefly or occasionally. Nor did I tell the two children then in my practice, a five-year-old girl who had been in analysis for a year, and a young adolescent girl whose once-weekly treatment had recently started. I chose not to tell the five-year-old, partly because I expected a negative effect on the shaky alliance with the parents, and also because at her age the concepts of serious illness and death are not developmentally available. The patient had fantasies that I was pregnant, probably stimulated in part by the changes she perceived in my body; my absences were experienced as going away to have the baby and were occasions for struggles with sibling rivalry. These issues were the focus of transference interpretations that seemed to make sense to her. I began to see the older girl in the second phase of my illness, and did not tell her of it because she planned to be vacationing at the time of my expected absence; I listened and never heard any reason to discuss the illness with her.

Reaction to my disclosure was unique to each patient, but generally it facilitated the process and deepened trust and confidence in me. Nearly all my patients were at times fearful of my dying and of losing me forever. In order of prominence, reactions included (1) a desire to help me, to find me the best doctor; (2) fear that talking about illness and death would hurt me; (3) anger at the potential disruption of their treatment; (4) pain and sadness about past experiences of illness and loss of important people; (5) reluctance, guilt, and shame about speaking of their own needs and problems, which they considered trivial compared to mine or those of other patients. An example of this last reaction was a patient's dream of sitting at her mother's table with lots of other children eating a meal, while she herself got only crumbs. As we discussed the dream, she revealed a fantasy that I would stop seeing her until the end of my treatments, while continuing to see my sicker and needier patients. This led to further exploration of her feeling not entitled to ask for and receive the nurturing she longs for.

In response to patients' reactions to my changed states and to information I disclosed about my illness, I tried to be alert to any troubles with the therapeutic alliance and other aspects of their experience of our relationship, and wherever possible listened and commented on the metaphor of the illness and its transference meanings. At other, less noble moments, distracted by my own terror of death, loss, and separation, I was silent or disruptively reassuring, rather than inquiring further and deeper into its meaning. I was usually successful in correcting these lapses later, helped by my own self-observing capacity and by my patients' openness in showing me my mistakes.

Concluding recommendations

It is possible to work through the phases of a life-threatening illness, and with most patients careful and deliberate self-disclosure can deepen and facilitate the analytic process. The analyst must be able to recover steadiness when it is shaken in the face of uncertainty and loss. The patient's awareness of and response to the analyst's inner states will enable the analyst both to attend to the patient's needs in the collaborative relatedness with the analyst and to hear references to the illness as metaphor and as the basis for transference exploration.

The analyst is able to work effectively throughout such an illness only if certain conditions are met. He or she must have confidence in the medical team, feel well cared for, and have an open and truthful relationship with them. To hear patients' concerns about abandonment, the analyst must have a powerful, safety-providing physician to meet physical and medical needs, with no danger of abandonment. Another condition for continuing analytic work is an ongoing treatment relationship with an analyst in which the ill analyst's inner state is understood and reactions to the illness and to patients are examined. A less adequate arrangement is provided by ongoing consultation about clinical practice, focused on decisions about disclosure and countertransference issues interfering with the recognition of the transference and the requirements of the therapeutic alliance and treatment process.

The analyst's self-object needs must be met and examined in a professional context, whether in treatment or in case consultation. This will be important in any case, but especially so if the analyst's medical condition deteriorates. Denial is a powerful force, easily mistaken for hope, and there is no way to distinguish them solely within one's own subjectivity. If the analyst is to continue working with a life-threatening illness, he or she has the ethical responsibility to enlist the support of a trusted yet profession-ally objective person. Friends or family members cannot fill this role, since their love and their identification with the potentially dying analyst prevent them from seeing and speaking what the analyst cannot. Sometimes the dying analyst needs intervention and help in planning the end of practice and discussing termination with patients.

Last but hardly the least of the conditions required for continuing practice is the love and support of family, friends, and colleagues. Feeling connected to and embraced by an interested and caring network of people is essential for withstanding one's fears and anxieties about death, with its attendant fantasies of separation, loss, and abandonment. When one is terrified, it is extremely difficult to help patients with their own fears.

Notes

1 Subjectively, Morrison felt healthy, though her doctors were guarded in their prognosis. Within a few years after the publication of her paper, the cancer recurred and she died. We do not know how she managed the end of her practice and the termination of her patients' treatments, which is an extremely important area for further discussion in the literature.

9

LIFE-LONG ANALYSIS?

Evelyn Carlisle

'But this won't be a life-long analysis!' With these words my training analyst pointed out his advanced age to me in the preliminary talks. At that point in time he was 63 years old. My analysis did not start until two years later. I experienced the analyst as a vital, experienced, intelligent and extremely helpful analyst.

In the second year of analysis, when I had to wait unusually long for his door to open, I had a fantasy that he had broken down and was lying helpless on the floor. I was relieved when I could understand this fantasy as a father transference since my father had become quite fragile at that time. The analyst commented on my own life situation in my early forties as 'the best time after which not much would happen anymore', and he was of the opinion that at the age of 60 the 'biblical age' was reached and it would be time to die. In my sixth year of analysis he turned 70.

In the following year he told me that his wife had cancer. In the subsequent months I felt a fading attention in him and noticed that he occasionally fell asleep, until he admitted in one session that I 'had a depressive analyst' and that he needed a much longer summer break. I increasingly entertained the thought of quitting, especially since I was close to the end of my training. Today I regret that I did not find the courage to detach from him against his will, as, in the following year, my analysis terminated with traumatic consequences. These caused me to reach my limits in my working capacity for the first time in my career.

I don't know when I actually noticed this. It began rather unnoticeably. It was not just the frequent falling asleep during the hours, which he called the 'sleep of a wet nurse'. It was more a gradual change in his personality that struck me, at first, in his changed appearance. Thus I noticed an increasing carelessness in his appearance: stains on his clothes, a bad shave, interrupting the hour to go to the toilet, an unsafe, increasingly wobbly walk. In addition, he would frequently begin the session late and even forget appointments, which had once led to my anger since I often undertook a long journey to make it to the sessions. He reacted to this in the subsequent hour by yelling at me so that I no longer dared to lie down on the couch. This outburst of affect on his part was never talked about but rather ignored, except for an attempt at a humorous interpretation in the following session.

I experienced this as a serious breach in the relationship. I became cautious, reserved and internally distanced myself, yet I wanted to maintain my good object.

This became more and more difficult since I felt an increasing transparency on his part. For instance, he told me about other analysands, cited them in part verbatim and wanted to hear my opinion about them. In particular, in the case of an analysand, a woman, who terminated her analysis although she had started after me, he was outraged and asked me what I thought about it.

In one of the sessions he began with the question of what it could mean that his wife was bleeding from the vagina and if I found this worrying. I could not talk to him about my being upset over this. This was not the only session when I had been pushed into the position of a counsellor; I felt increasingly tortured and shamed on the couch; I felt shame for him.

These transgressions became many: thus I involuntarily once witnessed a big fight with his wife. Another time, he asked me after the session to take his empty wine bottles to the trash. Once he called me before our session to bring him rolls from a nearby bakery since he was not able to leave his house. In the last months I experienced a reversal of roles where I cared for *him*. That was the time when my father died.

Because he was very experienced, there were now and again sessions that were helpful even if they tended to decrease. More and more I felt that my problems were put off and not taken seriously; I reacted with massive psychosomatic symptoms, which he trivialized and advised that I should drink a glass of red wine to relax. Although the wish to quit was clearly there, I was no longer able to address it against the background of his previous statements and my serious reactions. In talking to another analysand, I found out that she, too, had a similar experience, but she did not feel as impacted as I and hence I became unsure of my perceptions.

The analysis ended soon after with the death of his wife. I came to my session without any clue and he called out to me through the door that the session was cancelled that day. Afterwards I never got a message from his relatives or representative who might have informed me of the final ending of my analysis. For some time I was in the dark about whether and how I might have any further personal contact with him. Only indirectly did I find out that he had become very ill.

My experiences, briefly summarized here, have not only damaged the relationship to my training analyst in a major way, but they have also deeply shattered my professional identity and, periodically, my attitude towards psychoanalysis. After this incredible termination, I suffered from panic attacks, extremely high blood pressure, let alone the fundamental doubts about my practised and loved profession. I reproach myself for my inability to end the analysis much sooner. I am still ashamed about this. Since my analyst was able to maintain a façade for quite some time, the negative development occurred so unnoticeably and subtly that I did not become aware until much later how ill he had already been and for a long time. In retrospect I was surprised to hear how massive his health problems had been.

In my last year of analysis, and for quite some time afterwards, I experienced a persistent and soon severe conflict of loyalty. I felt paralysed, wanted to stop the analysis, but did not see any possibility without getting into a massive conflict with my analyst. This impediment was made worse by his special status at the institute. But when I, nonetheless, turned to an older colleague of his, someone who was on friendly terms with him, this colleague reacted by trivializing the issue. This, of course, did not encourage me to seek out further help at that point, for example through the ethics committee. My anxiety was too great that I would be seen as a traitor and discredit myself, especially as I feared for my training qualification. I was afraid that, if I declared myself, my analysis would not be recognized, or that I would have to undergo a supplemental analysis after all those years of analysis.

What was helpful was the support of my supervisors, once it became known that my training analyst had been ill. The supervisors encouraged me to complete the qualifying stage of my training at all costs. Also, several sessions with a female training analyst at the institute helped me to understand how ill my analyst had been and the effects this had on me and on my analysis. On the other hand, this experience was limited by the fact that for reasons of loyalty I had gone to a colleague whom I knew had herself been in analysis with my analyst. Finally I had to grasp that I had spent the last year of my analysis with an analyst who was suffering from progressive dementia and that I had become a victim of narcissistic abuse; and this with the known psychical consequences that such abuse entails.

In sum, the way the institute dealt with my situation and the situation of those with similar experiences has been extremely unsatisfactory, even in retrospect. Although I have proceeded on a very satisfying path over the last ten years, both professionally and privately, which is surely *also* a result of my training analysis, the ending of my analysis has left persistent marks on me. Thus, on the one hand, I am left with the mourning of an unsuccessful ending, on the other hand, I hold a grudge against the responsible people at the institute, for instance the education committee, or the executive board, that nobody proactively approached me although it was known how ill my training analyst had been. People looked away, denied or misinterpreted the miserable situation of the last trainees in analysis. As great as the empathy was in personal dialogues that I later sought out on occasion, as lost and left alone I was in the situation of the abuse. In my view, the denial of the events that concerned not only the trainees but also numerous group members of self-awareness groups continues until today. No working through took place at the institute. My motivation to become active and engaged in the institute has suffered from this omission.

I have written down these painful experiences with the hope that I would incite a reflection on how to deal with the ageing of psychoanalysts, and to raise the question of how derailments of this nature could be prevented or else caught at an early stage.

10

ANALYSIS LOST AND REGAINED

Tove Traesdal

Introduction

When I was asked to contribute to this volume, it was exactly ten years since I had lost my second analyst through her sudden and completely unexpected death from cardiac arrest. Five years earlier, I had lost my first analyst equally suddenly, from the onset of his pancreatic cancer, a cancer that had proven to be incurable and terminal. In the wake of these losses, particularly the second one, I went through a very painful period in my life, with a great deal of confusion and inner turmoil over what had happened to me and why I reacted as I did. After a period of waiting, I was lucky enough to be taken care of by another female analyst, with whom I fortunately was able to establish a relationship that allowed me gradually to dare to risk yet another attachment to an analyst, and to delve once again into the process of letting go of my less serviceable coping strategies in the hope of attaining a richer and more fulfilling life. As part of my working through and making sense of my situation I decided to write a paper, which was published in the *Journal of the American Psychoanalytic Association* (Traesdal, 2005).

The present chapter will revisit in more depth some of the issues addressed there. Other aspects will be left out, however, particularly theoretical considerations and the review of existing literature. The two articles, written some eight years apart, will thus supplement each other. Some of my points will have relevance primarily to psychoanalysis, but mostly they will also pertain to psychotherapies conducted with the aim of bringing about structural changes on a deeper level in a patient's personality.

Delving into this topic again, it struck me whilst reviewing the sparse body of literature available that, contrary to most psychoanalytic writing, these articles show an abundance of self-revealing reports from colleagues. Some recount how their own life-threatening illnesses interfered with their work, their feelings and reactions, and how successful or unsuccessful they were at handling these situations. Others explore in detail their reactions and processes after the loss of an analyst/therapist. It seems that the problems we encounter on the edge between life and death compel us to reveal more about ourselves than we are inclined to do otherwise. This inspired me to think: do I dare now, ten years later, to be more personal in my writing? At the time when my losses occurred, I deliberately chose to protect myself from bringing my own experiences to the forefront. My boundaries were flooded by the sudden breach in the analytic process; something I presume is a general problem in such a situation. Now, a decade on from these traumatic events, I have decided to share with the reader some experiences I had during my unusually long and cumbersome analytic journey, and I shall use these as a point of departure for discussing some important aspects of dealing with the aftermath of such an experience.

Some moments from my personal history

The premature loss of attachment figures, and the attendant consequences, were the most important reasons why I had sought psychoanalytic treatment in the first place. During the work with my first analyst, I realised at a certain point how vulnerable I would be if something serious were to happen to him; and it scared me. He was in his late sixties and planned to go on working for a few more years. I decided to discuss with him to whom I should turn if anything should happen to him unexpectedly, trusting that he could handle my focusing on his mortality. He suggested that I might consult one of the two colleagues with whom he shared his premises, and I confirmed that, in case of an emergency, I would contact his female colleague. I presume that neither he nor I thought that this precautionary measure would really ever become necessary. This two-minute dialogue, almost an aside, turned out to be of great significance to me when, a year or so later, I returned from a couple of days abroad and found a message on my answering machine informing me that my next session had to be cancelled. He said that he had some health problems that needed examination, and I would receive further information as soon as possible. It turned out to be cancer, and two months later he knew that there was no hope of being cured. He chose to close down his practice with immediate effect; I was able to take leave of him by exchanging a couple of letters, but I never saw him again.

My analyst decided to stop seeing his patients as soon as he realised that he was incurably ill. This is some of what he wrote: 'With this diagnosis, there has not been a moment of doubt that I have to close down my practice immediately. Even if I were able to work for a period, I could not expose my patients and particularly not myself to an insecure compromise-situation . . .' And about the possibility of meeting to take personal leave: 'It is not easy to judge the advantages and disadvantages that might have for you, but I know that for me it is out of the question, so are telephone calls. I think I might have coped with it, but to be frank, I need all my strength available to cope with what I have to face now . . . You are welcome to write a letter – if you have questions, I shall try to answer; in any case I shall read what you write.'

This letter was written shortly after my analyst received the message that his cancer was incurable and that he was facing the prospect of a dramatically shortened life span. During the two months it took to establish his prognosis, I was offered contact with his wife, also a psychoanalyst, in order to be informed about the result of an operation. I talked to her twice on the telephone. She was admirably capable of handling the situation and I still feel grateful for the way that my needs were thought about. The two colleagues sharing practice premises with my analyst prepared themselves to serve the possible needs of his patients, and as soon as his situation became clear, they made themselves available for emergency consultations.

Thus I was lucky to have my needs well taken care of when my first analyst had to leave his practice so abruptly. My relationship to him was, and still is some 15 years later, one of deep gratitude and love. His help had been invaluable to me, and my mourning was profound. When thinking of him, I still miss him. The two analysts who have seen me through the remainder of my analytic journey have, in their own quite different ways, been equally competent and helpful. So, it is not so much the analysis but him as a person that I miss amongst the living.

I was in no doubt about my need to continue my analysis and, after seeing her intermittently for a short period, I was able to enter a five-sessions-a-week process with the female analyst mentioned above. She knew my former analyst well and, during the following year until he died, she would inform me from time to time about how he was doing. This was not done in detail, but it was enough for me to rejoice at the fact that he was well enough to celebrate his 70th birthday, and to prepare myself for his death, which happened some nine months after I had started seeing my new analyst.

When I lost my second analyst, circumstances were not nearly as favourable. She was a vital and energetic woman who was only 60 when she died a few hours after my Friday session; a sudden death nobody could have been prepared for. I had been seeing her for four and a half years and I was probably in the middle phase of this analysis, an analysis that had been 'hard work'. When she died, she had just returned from a long summer holiday and, after that long break, I happened to have been summing up, perhaps on more of a meta-level than usual, where I felt myself to be standing. I had a new feeling of having reached calmer waters, which was my metaphor at the time. I felt that my analytic threads were weaving themselves together into a tapestry of (re)integration, even if I still felt far from termination.

Even today, it makes me shudder to think of my state of mind during the first few months after her death. Having decided to trust the idea that losing one's analyst will not happen twice, I had not discussed with her what to do in such an eventuality. However, as a consequence of our work I felt more certain about what my needs were and more able to act accordingly. On a couple of occasions I was lucky to be able to discuss my situation with a male colleague and friend, who gave me his support and advice. The analytic community in my country is small, and the number of colleagues to whom I could turn for help was therefore very limited. Some who had no time available to give me nevertheless sent messages of compassion and acknowledgement of my difficult situation, which I perceived as supporting and helpful. Meanwhile, however, I was in a state that even now I feel unable to communicate in words. I was vulnerable, confused, desperate. My loss coincided with the assault on the twin towers in New York, and I would watch the TV news for hours, identifying with people whose loss mirrored my own state of mind in their desperate searching for their loved ones.

For a long period, I was unable to express what had happened to me. My everyday life was surprisingly unaffected; it was as though my life went on in two distinctly separate dimensions, and in the area occupied by my interrupted analysis I was completely cut off from communication with others. After a while, I was offered therapy by a senior analyst whom I saw once a week for a year. I think we both tried to make it work, but I never really felt understood by her. I was not able to verbalise my state of mind and, indeed, it would take me a very long time to regain that capacity. In addition, she tended to interpret my reactions as pertaining to her rather than to my deceased analyst. It was as if she tried to make me attach myself to her, even though from the outset she had offered only a limited period of psychotherapeutic aid. I felt that she interpreted my attempts to express my mourning as some undesirable idealising transference attachment to my deceased analyst. I am in no position to judge what was 'mere transference' and what was 'real', but my contact with her led nowhere.

After I stopped seeing her I waited a while in order to decide what I needed to do next. Then after a couple of preliminary interviews, I had to wait for another year before starting work with the woman who would turn out to become my third and, thank goodness, last analyst. I am in no doubt that each of the two former treatments would have brought my analytic journey to a sufficiently satisfactory conclusion for me not to feel the need for further analysis. However, although the process was prolonged considerably, it may in the end have been more thorough.

Two aspects of the approaches of my second and third analysts have been of particular value. Both of them gave me ample space for my task of mourning the deceased; and neither interfered with my dialogue with those who were dead. Particularly during the first part of my second treatment, I was greatly helped to overcome possible loyalty conflicts and to integrate the gains of my first analysis so that they could be built on with the new analyst. I have no doubt that the second time I had to start anew was made easier by my second analyst's way of handling the first loss, which meant that I could dare to take some things for granted. Neither of the two later analysts intruded upon my relationship with their predecessor, but left it to me slowly to develop the capacity to express myself verbally about it. If they ever disagreed with their deceased colleague they kept it to themselves, leaving it to me to bring up residues of negative transference or to focus on the less beneficial aspects of the former work. My love and gratitude were never treated as idealisation, or otherwise interpreted as defensive, even if some aspects of my reactions may have been exactly that. They left me to discover such things in my own time. I stress this because I think it is of particular importance, for reasons I shall explain further on.

It has been reassuring to read that many analytic patients who are also professional therapists report that they have benefited from the support of colleagues within the analytic community. I am sorry to say that, with a few very valued exceptions, I have had the opposite experience. I shall not elaborate on this, except to emphasise the need to accord bereft colleagues the same courtesy and compassion that we would give to any other human being who has lost someone important. I had the idea that my non-professional friends, who were not familiar with the world of analysis, might not be in a position to grasp intuitively the situation I was in. However, in general they turned out to be better at this. To share just one colleague's comment: 'How will you ever get over this and move on? You must feel that you killed them!' In this situation, as in many others, it is a good idea to confine analytic interpretation to the boundaries of the consulting room!

Comments

Preventive measures

In what has been written about illness and death in analysts, testimonies of confusion and chaos in the wake of these events are abundant. Many authors have pointed to the danger of colluding with the need that patients may have for analysts to be invulnerable, omnipotent and immortal. The topic of the possible illness or death of the analyst may be circumvented, consistently interpreted as separation anxiety or treated as fantasy. It goes without saying that in most instances the theme of the analyst's death should indeed be treated as fantasy material but, in my view, the reality aspect of death should not be denied altogether when working with our patients. Death can happen to anybody at any time. It is of vital importance that we as therapists are able to handle the reality of our mortality and to work through our own fear of death and dying thoroughly, so that we can handle the topic in an undefended way when working with our patients. There are ample reports in the literature suggesting that the sudden, premature rupture of an analytic process is bound to be traumatic, and may cause iatrogenic injury to the patient. In my opinion, it is important that this topic can be discussed on the level of reality at least once during an analysis or psychotherapy – preferably the first time that it surfaces or at least early on in the process. This does not preclude the simultaneous discussion of the theme on the fantasy level. In my experience patients will often approach the topic of my possible death rather obliquely, probably fearing that I will not be able to respond to the harshness of a direct comment on the subject, and they are relieved when they experience that I am able to talk with them about this in a focused, matter-of-fact way.

As I myself experienced, it is extremely helpful for a patient to have already discussed how to handle the situation if what must not happen actually does happen. Dattner (1989) briefly explores the complications that may arise when a dying analyst assigns his patient to a colleague with whom to continue analysis. She believes that such an arrangement may not facilitate the establishment of a new therapeutic alliance and can in fact be counterproductive. I am in complete agreement with her about this. At this stage, what is important is to have someone to turn to for advice, to help think about one's immediate and long-term needs.

Handling the crisis

Even if this chapter is mostly about the aftermath of death, I shall allow myself a short excursion into the topic of prolonged illness in the analyst. In the literature, professionals have described how serious illness caused deterioration in their analytic capacities (e.g. Schwartz, 1990; Wong, 1990). They report, not surprisingly, how bodily pain, discomfort, worry and increased psychic vulnerability made them self-preoccupied and fragile. In cases where a serious illness will eventually be cured, it may merely be a question of not resuming work too early, which many analysts will undoubtedly feel under pressure to do. If the disease is incurable and will necessitate periods away from work, as well as serious uncertainty and worry for both parties, closing down the practice seems to be the most realistic and ethical solution. In my country we have very solid social security arrangements which ensure that there are fewer financial problems than elsewhere; we even have a system of third-party payment for the bulk of any psychotherapy undertaken. It is evident from what professionals and patients report, that the kind of 'compromise-situation' that my analyst judged as inadvisable does indeed happen, often because the therapist is financially dependent on continuing to work, whether his health allows it or not. Particularly in articles from the United States, which constitute the majority of papers written on this topic, the detrimental consequences of this situation are described. Authors point out that continuing to work during a prolonged illness can be tempting, as it gives meaning to life. Medical doctors will often encourage us to participate as much and for as long as possible in normal activities when we are ill, while not necessarily taking into account the special requirements of our profession. Patients, for their part, will often wish to stay in contact with their analyst and appreciate continuing the work. They may be reluctant to leave a sick therapist even if he or she is incapable of functioning well, caught up in the same oscillation between hope and discouragement that any family member or friend experiences, with all the implications this has for the deterioration of the professional aspects of this particular relationship.

Then how are these problems to be addressed? All caring professions have their own particular requirements. One of ours is to try, as far as possible, to arrange ourselves in a responsible way financially so that our survival will not become a burden that our patients will have to carry. A therapist who is periodically ill may perhaps alter his activities in favour of short-term work, assessment or consultative crisis intervention or, if absences are not frequent or of long duration, an experienced clinician may still be of use in supervisory activities. In any case, there should be no burden on patients to support the survival of the analyst, either financially or psychologically.

When an analyst faces an incurable disease there is an understandable need for self-protection. The task of handling in a professional manner the patient's reproaches, angry transference enactments or emotional reactions of sorrow and despair may be too great, and the avoidance of this may be fully justified as a means of protecting both analyst and patient. But if at all possible, some kind of personal communication will greatly benefit the patient. If this is asking too much, a colleague might write such a note on behalf of the therapist. Personally, I felt relieved by the fact that my analyst was so clear in letting me know honestly that he was in no position to continue to work with me professionally, and it made a huge difference to be able to take leave of him in the form of a letter.

It seems from the literature that it is usually family members who become the messengers of an analyst's sickness or death. Generally, I believe this to be a bad solution for both parties. One of the most difficult aspects of the sudden interruption of an analysis is the breakdown of boundaries between the analytic space and outside realities. A patient may populate an analyst's private surroundings with all sorts of idiosyncratic fantasies or ideas. To many former patients, reading obituaries and attending funerals can be quite overwhelming experiences, where the privacy of the professional dyadic relationship is ruptured and the analyst as a private person is brought to the forefront. It can be difficult for a patient to withhold strong emotional reactions towards the analyst's bereft relatives. The relative who contacts the patient, usually in a state of grief, may not be familiar with the dynamics of the analytic process and cannot be counted on to handle the task in a way that benefits the patient. It is much better, in my view, for an analyst in private practice to arrange for a colleague to take care of his practice in case of an emergency. In every workshop I have attended where this topic has been discussed, the need for committees within institutes, which can assist in situations of sickness and death among colleagues, has been highlighted, but to my knowledge, such an arrangement exists in very few places.

The aftermath

What, then, are the needs of patients who suffer the sudden loss of their analyst? Several authors have pointed out that when a therapist dies the patient loses not only the analysis, with its investment of hope for change and the alleviation of suffering, but also a very important real relationship. The literature (e.g. Rendely, 1999) suggests that this latter aspect is particularly overlooked. I will devote the remainder of this chapter to reflections concerning the handling of both these aspects.

Immediate needs

It is generally recommended that the first professional therapeutic contact follow-ing the death of the analyst should initially be concentrated on helping the patient to share the loss. Patients who are not therapists themselves may otherwise have no opportunity to speak about this loss with someone who can understand it. It has been recommended by several authors that the 'bridging analyst', as this function has been designated by Ziman-Tobin (1989), should be someone who knew the deceased. The patient's need for confirmation of his or her perception of the analyst as a real person is emphasised at this stage. This accords with my own recent experience with a patient: I knew of his deceased therapist, but I did not know him well enough to be able to help the patient to confirm or disconfirm hunches that I felt he needed to be able to sort out. The patient needs the opportunity to describe the impact of the loss, to reminisce, and to speak about what the analyst meant to him or her. I think at this stage not much more is demanded of the therapist than simply compassionate listen-ing. Such sessions will serve the purpose of dissolving some of the transference, and making the analyst more real.

Left speechless . . .

Following the sudden breach of an ongoing analytic process, writers tend to agree that the kind of immediate help the analytic patient needs should be in the form of con-tact with another analyst who will serve a bridging function. However, Ziman-Tobin (op. cit.) has pointed out that needs may vary widely, as may a bereft patient's capacity to assess what they are. In the wake of an analyst's death, free association comes to a sudden halt. Whereas everyone capable of reflective functioning has two levels of communication going on simultaneously – inwardly to oneself and outwardly with others – the analytic patient is in a unique situation. In the process of free association, the inner monologue is extended to include someone else – the analyst. This stream of shared thought lies at the very core of the analytic process. A whole vocabulary of 'shorthand' metaphors and expressions develops within the analytic dyad but this is devoid of meaning if communicated to somebody outside it. The analytic dialogue is unlike any other dialogue in the patient's life and is, as such, irreplaceable in the external world.

It is interesting to note how often patients who have lost their analyst speak about the experience as losing one's voice, becoming mute (e.g. Garfield, 1990; Wolman, 1990). Wolman describes it as 'an island of "alexithymia" locked within my own psyche'. In a recently-published article, 'A Voice Lost, a Voice Found', Robin Deutsch (2011) describes in detail how the death of her analyst rendered her unable to speak about her inner life in any meaningful way, and how dreams became the primary vehicle, so to speak, by means of which she slowly regained that capacity. Ogden (1997) writes: 'The analysand's experience of the death of the analyst prior to the planned ending of a fruitful analysis represents not only an experience of enormous personal loss, but, as important, an *experience of a type of insanity*. The analyst's death forecloses for the analysand the possibility of fully retrieving his mind (a mind that has not been exclusively his own personal possession for some time)' (my italics). This loss of voice, speech, language – whichever metaphor one chooses – is probably the least conspicuous but the most important aspect to be aware of when seeing someone who has lost his or her analysis. It is very likely that when they see another professional during the acute crisis following the loss of the analyst, patients will lack access to the expression of what it means to them on a deeper level, how they feel about it and what they need.

Moving on . . .

According to the above-mentioned considerations, the bridging phase may be of variable duration. Considerable time may be needed. The bridging analyst may have an already full schedule and little time available, and may therefore feel pressured to reach a conclusion that could be premature. If patients are in doubt about how to proceed, they should be offered low frequency contact with the bridging analyst for as long as necessary until they feel more certain about future needs. If a patient needs to continue analysis, it has generally been recommended that the second analysis should be with someone who does not know the deceased colleague, and that it should not be the person who dealt with the immediate crisis. Personally, I doubt the universal validity of both recommendations. I think that, whenever possible, the bridging function should be handled in a way that leaves the door open to continued analytic work, so as to protect the patient from having to see more new professionals than is strictly necessary. Even if this entails waiting for a permanent vacancy, this might be more desirable for patients than referral elsewhere, which may involve another painful loss. Neither do I think that it is necessarily a disadvantage if the two successive analysts have known each other. In my own country, where the analytic/psychotherapeutic community is small, this requirement would in any case be impossible to fulfil. What is important is whether the second analyst's personality structure is narcissistically tinged, with concomitant countertransference needs to be a rescuer or to compete with the former analyst. It is probable that a very strong personal attachment to, or dislike of, the deceased would complicate matters, as would any strong and incompatible theoretical differences. All these factors would make it inadvisable to accept a colleague's bereft patient for treatment. Sympathy and respect for a deceased analyst whom one knew can otherwise make bridging of the two processes easier, as I myself experienced.

As I have already mentioned, the technique of interpreting invariably in terms of transference within the new analytic dyad will probably be unproductive or even detrimental. Without exception, everybody who has accounted for their personal experience of this situation has emphasised the chaotic, frightening feeling of having lost the power of finding words for their feelings. It is as if that capacity got buried with the deceased. I strongly believe that the analyst's capacity to allow space and time for the bereft to regain that capacity, without intrusion, will be *the* most important factor in turning injury into growth, providing the patient with a new companion with whom to illuminate his/her inner landscape, with the aim of making it a better place to stay.

BIBLIOGRAPHY FOR PART II

Abend, S. (1982) 'Serious Illness in the Analyst: Countertransference Considerations', *Journal of the American Psychoanalytic Association* 30: 365–380.

Arlow, J. A. (1990) 'The Analytic Attitude in the Service of Denial', in H. J. Schwartz and A.-L. Silver (eds), *Illness in the Analyst: Implications for the Treatment Relationship*. Madison, CT: International Universities Press, 1990.

Clark, R. (1995) 'The Pope's Confessor: A Metaphor Relating to Illness in the Analyst', *Journal of the American Psychoanalytic Association* 43: 137–149.

Cohen, M. (2002) 'Commentary on "Mortal Gifts: A Two-Part Essay on the Therapist's Mortality" by Ellen Pinsky', *Journal of The American Academy of Psychoanalysis and Dynamic Psychiatry* 30: 209–210.

Dattner, R. (1989) 'On the Death of the Analyst: A Review', *Contemporary Psychoanalysis* 25: 419–427.

Deutsch, R. A. (2011) 'A Voice Lost, A Voice Found: After the Death of the Analyst', *Psychoanalytic Inquiry* 31: 526–535.

Dewald, P. A. (1982) 'Serious Illness in the Analyst: Transference, Counter-Transference, and Reality Responses – and Further Reflections', *Journal of the American Psychoanalytic Association* 30: 347–364.

Dewald, P. A. (1990) 'Serious Illness in the Analyst', in H. J. Schwartz and A.-L. Silver (eds), *Illness in the Analyst: Implications for the Treatment Relationship*. Madison, CT: International Universities Press, 1990.

Dewald, P. A. and Clark, R. (eds) (2001) *Ethics Case Book*. New York: The American Psychoanalytic Association.

Eissler, K. (1976) 'On Possible Effects of Ageing on the Practice of Psychoanalysis: An Essay', *Journal of the Philadelphia Association of Psychoanalysis* 3: 139–152.

Feinsilver, D. (1998) 'The Therapist as a Person Facing Death: The Hardest of External Realities and Therapeutic Action', *International Journal of Psychoanalysis* 79: 1131–1150.

Freedman, A. and Firestein, S. (1990) 'Death of the Analyst as a Form of Termination of Psychoanalysis', in H. J. Schwartz and A.-L. Silver (eds), *Illness in the Analyst: Implications for the Treatment Relationship*. Madison, CT: International Universities Press, 1990, pp. 299–331.

Galatzer-Levy, R. M. (2004) 'The Death of the Analyst: Patients Whose Previous Analysts Died while They Were in Treatment', *Journal of the American Psychoanalytic Association* 52: 999–1024.

Garfield, D. A. S. (1990) 'Manifestations of Grief and Grievance: A Therapist's Response to an Analyst's Death', in H. J. Schwartz and A.-L. Silver (eds), *Illness in the Analyst: Implications for the Treatment Relationship*. Madison, CT: International Universities Press, 1990.

Gurtmann, J. H. (1990) 'The Impact of the Psychoanalyst's Serious Illness on Psychoanalytic Work', *Journal of the American Academy of Psychoanalysis* 18: 613–625.

Junkers, G. (1995) *Klinische Psychologie und Psychosomatik des Alters*. Stuttgart: Schattauer.

Kaplan, A. H. (1994) 'Experiencing Aging: Separation and Loss', in G. H. Pollock (ed.), *How Psychiatrists Look at Aging, Vol. 2*. Madison, CT: Mental Health Library Series.

Lasky, R. (1992) 'Some Superego Conflicts in the Analyst Who Has Suffered a Catastrophic Illness', *International Journal of Psychoanalysis* 73: 127–136.

Linna, L. (2002) 'When the Analyst Falls Ill. Implications for the Treatment Relationship', *Scandinavian Psychoanalytic Review* 25: 27–35.

Little, R. B. (1967) 'Transference, Countertransference and Survival Reactions Following an Analyst's Heart Attack', *Psychoanalytic Forum*: 2107–2126.

Morrison, A. (1990) 'Doing Psychotherapy while Living with a Life-Threatening Illness', in H. J. Schwartz and A.-L. Silver (eds), *Illness in the Analyst: Implications for the Treatment Relationship*. Madison, CT: International Universities Press, 1990, pp. 227–253.

Ogden, T. (1994) 'The Analytic Third: Working with Intersubjective Clinical Facts', *International Journal of Psychoanalysis* 75: 3–19.

Ogden, T. H. (1997) *Reverie and Interpretation: Sensing Something Human*. Northvale, NJ: Jason Aronson Inc.

Pizer, B. (1997) 'When the Analyst Is Ill: Dimensions of Self-Disclosure', *Psychoanalytic Quarterly* 66: 450–469.

Ponsi, M. (2000) 'Therapeutic Alliance and Collaborative Interactions', *International Journal of Psychoanalysis* 81: 687–704.

Rendely, J. (1999) 'The Death of an Analyst: The Loss of a Real Relationship', *Contemporary Psychoanalysis* 35: 131–152.

Schur, M. (1972) *Freud: Living and Dying*. London: The Hogarth Press.

Schwaber, E. A. (1998) 'Traveling Affectively Alone', *Journal of the American Psychoanalytic Association* 46: 1004–1065.

Schwartz, H. J. (1987) 'Illness in the Doctor: Implications for the Psychoanalytic Process', *Journal of the American Psychoanalytic Association* 35: 657–692.

Schwartz, H. J. (1990) 'Illness in the Doctor: Implications for the Psychoanalytic Process', in H. J. Schwartz and A.-L. Silver (eds), *Illness in the Analyst: Implications for the Treatment Relationship*. Madison, CT: International Universities Press, 1990.

Schwartz, H. J. and Silver, A.-L. (eds) (1990) *Illness in the Analyst: Implications for the Treatment Relationship*. Madison, CT: International Universities Press.

Silver, A.-L. S. (1990) 'Resuming the Work with a Life-Threatening Illness—and Further Reflections', *Contemporary Psychoanalysis* 18: 314–326.

Traesdal, T. (2005) 'When the Analyst Dies: Dealing with the Aftermath', *Journal of the American Psychoanalytic Association* 53: 1235–1255.

Weyerer, S. and Bickel, H. (2007) *Epidemiologie psychischer Erkrankungen im höheren Lebensalter*. Stuttgart: Kohlhammer.

Wolman, T. (1990) 'The Death of the Analyst in the Post-Termination Phase of Analysis: Impact and Resolution', in H. J. Schwartz and A.-L. Silver (eds), *Illness in the Analyst: Implications for the Treatment Relationship*. Madison, CT: International Universities Press, 1990.

Wong, N. (1990) 'Acute Illness in the Analyst', in H. J. Schwartz and A.-L. Silver (eds), *Illness in the Analyst: Implications for the Treatment Relationship*. Madison, CT: International Universities Press, 1990.

Ziman-Tobin, P. (1989) 'Consultation as a Bridging Function', *Contemporary Psychoanalysis* 25: 432–438.

Part III

INSTITUTIONAL PARTS
OF ENDING

11

CONTAINING PSYCHOANALYSIS

The analytic institution

Gabriele Junkers

The twenty-first century confronts us with an entirely new demographic situation: Never before have there been so many elderly people, so many who live on until high old age. Never before have so many generations lived side by side. Since the early twentieth century, life expectancy in the western world has risen by an average 30 per cent. In about 20 years, every second person will be over 50, every third over 60. What we call 'old age' will encompass a lifespan that will last at least as long as childhood, adolescence and education together (Schirrmacher, 2004, p. 17). As a consequence four to five generations will be living at the same time, which means that on average ageing parents will figure in the lives of their adult children for over half a century.

We psychoanalysts also need to accept this reality as it will affect our future co-existence among colleagues. At present, over 70 per cent of our members are between 50 and 70 years old. On average, our teachers, the training analysts, are 10 years older. In other words, about half of all training analysts are older than 60 (Leonoff, 2012).

This situation and the changes we can expect to result from it confront institutional-ised psychoanalysis with considerable structural, administrative and ethical problems. We need to accustom ourselves to the fact that in the immediate future the number of international members will shrink, although we might expect more newcomers, less so in the western than in the eastern part of the world. Accordingly, we will have to rethink, reconsider and redistribute the usually honorary functions performed in our institutions so as to find new forms and structures for our joint efforts. For these changes we require ethically acceptable, clearly defined guidelines to which we can gear our concerted intergenerational objectives.

I am convinced that we psychoanalysts will continue to need a group – an institute or society – where we can experience togetherness and solidarity with our analytic siblings, colleagues, parents, children and grandchildren. We need the 'third' not least to open up the narrow 'dual' space of our consulting rooms and to reflect on our impressions and cogitations. We also need the organisation and its structure to assign psychoanalysis a rightful place in the public space and to carry it forward by providing psychoanalytic training. We need a group for the constant process of scientific and critical exchange without which psychoanalyses would be endangered by impoverish-ment and obsolescence. We also need the protective function of groups and organisa-tions to help guarantee the continuity of our shared philosophies and to help us insure the quality of training and of the analyst's work, both of which will provide the analyst with income and with successors.

For co-existence in an institution we need to share visions, philosophies, rituals and rules acknowledged as binding by all members. During our training we grow into the group. At the same time we internalise the legacy of our predecessors and weave it unconsciously, as Green (1997, p. 93) emphasises, in our treatment strategies. As soon as we have qualified as analysts, we are (mostly) officially welcomed to the association by our colleagues, become full members and acknowledge this commonality, usually without questioning it too much. After all, we are paying the organisation to represent our interests both internally and externally. In this way we acknowledge its raison d'être.[1] But as soon as we become active members of our institution, we adopt a constructive role and accept the rights and duties that we have agreed to either implicitly or explicitly.

Growing older as a psychoanalyst, with all its implications, has a very immediate significance for the boundaries we draw between the private and the public sphere, between private self-determination and inclusion in the group with its structure-giving rules and provisions. Some members reject the obligations and duties created by their membership and insist on the private nature of their independent profes-sional identity as a psychoanalyst ('I'm not going to let anyone tell me how to do my job . . .'). Others attribute major significance to the institution and to the clear struc-ture and rules represented and safeguarded by it. They consider the incorporation of their work into this institutionally established framework to be advantageous, if not downright essential (e.g. Danon-Boileau, 2011). In addition, the group as a whole must find a way of coming to terms with its own 'ageing' and the paucity of young analysts and ask whether and to what extent a reorganisation is necessary for the group structures that have existed so far.

In the tensions prevailing between the individual and the institution, a character-istic group culture takes shape (Bion, 1961, p. 39). But Bion also reminds us in no uncertain terms that the group almost always develops a feeling of frustration because the gratifications it has to offer can never live up to the expectations we place in it.

It is part of our group psychoanalytic culture that we have elaborated rules by which we learn or have learned our profession. We go through various examina-tions and initiation rites geared to more or less firmly established philosophies and by becoming analysts we acknowledge their validity. In addition, the group has agreed on joint objectives and standards for the exercise of the analytic profession with a view to assuring the quality of its members' work. Accordingly, the group should also ensure that it has resources and methods not only for supervising the compliance with these standards but also for keeping close tabs on the standards themselves and if necessary taking steps to restore the quality of our work, should it ever be jeopardised.

But there are few rituals marking the end of our careers, as there are in so many other professions. True, some prominent psychoanalysts may be feted on the occa-sion of their 70th, 75th or 80th birthday. But there are also members who indignantly reject even a word of congratulation from their own societies as impertinent interfer-ence in their private lives.

Let us take a look back at what we psychoanalysts have done – or failed to do – at a personal and institutional level about the issues posed by ageing. In the 1960s there were reports of a committee (Michaels and Schoenberg, 1966) elaborating 'policies of retirement' and making sure that they were written into the statutes in a binding manner. But for years nothing happened. No rules were set down to regulate professional practice in old age or intervals caused by age or illness. Some ten years previously, the Education Committee of the Boston Institute (1953) had proposed the following recommendation: 'Training Analysts who have reached the age of seventy-five should become Training Analysts Emeritus, and should no longer be engaged in active training matters'. In the years to follow, neither this recommendation nor reminders about the constant rise in life expectancy (Michaels and Schoenberg, 1966) had any appreciable effects at an institutional level. According to Klockars and Hooke (2009), inquiries about existing regulations in 26 European societies receive answers such as 'no fixed policies', 'we discuss it informally', 'we follow a gentleman's agreement'. Though many societies have suggested an age limit for the commencement of training analyses, this is frequently not adhered to, particularly when the colleagues in question are prominent figures. There is no age limit for work with patients in any of the European societies questioned. In Germany the age restriction (68) on running a practice, financed by health insurance (in which health-plan patients are treated), has just been revoked. With the multimorbidity beyond the age of 70 mentioned earlier increasing by leaps and bounds, what makes us so sure that we can complete an analysis we have embarked on at the age of 70 or older in complete possession of our mental faculties, physical health and professional competence?

Apart from the European survey quoted above, I have been unable to track down any sources indicating whether and how the regulations called for by the branch societies in 1953 have been introduced and implemented. To my knowledge, the IPA has yet (60 years later) to make any headway on this point. As far as I can see, the title 'training analyst emeritus' has never been officially accepted, that is by the IPA. All I know from the roster of the British Society is that emeritus members are listed there, but no ritual farewell ceremonies for such members exist.

As Kernberg (2000, p.100) noted in connection within his critical analysis of the training situation, the way we deal with each other in our psychoanalytic institutes and societies is marked by a culture of silence. Not only training analysts have difficulty confronting candidates with problems encountered in their training (Junkers et al., 2008). The problem of silence affects our dealings with our colleagues as well. We see and hear but we do not respond with words or deeds (e.g. Sandler and Godley, 2004). Is this perhaps a mistaken interpretation of abstinence in relation to our colleagues? Whenever members have found out about a colleague where something had 'gone wrong', their response has been extremely troubled and they have once again called for an institutional solution. The only conclusion we can draw from that is that here a multiplicity of unconscious wishes comes into conflict with perceiving reality and that personal/institutional denial is at work. If we continue to turn a blind eye to this, we run the risk of behaving unethically towards our patients, our candidates and '*vis-à-vis* our internal object "psychoanalysis"'.

The theory of psychoanalytically based organisational consultation is that unperceived repetitions and errors in the dynamics of organisations are denied or even erroneously taken to be an illusion. This increases the risk of their being shifted upward in the hierarchy of responsibility. But if those working at that level are themselves affected by the problems under discussion, it is very likely that individual defence strategies will be transferred to the group, as Jaques (1955), Menzies (1961) and others have shown. The leaders are then impaired in their capacity to perform their central function, which is to contain the tension within themselves and enable the members to project into them the undigested elements they have yet to come to terms with (anxieties, fear of exposure and helplessness, hatred, envy and the striving for power).

Bion has taught us that the welfare of the group is a higher value than that of the individual and that the most important objective is group survival, not individual survival. This helps us to understand why the topic of the 'ageing psychoanalyst' could not have impinged on our awareness before we realised that we are living in a time of a shortage of candidates and that the future of psychoanalysis is no longer assured. As a consequence, the material future of the psychoanalytic group has become more precarious. Members' dues are dwindling, so many societies can no longer permit their elderly members to pay less or possibly nothing for their membership. In short, the increasing number of elderly analysts brings into question the factual material existence of our psychoanalytic institutions and their ability to function.

We find ourselves at a crossroads. Should we attempt to interest younger potential candidates in a course of training as analysts at all costs? Or should we see the situation as an occasion to look inside ourselves and ask whether among the many potential reasons for loss of attractiveness there may be something within our own selves that makes the psychoanalytic approach we are presently living no longer attractive?

If we claim to learn from our experiences as an institution, then we must acknowledge that age-related withdrawal from work is not at all an exclusively individual matter. It also affects professional and public life. We have a responsibility towards our institutional philosophies, the representation of psychoanalysis to the outside world, towards our clients, our candidates and our colleagues.

How do we experience the institution we have helped to create and shape in terms of our own selves? As we grow older, we realise that many have very ambivalent feelings about their own institution. On the one hand, there is the fear that the younger colleagues may not be 'sufficiently good' at protecting and furthering the cause of psychoanalysis; that they will 'squander their heritage'. On the other, there are many colleagues who are sorely disappointed with institutionalised psychoanalysis, or to put it more precisely, disenchanted with some colleagues and members and their way of representing psychoanalysis to the outside world. Multiple group formations, friendships and enmities that have developed over the years can lead to an attitude towards the group as posing a threat or at least no longer sustaining us benevolently. This might explain why it is so difficult to enlist the aid of the group or members of that group in times of bad health when assistance would be so important.

The ideas set out in the chapters in this volume show that ageing is a highly individual process and that designs for living are more diversified in old age than at almost any other stage of life. Accordingly, we must be sceptical about a restriction of professional activity based solely on chronological age. But this restriction is the norm in other walks of life. Exceptions are hard to bring about, extremely rare and restricted to enterprises small enough to ensure close monitoring. If considerate treatment of this kind is to be a viable proposition in larger groups, we will need to create transparency and establish criteria that we can draw upon to devise a solution that is even-handed and acceptable for all concerned.

Should we turn to medical science for assistance on this point? Would it be a plausible guideline to proceed on the basis of our knowledge that on average illness frequency appreciably increases past the age of 70? In many institutes all over the world, the age of 70 is considered the limit beyond which no training analyses should be undertaken. Klockars reports on how restriction on the basis of chronological age is dealt with in Europe. If we compare this with the figures just under 50 years ago, we see that the average age at which training analysts were appointed at the time was 46 (Michaels and Schoenberg, 1966). It was a time when colleagues completed the average nine-year period of training at about the age of 40.

Should the institution impose an age limit restricting work with patients and training candidates? Is there any way of countenancing individual justified exceptions in the framework of such regulation? Or should we attempt to assure the quality of our colleagues' work by finding ways of ascertaining the working capacity of an older colleague, for example by asking him to give a public account of his clinical work every two years? Should we ask for evidence of supervision of his clinical work? Or might we make constructive use of the criteria Tuckett (2005) has elaborated for the qualification of candidates? In a personal interview, Betty Joseph told me that an analyst's working capacity should be subjected to continuous checks, just like the ability to drive a car (2003, personal communication).

What role should the institution, society or institute play when an analyst falls ill, cannot go on practising as usual or possibly even dies? The chapters by Carlisle and Traesdal are two of the many testimonies (see also Barbanel, 1989; Dattner, 1989; Savitz, 1990; Tallmer, 1989; Rendely, 1999; Galatzer-Levy, 2004; Deutsch, 2011; Robutti, 2010) indicating just how serious the injuries inflicted by an incapacitated analyst can be. The extremely painful wounds he leaves will hardly ever heal and these traumatic events will disfigure the lives of those thus harmed. In addition, psychoanalysis itself may suffer damage from this for generations.

'My friends will tell me when I am no longer in a position to treat my patients as they deserve.' This frequently heard statement is meant to reassure. But we all know that the closer we are to one another and the better we know each other, the more impossible it becomes to tell a colleague something that flies in the face of his own self-perception and is thus likely to hurt him or even make him fly into a towering rage and thus transform a friend into a potential enemy. Whole institutes lapse into silence, a silence that makes them guilty not only of conniving. By averting their eyes from a colleague whose actions and behaviour do not live up to the standards of the group and by failing to intervene, they become perpetrators; their active responsibility is just as great as if they had displayed those failings themselves. On the subject of boundary violations, Sandler and Godley (2004, p. 36) write: 'The relationships within analytic societies carry particularly powerful unconscious elements. This may help to explain why psychoanalytic societies have on the whole great difficulties in identifying acceptable behaviour and/or possible boundary violations in a member'. This is just as true of potential problems with an elderly colleague. The reluctance to address difficult, critical, personal problems is exacerbated by the endogamy in our groups and the unresolved transference problems associated with it. Utrilla notes that institutes attempting to function along the lines of a family are doomed to failure (Perdigo, 2010).

Finally, Mary Kay O'Neil broaches the important issue of the way an ageing analyst can take precautions to guard against the case of his own sudden death. If the institution were to impose a professional will, this would not only give patients and candidates greater protection, it would also prompt colleagues to think harder about the uncongenial topic of transience, their own ageing and death and the closure of their own practice.

Future-oriented thinking is necessary when we look at issues connected with ongoing psychoanalytic training. Can it be ethical for us to accept future trainees who are almost 60 if not older? Should we let younger candidates run up such debts for financing their training that no one can say whether they will ever recover sufficiently from the pecuniary strains to which they have subjected themselves? Will they be able to lay up reserves they can draw upon in old age rather than being forced to go on working when they are strictly speaking no longer in a position to do so?

Finally, let me repeat the questions asked by Michaels and Schoenberg back in 1966 and apply them to the entire group of psychoanalysts:

> What is the responsibility of an institute to those training analysts whose entire time has been devoted to training within the institute when their professional life is cut off with the termination of their role as training analysts? What consideration should an institute give to the training analyst who, at seventy years and over, is mentally intact? In general, training analysts have been much more aware of their responsibilities and obligations to the institute and to their candidates than the institute has been to the training analysts.

Note

1 In different countries and international societies, the practice of psychoanalysis is organised very differently. Thus the relationship between institutes and societies can also be very wide-ranging and the society as an institution may play a wide variety of roles.

12

AGEING IN EUROPEAN PSYCHOANALYTIC SOCIETIES

Psychoanalytic practice: Terminable or interminable

Leena Klockars

Introduction

Theory as well as psychoanalytic practice has developed tremendously over the past hundred years; regulations for individuals and institutional training programmes have changed as well. Since the early times of psychoanalysis we can trace back a steady increase of members: In 2006 there were 30 European psychoanalytic societies within the IPA, comprising roughly 5,000 members, 870 training analysts and 2,000 candidates in training (Erlich-Ginor *et al.*, 2007). But more recently psychoanalytic training has lost some of its popularity. We are now facing a dilemma, which could threaten the future vision of psychoanalysis. Specifically, this is true for the demographic changes of the members, the candidates and the applicants: all of these groups are now considerably older than they used to be. The heretical conversation amongst psychoanalysts themselves has voiced fears that the profession is becoming a gerontocracy. This general ageing of the psychoanalytic community, containing the risk of rigidity and sticking to old convictions, could contain the danger that psychoanalysis may not seem attractive for a younger generation of analysts because the training does not appear flexible or supportive enough and new ideas would be perceived as not welcomed.

The phenomenon of increasing of age in psychoanalytic applicants is separately discussed and evaluated (Hooke, 2009) and also taken up by Marino. Living in a multigenerational situation the young analysts and the very old ones are in danger of having difficulties in communicating and understanding each other. This highlights some of the fears about ageing and maturation.

One of the problems with ageing is that there is a higher risk of physical and mental changes and related illnesses. This may have negative effects on analytic work in private practice and training. Therapeutic as well as ethical consequences may result. For example, this is the case when an ageing member loses his/her ability to work properly without showing critical self-awareness. These issues create a dynamic that ends up holding the younger generations back and prevents the older members from thoughtfully and realistically addressing these conflicts.

Societies are presently struggling to try and examine these difficulties responsibly, especially understanding the ethical and practical implications. However, no mutual agreement or joint commitments on these issues have been developed by now. It looks as if the clinical practice seems to be interminable and it appears thus far that the psychoanalytic community has largely been turning a blind eye to these issues.

Ageing from the point of the societies

The IPA committee on ageing of patients and psychoanalysts (CAPP) chaired by Junkers took up the issue outlined above. The study by Klockars and Hooke (2010) was part of its research programme and aimed at building on the preliminary study by Junkers and Opdal in 2004, looking at age demographics within the structure of the European psychoanalytic societies. Second, the work was to understand the consequences of ageing on the societies, and third, to explore the difficulties of retirement from the profession. With the help of a specially designed semi-structured questionnaire, data about the distribution of age among the members, training analysts and candidates within European Psychoanalytic Societies were collected. The questionnaire was sent during the summer and autumn of 2008 to all the 30 societies presently existing within the EPF. Twenty-four societies replied. The response rate from the provisional societies was lower than from the component societies. Possibly this is a result caused by the higher number of ageing members and occurring age problems within the established societies than in the provisional societies.

Findings from a questionnaire investigation

Age distribution in psychoanalytic societies

Within the provisional societies the members are much younger than in the old, established component societies. Within these 70 per cent of the membership is between 50 and 70 years old, 16 per cent over 70; 50 per cent of the training analysts are between 60 and 70 years old. This is different, though, within the provisional societies: there are nearly 33 per cent younger than 50 and only 7.6 per cent are more than 70 years old (Table 12.2).

There has been a prominent change in getting older by average within the component societies. This also means that psychoanalysis is transmitted by much older training analysts: only 2.4 per cent of them are younger than 50; 66 per cent are between 60 and 80. Within the provisional societies, training analysts are much younger: here

Table 12.1 Age distribution of members in component and provisional societies

	<40	40–50	50–60	60–70	70–80	>80
Provisional Societies and study groups (n = 5)	0%	30.5%	36.6%	25.2%	5.3%	2.3%
Component Societies (n = 19)	0.5%	12.9%	37.2%	33%	11.8%	4.6%

nearly 11 per cent are under 50 and only nearly 11 per cent are over 70 (Table 12.2). This is relevant not only in terms of the risk of declining health with age but also concerning the risk of transporting the message that psychoanalysis is something for old people.

We see that candidates show the same general trend (Table 12.3): they tend to be younger in the newer societies: 42.2 per cent are under 40 in the provisional societies compared with 20.4 per cent in the component ones; and 17.8 per cent compared with 31.7 per cent who are over 50. The age difference is as big between candidates as among members and training analysts.

Like members and training analysts, candidates are reported to be older when they apply than they used to be ten years earlier (Erlich-Ginor *et al.*, 2007). Only some societies report having also accepted quite young candidates. Some of the problems evolving are discussed by Hooke (in this book). But this again contributes to the fact that the whole profession is in danger of becoming the profession of old people.[1]

Age limits and age regulations in the societies

Age limit for retirement, taking in or giving up membership or positions

In almost all societies no age limits exist for members to retire or to give up society positions. But there are limitations in place concerning training analysts: in most societies there is the wish to limit training analysts taking up new training cases after a certain age. In some societies there are definite rules, but mostly it is left 'in the air' or there is some sort of recommendation not to start new training analyses after 67 or 70 or 75 years of age. There are a couple of societies where the training analysts have to ask permission to start a new training case after 70 years of age; only one society requires training analysts to reapply every year after 70. On the other hand most societies mention the fact that there are always exceptions to the rules. These regulations seem particularly to concern the work of training analysts, but do not limit supervision or teaching.

Table 12.2 Age distribution of training analysts in component and provisional societies

	> 50	50–60	60–70	70–80	>80
Provisional societies and study groups (n = 5)	10.8%	37.8%	40.5%	8.1%	2.7%
Component societies (n = 19)	2.4%	23.5%	46.9%	19%	8.2%

Table 12.3 Age distribution of candidates in component and provisional societies

	< 30	30–40	40–50	50–60	> 60
Provisional societies and study groups (n = 5)	2.8%	39.4%	40%	17.2%	0.6%
Component societies (n = 18)	2%	20.2%	46.1%	27.7%	4%

Society fees

In little over half of the societies there are regulations concerning the society fees. In some societies the fees lower stepwise after 65–70–75 or the fees are only 50% between 68 and 77. In some societies a member doesn't pay any fee after 70, 75 or 80. But again there are many exceptions: for example if one is seriously ill or has no clinical practice, has a low income or has retired, then there is exemption from paying the society's fees; often this is regulated on an individual basis. Some societies mention that they have changed regulations during the last years; some have raised the age at which members don't pay fees because 'members do work longer nowadays' or because 'some old training analysts do want to support younger members'.

Retirement procedures

In none of the societies do formal procedures exist for retirement, either for members or for training analysts. In some societies there are some informal procedures, for instance the society sends a letter of thanks, the member is asked to give a 'last will' lecture, the members can be nominated 'honorary members' or 'full-term training analysts' or the society offers a special celebration when the member becomes 70, 80 or 90. But usually members and training analysts just stop working gradually without special retirement procedures. One society mentions a definite regulation for old training analysts: when reaching 75, she/he has to make a retirement plan with the institute.

Most societies consider this issue to be very important but difficult, delicate and sometimes even impossible to discuss. Many societies seem to be in the process of considering, planning, anticipating and working on rules, regulations and procedures for retirement.

Problems concerning ageing from the point of the societies

Members' position

Societies consider the ageing of their members to be a confusing issue; it brings different kinds of problems: societies have difficulties in finding active members and the decreasing income from lower fees may lead to further financial problems for societies. Some old members seem to withdraw from discussions and they lose contact with the institute; others wish to keep their former influence on the group so that some societies are afraid that ageing members contribute to a more conservative atmosphere and even some rigidity. Old age carries the risk of psychic and physical problems such as mental slowness, memory problems or different kinds of illnesses. There are however ten societies that do not report any problems with ageing members, most of them are provisional societies.

Ethical problems

Half of the societies report no ethical problems with ageing of their members. Again, the majority of these are provisional societies. Half of the societies report problems with elderly colleagues such as difficulties in keeping boundaries, settings and standards in clinical practice. They also mention memory problems, dementia and impaired functioning. Ethical problems when ageing can also manifest because of loneliness, narcissism and erotic transference. In one society a professional standards group cares for the investigating of illness and inability to function of the membership.

Discussions in the societies

About half of the societies express the wish and the intention to discuss ageing and retirement issues, but at the same time find the issue very difficult and problematic to raise. Most societies recognize the need and therefore the wish to have younger candidates, members and training analysts. A shared concern exists that the psychoanalytic career nowadays only follows a psychotherapy career. This happens for many reasons: because of the health professions' regulations and insurance companies' regulations in different countries, because of the difficulties in getting psychoanalytic patients and earning a living, because of the cost of psychoanalytic training, and because of the diminished status of psychoanalysis in the community and especially within psychiatry. In the French model, but also in some societies that follow the Eitingon model, candidates start their own personal analysis long before starting training so that in consequence they are older when starting training.

Psychoanalytic practice: Terminable or interminable?

The increasing number of old psychoanalysts causes problems for the future of the psychoanalytic societies. On one hand old analysts bring a huge amount of experience and wisdom, on the other hand there is the danger of bringing conservatism, inflexibility, sometimes authoritarian behaviour and more often than officially acknowledged physical and mental problems. It is truly surprising how rarely this topic, all round, is discussed. Whether this is potentially becoming a problem for societies depends on how this phenomenon will be handled practically and what guidance can be instituted responsibly to address these issues going forward.

The psychoanalytic societies and the individual psychoanalysts have different viewpoints: Societies are worried about the future of psychoanalysis, about the professional situations, positions and roles in the societies, about the quality in the practice of the ageing members and about the ethical problems possibly occurring in their practice. The individual elderly psychoanalysts are anxious and worried about losing their work, profession, their positions and patients, becoming worthless and lonely and possibly getting financial problems. This is one way the psychoanalytic community is considerably better than much of western cultural relationships with ageing populations where the elderly are often treated with discrimination or even contempt. It is essential that this other problematic extreme does not manifest within our dialogues about ageing.

Tallmer (1992) wonders why getting old and terminating our practice is so difficult even though we, the psychoanalysts, 'more than any other group of behavioral scientists, should offer us the most insights about the ageing process as it relates to professional life. No matter what their analytic persuasion may be, they are all trained to be exquisitely introspective, interpretative, and self-monitoring' (p. 382). Such constant self-monitoring should lead to recognition of changes in technique, changes in attitudes towards patients, and changes in affects related to the recognition of the ageing process by both the analysand and the analyst. Danielle Quinodoz (2009, p. 171) speaks about the importance of the 'clear-headedness' in our work because of our exceptional deep responsibility towards our patients and candidates.

One older psychoanalyst remembered:

> When we were fifty years old, some IPA colleagues visited our society and we also discussed the issue of ageing and retirement in our society and we all agreed that in the future, we would take ageing into consideration and retire when we are seventy or even sooner if we are becoming ill or unable to work properly and we promised to tell each other about our mental and physical problems whenever these appear. These IPA people went away and we never were able to talk about the issue any more.

Freud's example

Freud himself worked until the very end of his life (Schur, 1972) and many other of our analytic ancestors never actually retired. Working as a psychoanalyst was and is for many colleagues not only a job, not only a career, not even only a profession, it was and also is still a lifestyle, a way to exist, which contains their personal identity. Analysts are from the beginning and from their heart devoted to human life and are curious about the unconscious mind and its functioning. This way of being doesn't end or even diminish with age.

Freud wrote to Pfister on 6 March 1910:

> I cannot face with comfort the idea of life without work; work and the free play of the imagination are for me the same thing, I take no pleasure in anything else. That would be a recipe for happiness but for the appalling thought that productivity is entirely dependent on a sensitive disposition. What would one do when ideas failed or words refuse to come? It is impossible not to shudder at the thought. Hence, in spite of all the acceptance of fate which is appropriate to an honest man, I have one quite secret prayer: that I may be spared any wasting away and crippling of my ability to work because of physical deterioration.
>
> (Schur, 1972, p. 259)

Between the years 1923–1938 Freud had to endure more that 30 surgical operations because of his mouth cancer. His health must have had a significant influence on his work, yet he tried to go on with his practice. He wrote constantly to his closest friends about his health and his doubt about his ability to work. 'I am no longer the same man. In reality, I am tired and in need of rest, can scarcely get through my six hours of analytic work, and however cannot think of doing anything else. The right thing to do would be to give up all work and obligations and wait in a quiet corner for the natural end' (Freud's letter to Eitingon, 22 March 1924, Schur, 1972, p. 377). Freud replied to Marie Bonaparte after her letter containing an interpretation of something, which had occurred in her analysis with Freud. 'Superb! It must have been just the way you understood it. My comprehension was paralyzed by my preoccupation with the cancer' (Freud's letter to Marie Bonaparte, 21 December 1936, Schur, 1972, p. 486). And later, after one more extensive surgery on 27 September 1938, to Bonaparte again: 'It cannot be long as I can hardly write, any more than I can talk or smoke. This operation was the worst since 1923 . . . I am abominably tired and weak in my movements, although I began yesterday with three patients, but it is not going easily' (Schur, 1972, p. 510). Still, throughout July 1939 Freud continued with a few patients, but during August 1939 he went downhill rapidly, and on 23 September 1939 Freud died.

He had an extraordinary position, prestige and experience. To be analysed by Freud was of course very much appreciated and highly prized. Younger colleagues and established layman wanted to be analysed by Freud even though he was weak and ill. Analysis with him might have been experienced as a divine blessing. This kind of phenomenon is also well known after Freud. Established analysts are eagerly wanted as analysts, supervisors and teachers, even though they are old and not in full strength any more. How could it be otherwise? Yet this habit has its disadvantages. It keeps up the overvaluation and the omnipotence of the old, highly respected analysts and their individual, personal value and undervalues psychoanalytic method as such and younger generations' possibilities to get their opportunities. Freud also felt he had to work because of his financial duties towards his family (Schur, 1972).

He certainly has left behind a powerful model, a model of an analyst who is deeply devoted and committed to psychoanalysis and to psychoanalytic practice and whose other interests are secondary and subordinated to psychoanalytic thinking. On the other hand, it raises core ethical questions about self-care and the responsibility to our patients and by what standards we judge or compare best working practice versus what is passable or acceptable.

Changes in the surroundings of a psychoanalytic society

Since the time of Freud, the world has changed. We nowadays find a huge amount of all kinds of different psychotherapies and psychotherapeutic training programmes around psychoanalytic societies. Nearly all of them have their roots in early psychoanalysis, later claiming their independence from psychoanalytic thinking, seeing themselves as 'more modern' techniques, much quicker for less money. The post-modern 'theory of mind' underpinning 'modern psychotherapies' seems to be more easily reachable and therefore more tempting for many patients. Many of the values and issues that are basically important for psychoanalytic thinking, such as Oedipality and sexuality, are seen by the new psychotherapeutic disciplines as useless or antique. Psychic illnesses and their treatments are regarded more in terms of symptoms and behaviour than in terms of development and history.

Although we still meet respect for psychoanalytic achievements, the status of psychoanalysis and psychoanalysts has been diminishing. In this competitive situation psychoanalysts might tend to withdraw to their own circles and to their own old ways of professional practice with those patients they can still get and reach. The situation is different in the new societies in countries where psychoanalysis has only recently been established. Here psychoanalysis is still seen as revolutionary and refreshing. So it is not surprising that so many IPA psychoanalysts enjoy working with the East and Far East Training Programmes. On one hand we psychoanalysts watch out for new impulses and power for our theory and practice, for example via neuropsychology and neuropsychoanalysis, and yet many of us psychoanalysts have great difficulties in appreciating this kind of research.

In Freud's time, psychoanalysis was more a way to explore oneself and to get more insight into one's unconscious and internal world. Many of these new therapeutic disciplines are quite often interested mainly in the patients' possibilities to get rid of their symptoms and difficulties. Nowadays society in general wants to get quick therapeutic results, outcome research data have to be presented; only after getting these are the insurers and clients willing to pay for these treatments. We psychoanalysts have asked to get the same communal and financial advantages as the other treatment systems. The national health insurance systems and the insurance companies pay for our treatment and therefore they also want to intertwine with our dyadic relationships with our patients, control our settings and to get some outcome research data. Although this is contradictory to our method, we agreed to have this organizational and financial support from outside our consultation rooms. Nowadays psychoanalysts work much more under the pressures of governmental as well as insurance companies' agendas. Societies do not have a clear stance to manage the tension from external pressures and the internal aspirations to address these challenging ethical issues.

Changes in clinical practice

Our patients have also changed. There are less and less 'good, neurotic' patients and increasingly more difficult patients with borderline and psychotic features. It is unclear how well we can help these patients with our classical method and how much we should accept new models, new terms, and new techniques. Often these post-modern patients wish for shorter, quicker and cheaper treatment and less for an understanding of themselves.

As psychoanalysts, in our practice, working with the patients, we have to keep on believing in mutuality, in shared understanding, in deep emotional relationships, emotional interchange, even unconscious interchange. We have to be able to be timeless, to carry on with the illusion of regressive wish fulfilments, even the fantasy of immortality. We have to agree to wander on an unrealistic ground. We have learned to be needed by our patients. These professional qualities are in danger of also becoming part of our own personal identity and they are difficult to give up with age and with termination and retirement. Our professional work can perhaps heal our own ageing and our work saves us from uselessness and loneliness. As ageing analysts 'we are in danger of keeping analysands longer than necessary, either by binding them to the analysis or even by offering them a more friendship-like contact' (Junkers, 2007).

What can we do?

For those psychoanalysts who do other kinds of professional work as well, who do not work only as analysts in practice, termination and retirement from the work with patients might be easier, because they still feel needed in teaching, supervising, consulting, writing and giving papers. The training analysts are a good example of this, and ageing and retirement from practice might not be so problematic for them personally. On the other hand, they have been mostly committed to psychoanalysis and have maybe even less private lives to get into after retirement. For them, losing work because of age is difficult, because they have devoted their lives to psychoanalysis and have even made sacrifices when devoting all their energy to their profession. Often they have concentrated all their relationships on colleagues. If they can hold some positions, roles or tasks in the society, termination and retirement from practice might not be so difficult. Many societies voice an urgent need to find possibilities for elder members to keep up with their psychoanalytic identity and meaningfulness without working with patients. Could there be voluntary teaching, voluntary theoretical reading classes, theoretical reading classes for the elderly only, supervision, group supervision, group supervision for the elderly only, intervision groups, clinical groups, clinical groups for the elderly only, etc.? There are many possibilities, but it seems as if the societies have to organize these activities. Perhaps societies could provide some kind of 'ageing information' such as some financial advice about insurance companies, national health insurance systems, and so forth, for its older members, in order to make termination easier for them.

Nowadays, to become a psychoanalyst and to become a training psychoanalyst demands very long and expensive training, very many unpaid activities within the societies, extensive and intensive commitments with the psychoanalytic movement. Psychoanalysis has become a profession for the experienced, but also for the old. It has become a profession for those who have been working as psychotherapists for a long time already, a postgraduate profession. In the future, we have to open up more possibilities for the younger colleagues in order to be more attractive to them, our talented 50-year-old candidates have to reach rewarding positions before they are old themselves. In the societies we know that we also need younger candidates and probably also shorter training possibilities. If training takes from six to ten years (Erlich-Ginor *et al.*, 2007) it might not be attractive enough for many medical doctors or psychologists.

It seems obvious that the ageing issue has also to be taken up from the outside of the national societies in order to help societies and individual psychoanalysts to make proper evaluations and conclusions. We need the IPA's and EPF's oversight functions. Inside the societies the issue provokes too much anxiety among the old analysts, about their future. The younger colleagues feel irritated by how to be able to see and to encourage their own analysts and teachers to go. The older ones know how difficult it is to go to a colleague and friend and to try to persuade her or him to stop working, because she or he is so old, weak, has memory problems, is disoriented sometimes or not functioning well enough. For the younger ones this task is almost impossible. Yet the old analyst may need some help to find the right moment to terminate practising psychoanalysis in order to prevent them from spoiling their merits and important contributions. Discussions within societies might help the old psychoanalysts to become aware that the moment to stop analytic practice is coming closer. Discussions and proposals by the international psychoanalytic community could help in keeping the ageing issue in the air.

Retirement as a psychoanalyst is a difficult issue. We need studies to describe how psychoanalysts by themselves see this problem. How would they like to work when becoming older? How would they like to decrease their practice? Would they like to keep some work and duties in their societies? Would they like to retire at a certain age and could they afford to do this? Societies should propose some suggestion about the different age limits. Some societies do already ask their members at a certain age, yearly or every three years, to give some information about the work they are doing as psychoanalysts, some societies ask for this information only from their training analysts. Most of the psychoanalytic societies do nowadays have ethical guidelines and we could ask why we couldn't also have some kind of guidelines for termination.

Note

1 A comparison with North and Latin America shows the same general configuration of the demographics in Europe: In the Brazil Psychoanalytic Federation (FEBRAPSI) 82 per cent of analysts are older than 50; in the Psychoanalytic Association of Buenos Aires (APdeBA) 81 per cent are over 60; In Canada 68 per cent of the members are over 60 (Leonoff, 2012).

13

WHAT CANDIDATES SAY ABOUT PSYCHOANALYTICAL PERSPECTIVES ON AGEING

Luisa Marino

In 2009, the IPA[1] Committee on Psychoanalytical Perspective on Ageing (CPA) contacted the IPSO[2] Executive Committee and I was asked as president to contribute to their ongoing research on 'ageing'. The work of Maria Teresa Hooke and Gabriele Junkers on this subject matter impressed me as a critical topic that has been largely neglected. They mentioned in their letter that, as they were investigating this concept of age and ageing among IPA psychoanalysts, it would be very important to ask candidates to contribute with their own data and opinions on this significant theme. I felt very honoured by their request to contribute to this collection of work on ageing.

When we first began this work, asking the opinion of candidates was at that time a novel concept among IPA Committees: including or involving IPSO, the organization that represents analysts in training at IPA Institutes, was also unusual. IPSO is a relatively young organization, being only 40 years old while the IPA has recently celebrated its centenary. This data in itself is in my opinion very significant, particularly on themes like 'generations', transmission/diffusion of psychoanalysis and 'age/ageing' itself.

The IPSO Executive Committee accepted enthusiastically and agreed to submit the adaptation for candidates of the CPA questionnaire; this questionnaire was previously used for investigating psychoanalysts' view on ageing within the component Societies of the IPA. We submitted it to 65 IPSO members attending the IPSO *European* Annual Meeting in Italy, in February 2009. We received back 26 completed questionnaires; we added the results of 13 questionnaires from Australian candidates. These first results were presented in Brussels during the EPF Conference in April 2009 (see the IPSO website, research area).

In a second step, over two years we expanded the sample internationally and our IPSO vice presidents (Drew Tillotson, NA; Eva Reichelt, Europe; Adela Escardo, Silvia Pupo Netto, Valeria Nader, LA) distributed the questionnaire to candidates from each of the other two IPA/IPSO regions: North America, and Latin America. We also circulated questionnaires to PIEE candidates but none were completed or returned.

To sum up: 13 questionnaires were received from the Australian Psychoanalytical Society candidates; 26 from European IPSO Candidates; 25 from North America and 21 from Latin America. These results were presented during the last IPA-IPSO Conference held in Mexico City, 2011.[3]

In working to formulate some reflections based on the data that were received back from the ongoing research: first, there were low numbers of questionnaires collected compared to the numbers distributed from our IPA/IPSO candidates. It is important to contextualize that candidates are less likely to react to international research requests as they are just becoming immersed in their local analytical careers and there are more political sensitivities, which I shall address later within the chapter.

Still one further reason could be found in the last question of the questionnaire: 'Has this theme of age ever being discussed in the IPSO?' The highest rated answer is: 'I don't know', not: 'no, never'. If it is hard for older analysts to openly discuss issues of ageing, we must not be too surprised that there is a sort of taboo between new generations (so 'naturally' linked to older colleagues via their training analysis) to talk openly about possible fantasies underneath matters such as: 'When and why did you start the training? Why not before? Are there subliminal/clear messages of non-acceptance/benevolence towards young trainees in your institute?'

We believe that it is rather rare if not impossible to discuss at the beginning of the training themes that may seem to be in open conflict with that training; unless, we believe, they have been previously discussed by training analysts with their patients/ future candidates during their personal/training analysis. And at this point we come across a circularity rather than a vicious circle: if elderly analysts don't discuss themes of age/ageing among themselves, they probably don't consider it a theme to be discussed or worked through with candidates in analysis or during their training. So candidates themselves can't 'imagine' discussing it, as it would be dissonant with their analysts invested with a certain amount of transference libido. As we mentioned above, particularly at the beginning of your training, you wouldn't like or wish to be dissonant with the establishment as you may fear to harm somebody by doing so or worry that one's actions would be misinterpreted to the degree that it could socially ostracize one.

We will explore opinions/perspectives on 'age' of candidates themselves as future analysts, about differences among the three IPA-IPSO regions about the 'age of starting training'. The typical age for starting psychoanalytic training is between 40 and 60. It has been discussed several times in previous panels and other chapters of this book and has important primary and secondary effects on analysis itself, patients and analysts, as well as for 'now' and future institutional life. When we go through differences between regions we find that North American candidates seem to start their psychoanalytic training at a considerably higher age than Latin American ones. Most NA respondents (56 per cent) began their training when they were over 50, compared with only 19 per cent in LA. European data collected in 2008 reveal that 45 per cent of candidates start their training between their forties and fifties; 26.5 per cent of European candidates start their training after 50 years of age, meaning a bit later than LA candidates but much earlier than NA.

At this point we would like to attempt to relate these first 'row' data to those that concern the question: 'Do you think that there are subliminal messages in your institutes about the age to apply to the training?' Table 13.1 is the statistical table.

Table 13.1 Regional differences regarding the answers to the question: 'Do you think that there are subliminal messages in your institutes about the age to apply to the training?'

		Yes	*No*	*Maybe\Don't know\Some do some don't*
North America	Number	9	11	5
	%	**36%**	**44%**	**20%**
Latin America	Number	7	11	3
	%	**33%**	**52.4%**	**14.3%**
Europe	Number	15	15	4
	%	**44.1%**	**44.1%**	**11.8%**
Total (n–80)	Number	31	37	12
	%	**38.8%**	**46.3%**	**15%**

A possible explanation for this difference between regions might be based on the fact that European candidates are perhaps younger in general; when we look at what candidates from each age group think about the issue, we can see a clear difference between groups.[4] Most respondents who started their training when younger than 40 feel that such a message does exist. See Table 13.2 about age differences in considering the message as present or not.

It seems that the younger candidates who are the ones that would actually encounter such a message tend to feel that the message exists. For other candidates this might be more of a theoretical issue.

Interestingly, though, the three youngest respondents who started training before they were 30 didn't think the message exists. Probably the very fact that they were admitted at their young age is indicative of their specific societies' positive attitude towards young candidates. On the other hand, we could think that their training analysts who believe it is a good idea to apply at a young age have supported them to apply at that time. This would easily explain differences among the same regions (and hypothetically, the same institutes): we could assume that each institute may include people who believe one has to be older and wiser, as well as people who may openly support young applicants. At the same time we might think that fears to apply for an analytical training have been successfully denied to allow people to submit at their 'very young' age, avoiding a too-high level of anxieties, which could have compromised the admission interviews.

Indeed, back to results, some respondents believe the message existed only, or more so, in the past, and that today it is found only in certain societies. To illustrate

Table 13.2 Age differences regarding the answers to the question: 'Do you think that there are subliminal messages in your institutes about the age to apply to the training?'

All		*Yes*	*No*	*Maybe\Don't know\Some do some don't*
< 40	Number	6	3	2
	%	**54.5%**	**27.3**	**18.2%**
41–50	Number	4	10	3
	%	**23.5%**	**58.8%**	**17.6%**
> 50	Number	6	9	3
	%	**33.3%**	**50%**	**16.7%**

I wish to give some of the responses to the question: '*How is the (subliminal) message conveyed?*':

- Openly
- Through the actual age of members and candidates
- Through the requirement to have clinical experience
- Through the big investment the training requires
- The most prevalent reason mentioned was the need for maturity and life experience that may (or may not – as some asserted) come with age as for example:

    - *Time brings maturity and deeper understanding.*
    - *I have always heard about this. Life experience is better and essential to understand his or her analysands.*

In my personal experience over these years of working with candidates, I noticed that some people who refer to it are usually older and started their analytical training later in their life; she quotes the so-called 'mid life crisis'. Nevertheless, now that I have just graduated, I can see, looking back, how much I have been learning and changing within the training, thanks to it, but I am not sure it is because I wasn't wise or experienced before: it is that life changes you and the other way round, at each age you are capable of living it and receiving inputs and accepting them and recognizing them to grow your identity, professionally and personally speaking. Because of this idea, I believe that this need of maturity and experience is a symptom of some inner conflict.

I would like to make a hypothesis on where this defensive fantasy may take its origin from: it seems to me that part of the perception/existence or not of subliminal messages from institutes on 'age' could come more from the side of unconscious fantasies of applicants themselves. Although it could be that this idea is brought up in the institute by those who as candidates and later as members 'conceptualized/ believed' in it. In fact I think: there seems to be a particular 'clear/subliminal' message of accepting/wanting only older and experienced candidates, how is it that the age of applications to training is so high (i.e. in NA)? One among dozens of different reasons could also be due to candidates' fantasies and defences of *fear of failure while applying for training*, a fear that in some way we couldn't/wouldn't/haven't been able/helped to overcome or to manage differently other than by waiting longer.

To quote some respondents' words: 'I think that this training has to be considered the top one so I disagree with the idea of opening it for young people without any experience, this can reduce either the level of the group and expose the risk of the external image that a candidate can give of the institute'; 'I think it's both true and not. If you're young and you feel ready and convinced to become a psychoanalyst I think nobody will stop you. However, if you feel uncertain about your choice it's easier to listen to subliminal messages that can withhold you from applying'; 'I think this is one of the main faults of the psychoanalytic training, because it deters the most active from becoming analysts young enough to renew the psychoanalytic institutes.'

One of the counterparts of these candidates' more or less conscious feelings/ thoughts might have to do with:

1   training analysts' conscious/unconscious fantasies themselves;
2   unconscious unworked-through elaboration of identification with (transferred/ invested) senior analysts, except with the 'founders', who themselves were definitely older than our now second/third generation of senior analysts.

When presenting these data in Mexico City, the impact I had from the audience helped me enormously to link my thoughts; many of the analysts present were world-renowned within the psychoanalytic field. The shift from reading their work to assimilating my experience of them as 'real' people who were very much 'alive and kicking' transformed my appreciation of the static transmission of learning to one that was actually in apprehending and learning from the person themselves. What was discussed during the dialogue after my talk, related to the difficulties in managing 'ageing themes' at institutes, and when we started reading our papers I felt a growing discomfort and almost a feeling of shame for what I was addressing. I felt as if I was 'hurting' and metaphorically 'killing' these extraordinary thinkers and clinicians inside my inner world and – even worse – publicly. Right after these first thoughts, I started being moved by recalling to my memories my 'father/mother figures', senior analysts and good memories of that time passed learning from their certainly long experience. Most of them in their interventions demonstrated their wisdom and clarity.

At some point during the discussion with the audience a young analyst mentioned our own clear ambivalence on what I would call the 'letting-them-go issue': we were talking about older analysts retiring and different implicit or explicit rules among institutes. She said in a deeply emotional voice, we younger analysts are the first who don't want to 'let them go' and who might feel abandoned if they retire, asking them (consciously and unconsciously to avoid the 'talk on ageing') to stay longer, not to leave us . . . Or, I would add now, also to include this could be one way of avoiding our ambivalent 'love and hate' feelings derived from inevitable narcissistic investments, especially in connection with either analyst or candidate leaving the analysis. This intergenerational complexity rings through these issues of cycles of development.

I think I myself was experiencing what some of the statistical data roughly gathered and I reported it to give a more lively contribution to my opinion on the theme 'to be mature and experienced', developed – it seems – both by candidates and analysts, younger and older as they are. I believe that our deep transferential ineluctable and unworked-through feelings of love (and hate, quoting the traditional Freudian dualism on human ambivalent feelings) for our training analysts are some of the strongest reasons why we more or less consciously might believe that:

•   as we don't want to lose our old analysts, we support their long endless careers;
•   we ourselves become unconsciously strongly identified with them;

115

- we have to be more identified with (and the less we are helped not to identify with) the older and more experienced (in identification with their 'senior' age) to allow us to access the analytical training;
- as a secondary side effect of this chain of fantasies, we obtain a partial reduction of our anxieties of failure, which is juxtaposed with our desire for independence.

These debates about applying at an older age rather than when one is younger remains a possibly contentious issue. Equally, the professional identity of being a psychoanalyst may also be changing. The question I am dealing here with is: '*Do you think that among the traditional profession of medicine, psychology and social work, becoming a psychoanalyst is still seen as a feasible career choice, as far as earning a living is concerned?*'

While in LA a vast majority of respondents consider psychoanalysis a feasible career choice, the NA respondents are divided between those who do and those who don't, with slightly more of the latter. The picture in Europe was more like the NA one, with the same tendency appearing even clearer as a majority of European respondents did not consider psychoanalysis a feasible career choice.

But another difference, and in itself significant related to the previous one, comes to light when we go to the question: 'Do you think it might be difficult *to become a student again* after occupying another officer position in a previous career?'

Table 13.3 Regional differences regarding the answers to the question: 'Do you think that among the traditional profession of medicine, psychology and social work, becoming a psychoanalyst is still seen as a feasible career choice, as far as earning a living is concerned?'

		Yes	No	Maybe\Don't know
North America	Number	11	12	2
	%	44%	48%	8%
Latin America	Number	14	3	3
	%	70%	15%	15%
Europe	Number	13	18	2
	%	39.4%	54.5%	6.1%
Total (n 78)	Number	38	18	2
	%	48.7%	42.3%	9%

Table 13.4 Regional differences regarding the answers to the question: 'Do you think it might be difficult to become a student again after occupying another officer position in a previous career?'

		Yes	No	Maybe\Not sure\ Depends
North America	Number	11	9	5
	%	44%	36%	20%
Latin America	Number	6	12	3
	%	28.6%	57.1%	14.3%
Europe	Number	10	19	4
	%	30.3%	57.6%	12.1%
Total	Number	27	40	12
(n = 79)	%	34.2%	50.6%	15.2%

About one-third of the respondents believe that returning to 'student status' might be difficult for those who held formal offices in related organizations. More NA respondents see a difficulty than LA respondents in being students again. In fact we are back to previous significant responses: NA are the older to apply for training and of those 56 per cent had already occupied previous officer positions against 19 per cent of LA students and 18.2 per cent of Europeans. Indeed LA and European students are the same ones who were applying for training earlier and don't feel there might be difficulties in being 'students' again.

I presented some possible reflections on the theme of age/ageing, connected with raw data on the age of candidates. At the same time these ideas are in accordance with the difficulties mentioned elsewhere on the 'lack of young candidates' applying for the training and applying at an age that might contribute significantly to the growing of institutes themselves.

This last question on 'being a student again' is briefly mentioned to underline difficulties that students and candidates may face according to their age when they apply, if they have been a student already and if they have been occupying an important official position in previous careers. What are the feelings that may accompany or not their (our) capability of learning from new training experiences and growing their (our) ongoing professional and personal identity as analysts in being; how much the fear of failure has been worked through and how much it may affect people applying at later ages rather than before. Among others, that of learning from a new experience at every age/stage of one's life I believe is a fundamental requirement for training and for the profession of psychoanalysis. Each of us is far from being immune to unconscious defences, as we well learned from our common experience of analysands.

I hope the mixture of the quantitative findings, rather than being solely scientifically based results, could be met with my explanatory capacity of providing a unique perspective of representing candidates on an international level and beginning to find a voice for mutually enriching cross dialogue. On this occasion, this means being able to look into the profession to aid in that most time-honoured tool of psychoanalytic work, to hold up a mirror of reflection for the discipline itself. My hope is to facilitate questions that naturally emerge from this reflection on the unconscious motivation of the analyst-in-training and of those who already as members have been through these kinds of issues for both to reconnect more to one another to better understand the other's perspective. I strongly believe that we all – younger and senior analysts – need to face and feel free to discuss the inner conflict behind ageing matters among each other and between different generations, to avoid the risks of what Haydée Faimberg (2005) described as 'transgenerational transmission' of cumulative traumas that may affect the capacity to grow up as professional psychoanalytical institutions and as analysts.[5] This coming together and working through does heal what can be considered quite a significant fragmentation that for all of our sakes and for the future development of the psychoanalytic profession needs to be weighed and measured so the true heart of these ideas can find some helpful and fruitful expression.

Notes

1 The International Psychoanalytical Association.
2 The International Psychoanalytical Studies Organization (IPSO) is comprised of candidates who are training in the Institutes of the International Psychoanalytical Association. IPSO is comprised of three regions: Europe (including Israel and Australia), North America (plus South Korea and China) and Latin America.
3 Results can be found online on IPA (www.ipa.org.uk) and IPSO websites (www.ipso-candidates.org.uk).
4 Nurit Fishman, CAPP statistical expert.
5 I wish to thank Maria Teresa Hooke, Gabriele Junkers and Leena Klockars for inspiring these thoughts and the precious help of the IPSO Executive Committee, with whom I had the honour to collaborate between 2008 and 2011.

14

GIVING UP AN IMPORTANT ROLE IN PSYCHOANALYTIC ORGANISATIONS

Cláudio Laks Eizirik

Introduction

What makes us analysts? When do we feel that we can call ourselves analysts? What is the role of our institutions in this process? And when (if this is at all possible) do we stop feeling that we are analysts?

These questions, which could be answered by taking into account chronological or procedural circumstances, deal with the complex issue of identity and, more precisely, analytic identity, both the subject of a considerable analytic literature.

In order to feel that we are analysts, we have naturally travelled across many relationships; through analysis, supervisions, seminars, the long hours and years of analytic practice and the much-needed exchanges with colleagues. In short, we have established an inner world of objects with which we relate and are in continuous dialogue, beginning with Freud, as a person and an author; the other authors with whom we identify more; our former analysts, supervisors and colleagues; but perhaps mainly with our patients, past and current, and with the specific analytic field that we have built with each of them.

In any case, all these external and internal relations take place in a particular setting, that of our institutions. This is where we become analysts, then develop our analytic career and, after decades, begin the often painful process of giving up important roles. What is more, all this takes place in the world we live in, as citizens and part of our Zeitgeist.

In this chapter, I will revisit some psychoanalytic ideas and other reflections on our current culture, then some contributions to the understanding of identity and analytic identity. After that, I will report some personal experiences and observations on having an important role in our institutions and, finally, discuss the impact of this specific part of analytic identity on the process of ageing and living; described by Junkers with the term 'the empty couch'.

Contemporary psychoanalytic views on culture

Several authors, both analysts and thinkers from other fields, have tried to offer insights on our complex and changing world (Eizirik, 2008). I would now like to summarise some of these views.

Van der Leeuw (1980) characterised our Zeitgeist as being constituted of: (1) a great flood of information, quantification and massive growth that leads to superficiality, hampers independent thinking and is accompanied by a levelling process, as a consequence of which silence, solitude and privacy become endangered and congestion disturbs man's consciousness of space and the experience of space he needs for his life; (2) changes in the role of the family as the basis of society, motherhood being increasingly neglected; (3) the dominant role of seductive advertising, encouraging immediate gratification and creating the illusion that total gratification is possible; (4) the increasing search for excitement, stimulation, brief and often violent explosions of emotions and the urge for rapid recharge instead of the cultivation of warm, tender feelings, in particular where children are concerned.

From a wider perspective, Lasch (1978) coined for our era the expression 'culture of narcissism', resulting from the breakdown of the family and the accentuation of instinctive gratification. As social pressures have invaded the ego, it has become harder to grow up and acquire maturity. This leads to a failure of normal superego development. Thus, in a world dominated by images, individual progress can only come from projected images and erroneous impressions produced by insecure egos. In this world, it is difficult to discriminate reality from fantasy, and what we really are from what the products we consume suggest that we are. The 'culture of narcissism' has abolished collective discipline and concentrated work in favour of a world of impressions, appearances and disguises.

Kernberg (1989) explored the nature of the appeal of mass culture, particularly as it is communicated by the mass media. He examined the regressive effects of group processes on the recipients of mass culture, and the striking correspondence between the conventional aspects of mass culture and the psychological characteristics of latency. Among others, he stressed the following trends in contemporary culture: the simultaneity of communication; the illusion of being a member of the crowd connected with a central figure who communicates what is important and what one should think about it; the denial of complexities; the predominance of conventional assumptions over individual thinking; the stimulation of a narcissistic dimension in the receiver, and also a paranoid one, in the form of justified suspicion or indignation; the application of a simplistic morality to social and political matters in the form of clichés (for instance, that good people will, together, be able to solve problems). In his view, conventionality may be the price of social stability, in spite of the danger of more severe group regression. More recently, Kernberg (1998) described a striking tendency in large groups to project superego functions on to the group as a whole in an effort to prevent violence and protect ego identity by means of a shared ideology.

The post-modern condition, a term coined by Lyotard (1979), has become an essential part of any discussion of our culture. In spite of the controversial acceptance of this concept, several trends in our era are often described as typical of the so-called cultural crisis: complexity, scepticism, challenges to all meta-narratives that were a central part of the project of the Enlightenment; acculturation through images in more and more virtual realities; claims to the right to difference and to following alternative lifestyles; the social demands for participation and for the rights of women, pacifists, homosexuals, the elderly and other minorities; the growing presence of the so-called pathologies of immediate gratification; the idealisation of ambiguity; an era of simultaneity and immediate accomplishment of ideas, wishes and purposes (Ahumada, 1997; Arditi, 1988; Baladier, 1995; Carlisky and Eskenazi, 2000; Castoriadis, 1996; Eizirik, 1997).

In the late 1980s and early 1990s, Zygmunt Bauman published a number of books that dealt with the relationship between modernity, bureaucracy, rationality and social exclusion. Bauman, following Freud, came to view European modernity as a trade-off; European society, he argued, had agreed to forego a level of freedom in order to receive the benefits of increased individual security. Bauman argued that modernity, in what he later came to term its 'solid' form, involved removing unknowns and uncertainties; it involved control over nature, hierarchical bureaucracy, rules and regulations, control and categorisation – all of which attempted to gradually remove personal insecurities, making the chaotic aspects of human life appear well-ordered and familiar. However, Bauman began to develop the position that such order-making efforts never manage to achieve the desired results. When life becomes organised into familiar and manageable categories, he argued, there are always social groups who cannot be administered, who cannot be separated out and controlled. In his article 'Modernity and Ambivalence' (1991), Bauman began to theorise such indeterminate individuals by introducing the allegorical figure of 'the stranger'. Drawing upon the sociology of Georg Simmel and the philosophy of Jacques Derrida, Bauman came to write of the stranger as the person who is present yet unfamiliar, society's *undecidable*.

In 'Modernity and Ambivalence' (1991), Bauman attempted to give an account of the different approaches modern society adopts towards the stranger. He argued that, on the one hand, in a consumer-oriented economy the strange and the unfamiliar are always enticing; in different styles of food, different fashions and in tourism it is possible to experience the allure of what is unfamiliar. Yet this strangeness also has a more negative side. The stranger, because he cannot be controlled and ordered, is always the object of fear; he is the potential mugger, the person outside of society's borders who is constantly threatening. Bauman's book, *Modernity and the Holocaust* (1989), is an attempt to give a full account of the dangers of these kinds of fears. Drawing upon the books of Hannah Arendt and Theodor Adorno on totalitarianism and the Enlightenment, Bauman developed the argument that the Holocaust should not simply be considered an event in Jewish history, or a regression to pre-modern barbarism. Rather, he argued, the Holocaust should be seen as deeply connected to modernity and its order-making efforts. Bauman argued that procedural rationality, the division of labour into smaller and smaller tasks, the taxonomic categorisation of different species, and the tendency to view rule-following as morally good all played their role in the Holocaust coming to pass. And he argued that, for this reason, modern societies have not fully taken on board the lessons of the Holocaust; it is generally viewed – to use Bauman's metaphor – like a picture hanging on a wall, offering few lessons. In Bauman's analysis the Jews became 'strangers' *par excellence* in Europe; the Final Solution was pictured by him as an extreme example of the attempts made by societies to excise the uncomfortable and indeterminate elements existing within them. Bauman contended that the same processes of exclusion that were at work in the Holocaust could, and to an extent do, still come into play today.

In the mid- and late 1990s Bauman began to look at two different but interrelated subjects: post-modernity and consumerism. He began to develop the position that a shift had taken place in modern society in the latter half of the twentieth century – it had altered from being a society of producers to a society of *consumers*.

This switch, he argued, reversed Freud's 'modern' trade-off: this time security was given up in order to enjoy increased freedom, freedom to purchase, to consume, and to enjoy life. In his books in the 1990s Bauman wrote of this shift as being one from 'modernity' to 'post-modernity'. Since the turn of the millennium, his books have tried to avoid the confusion surrounding the term 'post-modernity' by using the metaphors of 'liquid' and 'solid' modernity (2000). In his books on modern consumerism Bauman still writes of the same uncertainties that he portrayed in his writings on 'solid' modernity, but in these books, he writes of these fears being more diffuse and harder to pin down. Indeed they are, to use the title of one of his books, 'liquid fears' (2005). According to Bauman, at the dawn of the twenty-first century, we live again in a time of fear. Whether it is the fear of natural disasters, the fear of environmental catastrophes or the fear of indiscriminate terrorist attacks, we live today in a state of constant anxiety about the dangers that could strike unannounced and at any moment. Fear is the name we give to our uncertainty in the face of the dangers that characterise our liquid modern age, and to our ignorance of what the threat is and our incapacity to determine what can and cannot be done to counter it.

This new culture that presents permanent change and complexity produces increasing perplexity, anxieties, and losses of models and values that are felt as a threat to the integrity of the self, and to psychic identity. And yet, at the same time, it poses the challenge of learning to live in and to share with others this admirable new world (Huxley, 1932).

It is in this wide context that we, as analysts, live and have to face current growing challenges to psychoanalysis, which in many respects presents another version of the empty couch, in the sense that we have a world in which the analytic method is challenged by new therapies of all kinds, as something old fashioned and unsuitable to current liquid fears and psychic suffering.

Contemporary clinical practice makes psychoanalysis suitable for different kinds of patients with varying degrees of psychic suffering or different forms of personality disorders, but also, as has been amply described, presents a specific sort of patient – showing more severe conditions with the growing presence of pathologies of immediate gratification or, as Kristeva (1993) puts it, *the new diseases of the soul*. Living within a culture of narcissism (Lasch, 1978) or of immediacy, or 'liquid modernity' (Bauman, 2000), patients are offered the promise of faster methods, whose effectiveness is proven and guaranteed by so-called evidence-based psychiatry. Widespread socio-economic crisis and unarguable problems such as that of distance in urban centres might render it difficult to put into practice the psychoanalytic method in its full scope. Taking into account what was previously described, one can expect that an unavoidable tension might be present in the analytic process or in the analytic field

(Baranger and Baranger, 1961) considering that these somehow more stable psychic elements like identity will get in touch with the changing world of our time.

Current patients, living in a globalising world, might feel it difficult to adapt to the analytic setting, where silence, intimacy and a long, joint work-through of emotions and memories might be seen as strange or old fashioned. Usual analytic procedures such as the couch and several sessions a week might also be seen as different from what is more widely publicised about other methods.

Despite the long clinical experience of more than a century and a lot of effectiveness studies showing the strength of the analytic method, one cannot forget that scepticism and challenges to meta-narratives are common trends of our culture.

Ricoeur (1970) mentioned that Freud, Marx and Nietzsche were masters of suspicion, in the sense that they did not accept well-established truths.

As I have tried to show, several psychoanalytic insights are useful for understanding the globalising world in which we live.

But, in any case, questions remain concerning the relevance of psychoanalysis itself, with all its complexities and requirements in a world dominated by 'liquid modernity' (Bauman, 2000), and in which human relations seem to be so provisional and very often meaningless; or in which some recent examples of the demonic power of the compulsion to repeat, so well described by Freud, something that, according to Green, assassinates time, can be found in the different expressions of fundamentalism, as well as in brutal social and economic differences that keep millions of people condemned to famine, disease and early death; or in which systematic attacks on the environment threaten our shared world; or in which new and fascinating possibilities have changed forever our methods of communication, information systems, science and the humanities; or in which new methods of expression or language are created in the arts, and new meanings are found to symbolise and deepen our understanding of the human mind and body (Eizirik, 2008).

In this changing world, psychoanalysis responds to change with change. Not only are our different theoretical schools in full development, but we are also more than ever in a position in which we are able to work analytically in closer emotional contact with our patients, as well as more equipped to analyse patients with severe conditions.

We faced the main challenges of analytic education while acknowledging the existence of different methods of analytic education and developing studies on how to obtain analytic competence. As for our relations with the outside world, we can see that in each society, country or region new and stimulating initiatives show that, after a period of a sort of 'splendid isolation', psychoanalysis is again, as in Freud's time, in the forefront of the international struggle for the freedom of critical and independent thinking.

Identity and analytic identity

It is widely recognised that an individual's capacity to remain himself during periods of change is fundamental to his sense of identity, something that he experiences emotionally. Establishing a sense of identity means maintaining stability in the face of changing circumstances and the successive stages of the life cycle. But how much change can an individual tolerate before it works irreparable harm on his identity?

Grinberg and Grinberg (1989) suggested that the establishment of a sense of identity depends most importantly on the internalisation of relations with meaningful persons and their assimilation by the ego. The ego assimilates objects by means of authentic introjective identification, not by manic projective identification, which creates false identities and a false self.

In their book on migration and exile, the Grinbergs report that events such as migration (and here we could also consider old age, retirement and giving up important positions) which cause drastic changes in individuals' lives can pose threats to their sense of identity. Victor Tausk, who introduced the term *identity* in psychoanalytic literature (1919), maintained that just as a child discovers objects and his own self, so an adult in his struggle for self-preservation frequently repeats the experience of 'finding himself' and 'feeling like himself'. The immigrant in his struggle for self-preservation needs to hold on to various elements of his native environment (familiar objects, music, memories, and dreams representing different aspects of his native land) in order to be able to feel like himself.

It is interesting to note that in all his writings, Freud only once used the term *identity* (1926), and he gave it a psychosocial connotation. In a speech in which he tried to explain his connection to Judaism, he spoke of 'obscure emotional forces' that were 'all the more powerful the less easily articulate they were' and of 'the clear consciousness of an *inner identity* based not on race or religion but on an *aptitude common to a group* to live in opposition to and free of the prejudices that undermine the use of the intellect'. Thus, Freud refers to something in one's core, one's interior that is crucial to the internal cohesion of a group.

Erikson (1956), commenting on Freud's statement, deduced that the term identity expresses 'the relation between an individual and his group', suggesting a certain consistent sameness and shared character traits.

In *Identidad y cambio* [Identity and change] (1971), the Grinbergs introduced the notion that one's sense of identity is born of the continuous interaction between spatial, temporal and social integration links. They have had ample opportunity to study these links as they appear in the relation between patient and analyst. What follows is a synthesis of the complex permutations that set the stage for the acquisition of a sense of identity in the psychoanalytic process; from these we may infer the ways in which identity comes to be formed and how its disorders affect individual development, the relation between the individual and society, and, most important, the individual's experiences of change.

One should take into account that a patient generally comes into analysis with conflicts that to some degree affect his sense of identity, and his conscious or unconscious motive for seeking analysis is the need to consolidate his sense of identity.

The sense of identity expresses, preconsciously and consciously, a series of unconscious fantasies which, once integrated, constitute what could be called the unconscious fantasy of the self.

The process leading to the acquisition or maturation of one's sense of identity can be developed, in fact, with the psychoanalytic process, for the analytic framework itself provides a 'container' to hold and keep within bounds the projections made by 'pieces of the self'. The container, at the same time, becomes the crucible in which complex operations are performed on these pieces before they can become integrated in a whole.

Another image that helps to illustrate the analytic process and the framework as boundary and container can be found in the notion of the analyst as the arms or, more regressively, the skin that holds together the parts of the baby/patient.

Inspired by the contributions of Melanie Klein and Wilfred Bion, the Grinbergs suggest that object relations and identification mechanisms at work in the analytic process and manifested in the relationship with the analyst are worthy of attention. The analyst's container function, together with his interpretive role, allows the patient to work through and consolidate his sense of identity. In this process, the patient accepts the infantile parts of the self and detaches from those regressive aspects that block the path to the firm establishment of an adult self.

Analytic identity was the object of an international symposium, held in Haslemere, England, in 1976, whose papers and discussions were published by Joseph and Widlöcher (1983). In my view, this is a unique and relevant contribution to the understanding of the many dimensions of our specific identity, including a precious discussion of Grinberg. Throughout the chapters of this book, analytic identity is connected with previous life experiences, and mainly successive identifications with the analytic function, training analysts, supervisors, authors, and the basic values of psychoanalysis. But in my view, the most stimulating contribution was that offered by Pearl King (1983), who examined the analyst's identity crisis through his life cycle. In her view, the fourth critical phase in our professional life cycle occurs when we become aware of our own ageing, the depletion of our skills, capacities and abilities, and possible retirement from professional life.

Despite so many differences concerning our culture and our language, we all share the unique experience of working with words. The most important Brazilian poet Carlos Drummond de Andrade once wrote in a poem: 'Come closer and stare at the words / Each one has a thousand secret faces hidden under the neutral one / and asks, without caring about the poor or terrible answer you were supposed to give: / Have you brought the key?' (See Nist and Leite, 1962)

The psychoanalytic key has been used to open many doors, but there are still a thousand others waiting for us.

A personal experience

To my knowledge, what we usually know about each presidency of the IPA (as well as societies or other institutions) comes from reports from previous presidents, documents and evaluations from other people involved in the experience, as well as historical references that can be found in several dictionaries and books. The most recent one is the wonderful book edited by Loewenberg and Thompson (2010) to celebrate 100 years of the IPA, where one can read chapters in which Leo Rangell,

Robert Wallerstein, Horacio Etchegoyen, Otto Kernberg and Robert Tyson, Daniel Widlöcher and myself report the main events, achievements and problems of the administrations under our presidencies. With a few exceptions, these are or try to be objective reports. At the same time, Widlöcher offered a candid account of his lifelong experience of becoming and remaining an analyst, with precious notes on his personal experience as president of the IPA.

It seems to me that the readers of this book will perhaps be interested in knowing some facts and, mainly, feelings of the immediate past president of the IPA, at a point when the process of mourning for the presidency is practically over and at the same time is not so distant as to prevent the memory of what was felt.

Several times, when I am invited to lecture and supervise in different societies of the three geographical regions of the IPA, there is a moment, during a car ride, or a quiet conversation with one or more colleagues, that this question arises: what was the experience like of presiding over the IPA? Each of these moments asks for a different answer, according to what comes to my mind in free association: faces, situations, congresses, challenges, achievements, problems, joys, sorrows, nostalgia, but, after thinking about it, I usually say that it was a positive and rewarding experience.

Danielle Quinodoz (2009) described what she calls the small second of eternity, those moments of intense emotion where we perceive the shock of beauty, love, certain pains, and key decisions and which seem to escape from measured chronological time, without actually denying it. In her view, older people who are able to learn from their experiences can attest to the complexity of each event, which can help in achieving an overview, avoid hasty judgements and give time to time. They also feel the importance of rebuilding their internal history by integrating the emotionally important moments of their lives into a coherent overall story. They can perceive that it is sometimes those events that were very simple but loaded with emotion that have, in fact, been an underground guide all their lives, and thus recognise what she calls, precisely, these seconds of eternity.

To understand why I was fortunate to live several seconds of eternity during my four years as IPA president, I must quote what I wrote in the IPA Festschrift:

> I was born, grew up, and undertook all my studies and analytic training in Porto Alegre, a lovely city in the south of Brazil, the capital of the state of Rio Grande do Sul, which borders Uruguay and Argentina. Since childhood, I have had, in many respects, the feeling of living on the border: our state is part of Brazil, but different in the sense that we also have much in common with our neighbouring countries, and are a state with a lot of descendants of European immigrants. I am, at the same time, a Brazilian and a Jew, a psychiatrist and a psychoanalyst, a clinician and a researcher, a medical doctor and a lover of the arts, mainly literature and films, an inhabitant of my country but often feeling at home in so many different places. Despite some initial anxieties and doubts about what would happen in my position as IPA president, I was always able to count on constant love and support, making my experience mainly a very positive and rewarding one.
>
> (Eizirik, 2010)

Over the last few decades, since I was a candidate, I have felt a great interest in institutional activities. I have the impression that this is connected, naturally among other factors, with a certain tradition in my own family, as my grandfather was the president of the main synagogue in town during the construction of its then impressive building and my father was the president of the local Zionist organisation; institutional issues were always part of family conversations. Thus, it seemed natural to me to be an active member in student organisations, even during the 20-year dictatorship that dominated Brazil, and after that always to be an active player in different institutions of MDs and psychiatrists, then in psychoanalytic institutions. Despite the fact of being the first Brazilian to become president of the IPA, if I look back to my previous engagements at local, regional and international levels, for instance Dean of the Medical School, president of my own Society and of the Latin American analytic federation, chair of several IPA committees and so on, I could feel that this was almost a natural consequence of this progression. When I took over the presidency of the IPA, in the Rio Congress of 2005, what came to my mind was the feeling that Churchill reported when he became prime minister of Britain during World War II: I felt that all my previous life had been a preparation for this moment.

The task of presiding over the IPA was present in my mind for at least three years before it formally began, then, if one takes into account the fact of running for the position, being president-elect for two years under the leadership of Daniel Widlöcher, the four years of presidency and at least two following years of working through all these complex experiences, the total amount of time comes to more than 10 years; an important part of my adult life.

So, as I try to integrate some of these seconds of eternity into my whole identity and life experience, what comes most often to my mind are the following situations: the opening speech in Rio, looking at my parents and my family in the first row; being the first Brazilian in this position and a son of immigrants; the opening speech in the Berlin congress (the first time there since Freud's last congress in 1924) beginning with a quote, in Yiddish, of the Partisan anthem, and the emotional atmosphere that mixed together Germans, Jews and so many other people; and the few moments later during the unveiling of the Gradiva statue in a square when I was able to say that Nazism lost and psychoanalysis was alive and strong almost all over the world; the speech at the UN on behalf of the IPA celebrating Freud's 150th anniversary; the board meeting where we, after so many years of discussions and arguments, fears and threats, were able finally to approve the three training models; the meeting in Beijing where we formally began the analytic training in China; the breakfast in a Porto Alegre hotel where Monica Siedman de Armesto agreed to run as secretary general and I felt that with Brazilian and Argentinian support we had a real chance of being elected, and so on.

To preside over the IPA was mainly rewarding, not only because it fulfilled narcissistic wishes, or had Oedipal resonances, or offered strong emotions, but mainly because it offered the opportunity of doing several things that I was convinced were good for psychoanalysis and the IPA, and of doing them jointly with so many colleagues in what was very often a real work group. Just one example was the idea of creating a committee to study the ageing of patients as well as the process of ageing in analysts, and to invite Gabrielle Junkers to chair it. From what I can see at this point, the committee is doing very relevant work.

In short, I really enjoyed these aspects of the activity, and felt able to perform them with enthusiasm and to achieve the main objectives we, as a work group, had jointly planned together.

And then, when I knew almost all the regional and local presidents, when things were moving forward, when new and stimulating committees were fully working, when it seemed so natural to be the president of the IPA, the end of the term was on the horizon; small signs of the end were appearing and then stronger ones, and then it was over. I could fully understand King Lear's question in the months after the fall: does anybody know me? Half-jokingly, I used to ask close friends, immediately before and after: is there life outside the IPA? I then realised that I had spent my last 15 years in several active roles in the IPA, and that now I had none.

Despite conscious knowledge of this process and active procedures to transfer the position to the president elect, and all sorts of administrative actions to make it happen in the best way possible, and, even despite all previous experiences of holding and then leaving important roles in institutions, I was able to observe in myself feelings of loss, emptiness, sadness and an apparent lack of perspective that appeared in very expressive dreams as well as in conscious ideas. There were associations with death, illnesses, as well as historical associations, again Churchill, for instance, who lost an election after winning the war, and so on.

First of all, it seems to me that the first step in this process is not to deny it, nor to try to keep any small part of power, or to become paranoid or bitter, but rather to take into account that it is a process of mourning along the lines so well described by Freud and Melanie Klein.

And, as in all processes of mourning, the lost object after some time is installed into the self, as one of the many objects that constitute our internal world.

The IPA became one of my good internal objects, but at the same time one of the external objects with which I have and will always have a relationship. This implies a feeling of a certain amount of responsibility for its history or subsequent developments, and a natural tendency to take some action, at a limited level, if needed to protect its structure and achievements.

After a certain period of mourning, the core of my analytic identity, namely working with patients, supervising, teaching, both at the institute and at the university, reading and writing, all regained their prominent role in my mind and in my daily activity. And this leads me to the last part of this chapter.

What is the role of institutional positions in the analyst's identity?

The considerations by King, Junkers and Quinodoz seem very relevant to this topic. According to King (1983), when analysts are over-dependent or even parasitical towards their role as psychoanalysts, using their patients and professional activities as extensions of themselves (which are the main sources of their identity as human beings), then the process of retirement or withdrawal from full professional activity can threaten the stability of their personalities and lead to an inability to face their own identity crisis in a creative and constructive way. Junkers (2011) stressed that the most difficult task when growing older seems to be to deal and cope with all the narcissistic blows and losses; feeling forced to accept more and more limitations. The work on the ageing process demands the conscious and active giving up of something familiar and narcissistically highly important, to abstain from wishful thinking whilst the internal world of wishes remains as lively as ever before. Quinodoz (2013) states that what is lost in external reality can be kept in psychic reality as an internal object. When she finishes an analysis, she says, her couch is empty in connection with external reality, but it is occupied in regard to her internal world. While reading their stimulating papers on this subject, what came to my mind was the idea put forward by Melanie Klein regarding how to live well as an elderly person: if envy is not very strong, gratitude for what was lived throughout life predominates and the old person is able to identify with the young. This is very similar to the function of generativity described by Erikson.

In my view and in my experience, as well as from my observation of what happened with other colleagues who held important institutional roles, when this position was accepted as a transitional or ephemeral one, and when the process of mourning was not denied and all its painful feelings were faced, after a certain period of time the core of analytic identity regained its relevance. When these positions were invested with a great amount of narcissistic gratification, or they meant Oedipal triumph or feelings of omnipotence, the risks of bitterness, envy and destructive actions towards other colleagues and even the shared institutions prevailed; during my term, and even before and after, I witnessed several sad situations in which these later feelings lead to crises and painful splitting/separations.

As I am currently working very actively as an analyst, and institutions have become good internal objects with which I have a certain critical distance, and feel that I can see and accept their possibilities and limitations, I wonder what will happen when I arrive at a moment when I will stop working so actively and, in fact, will cease my analytic activity.

What I imagine is that my internal couch will not become completely empty; in my view, our analytic identity is more a matter of an internal world than of external facts. I cannot imagine myself as someone not thinking as an analyst and seeing the world through this prism, or this way of thinking and feeling.

More and more, I am asked for advice on clinical or institutional situations; it gives me a real pleasure to use my past experience to try to help younger colleagues, and it is a real joy to listen to a good clinical material, or to see someone who was my student, supervisee or patient take over institutional positions or show good clinical or theoretical skills. It is similar to seeing the way my own children move forward in their personal or professional lives.

Despite all the challenges and problems faced by psychoanalysis and its institutions, it is rewarding to feel that once I was able to contribute to its vitality and human and social relevance; but it is even better to witness how many younger and talented colleagues are doing even better, and to be able to trust them in their mission of protecting our common legacy.

15

PSYCHOANALYST ASSISTANCE COMMITTEES
Philosophy and practicalities

Audrey Kavka

Introduction and overview

Through our clinical work, we analysts help our patients develop a greater capacity to bear the unbearable. More accurately, we work from the knowledge that what seems to be psychically unbearable can be transformed into something psychically bearable. As analysts, our own capacity for bearing psychic pain most often expands as part of lifelong development and through our experiences as analysts. Yet, analysts are not immune from overwhelming psychic pain, and when an analyst cannot bear the pain of his or her own inner and outer reality, this will have an impact on his or her capacity to function as an analyst. Psychoanalyst Assistance Committees (PACs) recognize this very human vulnerability and are empowered to serve the analytic community's obligation to our patients, colleagues, families and ourselves to help analysts who may be struggling with the specific pain of diminished capacity to function as an analyst.

What is a PAC? Concretely, a PAC is a committee of psychoanalysts charged by the regional psychoanalytic institute, society or centre to develop, implement and maintain a programme responsibly to identify and provide assistance to analysts who may be functioning at an impaired level due to illness. The chapter title, 'Psychoanalyst Assistance Committees: Philosophy and practicalities', reflects my conviction that a theoretical framework for understanding the position of the impaired analyst enables us to develop a picture of what is appropriate and what is achievable in terms of 'assistance' for troubled colleagues. The practicalities of who will be on the committee, how the committee fits into the overall structure of the analytic organization, what procedures will be followed to 'assist' and other such key matters must flow from a coherent understanding of how to think about the impaired analyst and, in turn, how to formulate a theory of assistance.

I will present the view that the diminution of capacity to function as an analyst, due to somatic illness, cognitive decline or psychological frailty, poses a psychic and pragmatic challenge to the impaired analyst. Some analysts will make adaptations demonstrating that they have been able to integrate the external demand to maintain a satisfactory level of analytic functioning with an internal awareness of personal changes in capacity. For some analysts, a change in analytic capacity may be experienced as psychically unbearable and this will interfere with their ability to develop an appropriate and necessary adaptation.

Elliot Jaques introduced a broad and supple theory of adult development in the 1965 article, 'Death and the Mid-Life Crisis'. He placed a psychoanalytic focus on the psychic challenges brought on by the conscious and unconscious mid-life confrontation with the inevitability of ageing, decline and death. He termed this a crisis and explicated the crisis as a model of potential adult development or developmental stasis. From the vantage point of Jaques' broad theory, I have developed a conceptual model of the impaired analyst as an analyst in a crisis of personal development. Like other crises of personal development, impairment for any reason, whether it be physical, mental, emotional, temporary or chronic, may either be worked through or dynamically place the analyst in a defensive state in which they are unable to develop a flexible, dynamic integration of inner and outer reality.

Key to acceptance of and response to temporary or lasting impairment is the successful working-through of threatening internal psychic configurations, associated fantasies and affects that emerge with change in capacity. The 'assistance' provided by PACs can be understood within the conceptual frame of the growth-promoting qualities of container-contained engagement and function.

Having addressed why a colleague may need help and the theory of how a PAC can help the analyst of concern (A of C), I turn to the organizational path to development of local PACS. Clarity about the theoretical frame for the fundamental mission of the PAC is crucial, as experience indicates that serious resistances to the formation of a local PAC will arise from multiple directions. I will develop several trains of thought about the unconscious forces that contribute to the individual and community resistance to PACs.

The following section on the history of PACs in the Institutes and Societies of the American Psychoanalytic Association provides a model for the development of national policy to stimulate awareness of the problem of analysts in need of assistance and promote the development of local PACs. This history demonstrates that a conviction about the potential widespread harm of neglecting or haphazardly addressing the problem of troubled colleagues and a conviction about the organizational capacity to formulate and enact appropriate processes of intervention are instrumental in working through the resistances to PACs.

Last, I will identify some of the key elements to be considered in the formation of a local PAC. The structural and procedural elements of a local PAC will shape the PAC experience and should reflect the goals and mission of an individual PAC.

At the outset, I wish fully to disclose that I have chosen to offer illustrations in the form of composite, probable but fictionalized accounts unless the example includes a full identification of the actual person. Analysts are the subject of this chapter and book, and the possibility of disguise is limited. For the most part, the illustrations depict analysts in painful internal and external situations that demand our utmost attention to their dignity and distress.

The impairment crisis

In the course of the development of the individual there are critical phases which have the character of change points, or periods of rapid transition.

(Jaques, 1965, p. 512)

The loss of capacity to function as an analyst is one such critical phase. It may be anticipated and prompt the decision to retire pre-emptively, or it may appear unexpectedly with the sudden onset of a debilitating illness such as the rupture of a brain aneurysm or the occurrence of a traumatic event precipitating a persistent anxiety state. It may develop gradually, such that the moment of loss of the capacity to work as an analyst is perceptible only retrospectively, as in the development of a serious depression, substance abuse or Alzheimer's dementia. The transience or permanence of the loss of capacity will distinguish different situations requiring analyst assistance.

As observed and formulated by Jaques, psychic development is a lifelong process during which various crises and psychic challenges arise in relation to the internal meaning of bodily and external changes. Like motor development or puberty, the bodily changes of ageing or illness introduce new elements into the complex inner world. Jaques focuses on the transition point in life when the adult perceives a transition from 'growing up' to 'growing old' and famously dubs this the mid-life crisis. This brilliant choice of words efficiently and dramatically conveys an inner state of disturbance that may stimulate or interfere with ongoing personal development.

According to Jaques, the intrusion of the painful reality of death approaching precipitates the mid-life crisis and forces depressive anxieties into the present. To further understand the internal situation of the mid-life individual with a new load of depressive anxieties thrust upon him or her, Jaques turns to the studies of Melanie Klein. Klein's theories of the paranoid and depressive positions serve Jaques very well as the theory of 'positions' offers a fluid view of development throughout life. Jaques reports that if the individual is able to rework the depressive position during the mid-life crisis, he or she will transition from youthful 'hot from the fire creativity' to 'sculpted creativity'. This is an instance of successful maturation.

Things do not always proceed so well in the mid-life crisis. Jaques attributes this to the difficulty, for some, of bearing the grief of his or her infantile destructiveness in order to re-establish good internal objects. I interpret this from my own experience treating older adults to mean that the re-establishment and presence of reliable good internal objects enables the ageing individual to face the losses and unknowns of the end of life with psychic integrity. For those individuals who are unable to work through the depressive anxieties of the mid-life, Jaques proposes that the turn towards death will be experienced as a period of persistent psychological disturbance and depressive breakdown. He further observes that 'breakdown may be avoided by means of a strengthening of manic defences, with a warding off of depression and persecution about ageing and death, but with an accumulation of persecutory anxiety to be faced when the inevitability of ageing and death eventually demands recognition' (p. 511).

Like Jaques' mid-life crisis, the situation of impairment is a crisis of adulthood with a complex and dynamic interplay of bodily change, neuro-cognitive change, change in life circumstances, internal world representations and psychic meanings. Body-embedded and mental/cognitive health changes will themselves have an inner meaning with both conscious and unconscious representations, fantasies and anxieties in the mind of the analyst. Likewise, the impact on capacities will disturb the inner world with perceived meanings, fantasies and anxieties. Throughout life, our changing bodies and circumstances present crises of personal development of various magnitudes and difficulty. Some are rather universal and some are highly specific and individual. The internal meaning will always be specific and individual.

The issue of 'bearing the unbearable' enters into the understanding of the crisis of impairment, for psychic pain that is perceived as intolerable leads to psychic defence activities that disrupt thinking and development whereas working through what seems to be unbearable pain enables thinking and development. Whether temporary or permanent, real or imagined, the impaired analyst's confrontation with the transition from able to work to not able to work is a dramatic challenge to identity integration and stability. Joffe and Sandler (1965) write of the mental pain of discrepancy between one's actual state of being and one's ideal state of being. With professional impairment, a marked discrepancy between ideal and real exists. Professional competence is some part of the ideal state of the analyst. In health, the perceived discrepancy between the actual self and ideal self in terms of competence is wide enough to inspire ongoing growth but narrow enough to evade self-depreciation and hopelessness. When significant impairment develops, the perception of the discrepancy between the actual and real self may produce mental anguish and may pose a threat to the integrity of the self.

This is the narcissistic component of the adult impairment crisis. Painful inner states of helplessness, dependency, impotence and hopelessness may be revived with the experience of diminished capacity. The pain of such states may be difficult to tolerate, especially as the development of adult competence, and specifically, competence as an analyst, may have been crucial to the earlier building of an inner world of whole objects and a whole, autonomous self. If overpowering, defensive states of pathological narcissism may emerge characterized by denial, disavowal, omnipotence and manic qualities.[1]

Impairment intrudes into and upsets the existing inner narcissistic state of the individual analyst. Some degree of inner confrontation with the inevitability of decline and death and the timeless wish for omnipotence and immortality will evoke new or revived unconscious fantasies, anxieties and affects. Acceptance of the grief of the loss of omnipotence and immortality will be highly influenced by the state of one's internal object world. For some, the internal object world may become so dominated by schizoid, paranoid, primitive anxieties that the pain is psychically unbearable.

For others, this crisis offers the opportunity for reworking of the depressive position and creative maturation. Again, I quote Jaques:

when, by contrast, the prevailing balance between love and hate is on the side of love, there is instinctual fusion, in which hate can be mitigated by love, and the mid-life encounter with death and hate takes on a different hue. Revived are the deep unconscious memories of hate, not denied but mitigated by love; of death and destruction mitigated by reparation and the will to life; of good things injured and damaged by hate, revived again and healed by loving grief.

(p. 512)

An analyst who comes to the attention of a local PAC is quite likely to be unconsciously struggling with the transformation of his or her internal world in relation to bodily and/or mental changes affecting the capacity to work as an analyst. This is illustrated with the composite of Dr F whose case will probably evoke memories of real experiences within your own community.

Dr F was a most excellent and well-respected analyst. He could at times be criticized for some rigidity of standards, expecting more from candidates and colleagues than they could reasonably deliver. The analytic community could count on Dr F to raise issues of practice and ethical standards. When a study group colleague developed a chronic form of cancer, Dr F openly raised the question as to the afflicted analyst's responsibility to inform patients of the illness and the uncertainties associated with the illness. Privately, Dr F criticized the afflicted analyst for choosing not to inform patients of this medical situation.[2]

Some time later, Dr F developed an illness not unlike the study group colleague in that the illness was known to be ultimately fatal preceded by a long chronic course. He showed no inclination to reveal this to any patients and brought it up rather casually to just a few colleagues. In fact he was disdainful of any inquiry from his cohorts as to the illness and its possible impact on his capacity to function. With some unease, the informed colleagues tacitly agreed to respect the boundaries of privacy demanded by Dr F.

When the disease had progressed to the point that Dr F's supervisees were asked to meet him at his home where he met them in his sleepwear, the supervisees began to talk about it to their other supervisors, training analysts, and fellow candidates. This was not gossip. Dr F's supervisees were disturbed by the change. Now on the alert that something was amiss, the supervisees noted increasing frailty and a lack of consistency in Dr F's supervision.

Still no acknowledgement or explanation was forthcoming from Dr F, and the candidates were awash with uncomfortable emotions. Some changed supervisors, some felt a kind of sympathy that led them to stay and take care of Dr F by helping him maintain his revered analytic identity, others painfully worked through a rather rapid de-idealization of the person and for some, of the analytic profession itself. Many felt that 'something needed to be done,' but none knew what that something might be.[3]

The Dean of Training was not a close colleague of Dr F, but he was observant and noted that several supervisees had changed to other supervisors. At around the same time, the informal talk within the candidate group started to reach the ears of responsible graduate analysts. The local Psychoanalyst Assistance Committee received several reports of concern for and about Dr F. Each informant offered what information he or she could but also asked to remain anonymous to Dr F.

At first, Dr F was highly defensive and took a superior attitude towards the PAC members. With the firm insistence of the PAC, Dr F reported to his own medical team that he was being questioned about his ability to keep working. This resulted in a phase of direct and clear communication between Dr F, the medical team and the PAC. In this phase, Dr F began to develop episodes of panic as he confronted his prognosis. He reported to the PAC that he had decided to resume analytic treatment to help him with the panic. In practice, the PAC only learns about the A of C's internal dynamics if the impaired analyst elects to share at that level with the PAC.

In this illustration, Dr F reported back to the PAC that he had developed a plan to reduce his clinical hours to two daily and to inform all patients of the uncertainty about how long he would be able to practise. He explained that he had been struggling with a rigid sense of 'all or nothing', 'perfect or shit'. In his states of panic, he felt persecuted by fears of abandonment by internal objects that found him to be vile and disgusting in his state of illness. He had tried to find a safe haven by holding on to his idealized position with patients and supervisees. This was not entirely new; it had been a tremendous life-long effort to evade internal persecution and manage anxiety with idealized standards and performance. For Dr F, the diminution of capacity was experienced as a catastrophe of being frighteningly taken over by the harshly, critical persecutory objects. Feeling internally on the brink of breakdown, including suicidal ideation, Dr F had been unable to maintain concern for the patients as separate objects. He had been severely compromised in his work. The reality of ill health had seemed internally unbearable. In this composite illustration, the PAC was successful in linking Dr F with his medical team, with crucial information, with the availability of analytic treatment that could help him regain his capacity to mourn his losses and more fully use his mind.

Jaques's wisdom has been confirmed in my own clinical work with ageing patients over the last 30 years. This theoretical frame provides a vision of analyst assistance committee work as an opportunity to enter into a relationship with the expectation that the A of C is a troubled analyst mired in a crisis of personal development and mental anguish. Informing the troubled analyst of the concern initiates an important relationship between the A of C and the PAC and initiates a process of assisting the troubled analyst to make contact with the destructive aspects of their restricted working through of their troubled inner and outer situation. Through its actions and the development of the relationship, the PAC will provide strong support to the A of C to seek all appropriate help in order to better bear the pains that come with this contact.

PAC as container

> Working through again the infantile experience of loss and of grief, gives an increase in confidence in one's capacity to love and mourn what has been lost and what is past, rather than to hate and feel persecuted by it.
>
> (Jaques, 1965, p. 512)

This is the silver lining of the painful work of psychoanalysis, the work of PACs and the work of life. PACs can and do play an important role in assisting analysts who seem to be unable to 'work through' a significant change in capacity. In every PAC engagement, the PAC brings to the conscious attention of the A of C the possibility of some existing diminished capacity to work as an analyst while conveying a conviction that the A of C will be able to develop his or her existing capacity to bear the destabilization and emotional pain of working through the inner and outer changes.

The relationship forged between the A of C and the PAC is crucial to the outcome of the PAC process. PAC work calls upon our psychoanalytic understanding to appreciate suffering, the defences of the mind used to avoid suffering, the troubling consequences of psychic avoidance of suffering and the possibility of bearing suffering and staying in contact with one's internal and external reality. With these analytic capacities engaged, the PAC itself and the individual PAC members may be able to provide a container-contained structure with the A of C such that an apparent uncontained state of psychic distress can be modified.

'Working through' the adult crisis of impairment is a complex experience including grief in multiple dimensions. There is grief over the loss of the satisfaction of the function itself and grief for the inner stability associated with the experience of proper functioning as an analyst. The impact on the internal world is likely to be quite serious. The way in which 'able to work' has been essential to the stability of the inner world, essential to the capacity to experience oneself as an integrated whole of good and bad in a world of integrated good and bad objects becomes at least partially unavailable in situations of impaired functioning.

To convey the aptness and utility of the containment theoretical construct for PAC work, I turn to an illustration. A first-person account of the process of painful discovery of the need to retire comes from Mervin H. Hurwitz in his chapter, 'A psychoanalyst retires', in the 1992 book, *How Psychiatrists Look at Aging*. It is worthwhile to read his account in full, but for the purposes of this chapter I have selected these excerpts:

> I had never planned to retire from practice. In my mind my abilities as analyst would go on forever. In fact, I expected them to improve with experience ad infinitum. I had the sense of invulnerability.
>
> (p. 98)

> But a succession of treated medical problems including hip arthritis, hip replacement surgery, prostate cancer diagnosis and treatment, and triple bypass over the course of his 60s led Hurwitz to ask himself: 'Could I conduct an adequate analysis? . . . I continued to work, I soon realized that what bothered me most were my narcissism, anger and guilt. I constantly evaluated my work and as best as I could judge it, it was better than just adequate. However, in order to keep it good an intensity of self-analysis was necessary that I had never required before.
>
> (p. 99)

He reports that an 'infantile grandiosity' emerged at first to protect him from the 'terrible sense of defectiveness' in relation to his compromised health and very real mortality. It was the mental exhaustion of managing these emotions that resulted in his decision to retire.

> Losing the status of physician meant to me the loss of my mother's love and her adoration. The threat was of becoming nothing and this was a terrible thing to face. Although this now seems so obvious in retrospect, it was very difficult to acknowledge and analyze, and there was a lot of coming and going of the awareness of this problem until it became obvious and simple.
>
> During this period of self-analysis I discovered something that was a great surprise to me. It had never appeared to me in my training analysis. I really owed a great deal of the emotional strength that I possessed to my father . . . Thus my self-analysis brought more balance to my knowledge of my Oedipal conflicts.
>
> (pp. 102–103)

This personally revealing account of his decision to retire does not come across as glib and in search of a fairytale ending, but it does suggest that for some, there are internal objects that pressure and internal objects that inspire. For Hurwitz to work through his adult development crisis, he made contact with both these internal objects and the associated fantasies. He demonstrates a capacity for self-containment in making contact with various fantasies in such a manner that he was able to transform his experience of the painful reality of attempting to maintain analytic practice in the face of diminished physical health.

In Bion's description of the containing process between mother and child, containment is easily pictured as natural and welcome. Perhaps this is so for a well-matched infant and mother, but it may not be so for a functionally challenged analyst and his or her local PAC. If the A of C's behaviour suggests that he or she has been operating 'as if' there has been no change in capacity despite evidence to the contrary, it is an indication that the analyst is under tremendous internal pressure not to know what seems to be true. In this case, the contact with the PAC is likely to be experienced initially as a poorly timed and most unwelcome intrusion. This may be understood as an immediate projection of the intrusive, painful aspect of the impairment on to the PAC.

Members of the PAC may anticipate that the A of C may or may not be consciously aware of the crisis state. Although exact procedures will vary from organization to organization, after receiving a credible notice of concern, the PAC will have the duty to contact the A of C to inform him or her that concern about him or her has come to the attention of the PAC. In so doing, it should be assumed that the A of C would enter some form of a disturbed state of mind. The act of identification of a possible problem may unleash anxiety, dread and defence. For the A of C, this may be a moment of confrontation with imagining the unimaginable. Painful fantasies seem to emerge almost instantaneously and suffuse the call with intensity of emotion. It is an awkward and painful moment for both the A of C and the PAC member.

Based on experience, it is best not to go into any detail of the specifics in this first contact but calmly to keep to the task of informing the analyst that in accord with the established procedures, they would like now to set up an in-person meeting to begin a discussion based on the concern raised (how to designate who exactly will speak to the A of C will be a matter of locally determined procedures). Outrage, accusations, breakdown, panic, coldness may emerge in this brief contact. This is the beginning of the containment process. The PAC member should also expect to be disturbed by these immediate anxiety-laden characterizations but hopefully can benefit from the advance understanding that elements of fearful fantasies are entering the interaction. Ideally, the PAC member caller allows him or herself to experience the unleashed disturbance while holding steady with the guidance of a firm conviction of overarching intention to assist. How many of us have had to hold a truly terrified child still in order to have an injection administered for a vaccination or treatment? Only our conviction that it is in the best interest of the child enables us to submit the child to such states of terror. PAC work requires the same capacities and convictions.

The container-contained model is a bi-directional model of contact with something painful that is transformed from something raw into something with meaning. In this process, both the compromised analyst and the PAC will have to assimilate something unique and not previously experienced. Some degree of identification with the disturbed and disturbing A of C is inevitable and will be interacting with a more separate identification as an autonomous containing object with a complex relationship to psychic pain and suffering. To explicate the nature of this containing object identification I turn to Cartwright on Bion (2010). He writes: 'Bion thought that analytic goals should be orientated toward increasing the patient's capacity for suffering. Although at face value this may appear unduly pessimistic, his emphasis lies on the assumption that through "suffering" emotions, sustaining mental contact with them, we are able to transform such states into meaningful experience' (p. 17).

Cartwright goes on more specifically about containment: 'In this way Bion's view of analytical containment concerns a process of transformation whereby previously unbearable states of mind that prevent thinking and development are made more bearable and thinkable. As Bion put it, the containing process works on parts of the individual (or the analytic couple) that 'feel the pain but will not suffer it and so cannot be said to discover it' (p. 25).

Through its function of containment, PAC work offers the possibility of therapeutic benefit to the A of C, but PAC work differs in its nature from 'therapy' in several important ways. Most PACs are organized in such a way as to provide for the (albeit unlikely) possibility that troubled analysts might self-refer, but for the most part someone other than the A of C initiates PAC engagement. Certain privileges and responsibilities accrue to the analyst when entering into a tacit or explicit treatment agreement with a patient. There is no such agreement for therapy in a PAC engagement. I state this in order to emphasize that the PAC is not empowered to analyse or make interpretations.

PACs do *not* perform diagnostic examinations or treatments of the impairment condition, whether it be somatic, cognitive or psychological. PACs do identify the possibility of a problem based on received information and proceed from there to direct the analyst of concern to utilize outside experts to assess health status as it relates to their capacity to function and to arrange for treatment. The PAC will receive information from outside experts that pertain to diagnosis, treatment and prognosis as the basis for processing this information with the A of C in terms of appraisal of the capacity to function as an analyst. This could be as simple as the PAC hearing that the analyst falls asleep in afternoon supervisory sessions. The analyst reports to the PAC that she takes blood pressure medication at lunch that may be somewhat sedating. The PAC recommends that the analyst speak to her cardiologist about this problem and send a report to the PAC. The cardiologist may change the medication, the dose or the schedule of the medication with full resolution of the afternoon problem. Such a case would be resolved without exploration or interpretation of why the analyst had not made such a contact with the cardiologist on her own. The PAC might let the experience speak for itself or suggest this might be a warning of a psychic fault line and recommend/advise further psychological exploration if that seems to be the case. Even in such a simple case, the PAC functions to transform a fantasied state of helplessness (I have to take blood pressure medicine and cannot do anything about the adverse effects) into a state of awareness of the availability of assistance.

Experiences of immense grief are unavoidable in the course of life. Decline in the capacity to function properly as an analyst may be one of those deeply painful experiences. When such a decline elicits multiply-determined conscious and unconscious fantasies of loss, danger and other dreadful states of mind to an extent that seems to overwhelm the analyst's capacity to cope, PACs may be able to serve a containing function such that the analyst gathers the appropriate information and assistance to face inner and outer reality, act in accord with those realities and resume the course of lifelong personal development.

Understanding the resistance to PACs at multiple levels

In order for a PAC to function, there must be sufficient support within the analytic community to form a group to develop the committee and programme structure, to recruit members to the PAC once established and to have appropriate referrals to the PAC. It sounds straightforward, yet there is often much resistance at the community level in terms of lack of enthusiasm by the organizational leadership and at the level of individual members. This may result in little promotion of the committee and its goals. Individuals may be reluctant or unwilling to use an existing committee so that problems of impairment go ignored or are handled ad hoc as they were before the PAC was established.

Every community has its stories about the problem that was ignored until some kind of professional disaster took place followed by guilt and regret throughout the community. This can be very damaging to an analytic community. Surely, it would be more desirable to intervene at an earlier point in the functional decline of the analyst in order to protect patients, students and the analyst him or herself from the loss of professional dignity and jeopardy of potential malpractice or ethical violations. How are we to understand the resistance to PACs?

We can benefit from understanding the resistances of well-functioning analysts and of analytic communities as parallel and reciprocal to the resistances of the impaired colleague. The Hurwitz account introduced us to several of the powerful fantasies associated with the inevitability of personal decline that may be projected into the PAC. PAC as persecutor, PAC as abandoner and PAC as destroyer are powerful fantasies that may arise in the course of a PAC process. There is evidence that these fantasies are aroused in well-functioning analysts and in analytic communities merely by the proposal of a place for a PAC in the local analytic organizational structure.

Over the years, I have heard many sincere objections to the formation of PACs. These objections tend to cluster into groups. One cluster conveys hopelessness, 'What's the point? . . . Nothing will come of it' are common responses. Another cluster suggests fears of coming into contact with something disturbing, 'Why get involved in a mess like that?' Another cluster is the fear of knowing and is articulated in comments such as 'How do we know what he is like with his patients?' This is a valid question but seems to take the position that we should not try to know. In a similar vein is the oft heard 'He has always been like that; everyone knows he's a bit of a character'.

At times, there is explicit characterization of the PAC as a persecutor. This is usually in the form, 'Leave him alone. He has enough problems'. Apparently, the well-functioning colleague equates bringing the possibility of analyst impairment to consciousness with making trouble. A message emerges from the community, 'It feels persecutory to be presented with knowledge of things that arouse feelings of loss, despair and hopelessness'. Thus, denial of existing impairment and denial of even the possibility of an impairment problem that is serious but not hopeless operate as significant resistances to PAC work at multiple levels.

In his 1936 letter/paper 'A Disturbance of Memory on the Acropolis' Freud explored denial in relation to unbearable internal and external states. He quoted the last Moorish king of Granada immortalized for burning the bad news letter and having the messenger killed:

> You remember the famous lament of the Spanish Moors 'Ay de mi Alhama' ['Alas for my Alhama'], which tells how King Boabdil received the news of the fall of his city of Alhama. He feels that this loss means the end of his rule. But he will not 'let it be true', he determines to treat the news as 'non arrivé' . . .
>
> It is easy to guess that a further determinant of this behaviour of the king was his need to combat a feeling of powerlessness. By burning the letters and having the messenger killed he was still trying to show his absolute power.
>
> (1936, p. 246)

Is the PAC a dreaded messenger? Is there a fantasy that if there is no messenger, there is no bad news? I suspect this is so. And alas, when we do bear the unwelcome news, we become the Cordelia to our declining colleague Lear as so beautifully explicated by Junkers in the introduction to the chapter on ageing.

In 1923, Freud had already introduced his thinking about disavowal, the phenomenon of not seeing what is there to be seen. In 'The Infantile genital organization,' he wrote, 'We know how children react to their first impressions of the absence of the penis. They disavow the fact and believe they *do* see a penis all the same' (p. 143).

I suspect that for many, the spectre of analytic disability arouses a field of dreadful losses including castration, loss of love and dissolution of the self. The PAC must move forward with the knowledge that it may be perceived as a persecutory object while maintaining the hope that it will serve as a good enough object that can help the individual A of C and the community to make contact with the painful truth, the existence in our very midst of impaired analytic functioning.

A candidate, still in analysis, reacted negatively when I mentioned my work on PACs. She commented, 'I think it is terrible that you force them to give up something they are holding on to for dear life and then you drop them. Why would you want to do that?' Of course, I would not want to do that, but I learned a great deal from her comment. I learned that at times we probably do, and we certainly should not enact the role of abandoner. Once having 'helped' a colleague to retire appropriately, what do we do to stay in contact? There may be a tendency of the analytic community to turn away from impaired and retired colleagues. It may be threatening to the practising analyst's omnipotence to have an ailing analyst in its midst, and it may also arouse fears of somehow having damaged the impaired analyst.

Steve Firestein personally recounts visiting Edith Jacobson at home towards the end of her life. He found her to be welcoming of the visits and the analytic company. Presumably, many analysts would have loved to have a private visit with this esteemed analyst during her prolific and powerful years. And yet, in poor health and analytically inactive, it was virtually impossible for him to recruit anyone else to visit her.

PACs can play a role in staying in touch with colleagues who have been part of a PAC process. By staying in touch, they may be able to identify and encourage ways to stay involved in the life of the analytic community during sickness or after retirement. Keeping these analysts in our midst may be beneficial to the community in terms of mitigating our defensive blindness to the inevitability of decline.

I also learned from the candidate's remark how PACs may be perceived as destructive robbers of valued idealizations. This may be especially so for candidates still in analysis, but post-termination idealizations of former analysts, supervisors, teachers, mentors are widely in evidence.

In his most recent book, *Seeing and Being Seen: Emerging from a Psychic Retreat*, John Steiner (2011) addresses the formidable disturbance caused by an analyst 'seeing' the analysand. His observation about this aspect of analytic work is equally informative about the PAC perceived as destroyer: 'Of course narcissism involves a degree of self-idealization that is reflected in the idea of being admired; when this collapses, the patient has to face the experience of being seen with his narcissistic self-admiration exposed. With the collapse of admiration, narcissistic pride is replaced by feelings of embarrassment, shame and humiliation that demand to be dealt with. The patient may be exposed to a persecutory state in which pathological splitting and paranoia predominate' (p. 6).

And PAC perceived as persecutor: 'intended to weaken and demoralize him so that he can be destroyed and eliminated . . . an attempt is made to undermine his sense of worth and to destroy the very essence of his identity for someone else's benefit' (p. 7).

In a reciprocal way, members of the PAC are likely to be at least transiently emotionally captured in various troubling fantasies of self as a persecutor or persecuted, as destroyer or he who will be destroyed. Potent intervention that awakens dread and suffering in another can create inner turbulence for the PAC members, who are likewise forced to struggle with inner constructive and destructive forces.

Members of the analytic community and the PAC members themselves may have questions about the capacity to balance these inner forces. This uncertainty may contribute to doubts about the necessity or safety of PACs. If PAC work emanates from hatred, it is to be feared. PAC work will fail or flounder if it loses contact with loving capacities and/or does not maintain contact with the conviction that facing painful reality allows for ongoing personal development and adaptation (with or without additional psychological treatment) and therefore is in the best interest of the analyst of concern. It is not enough to have in mind the protection and safety of patients, students and the analytic community itself. The best interests of the troubled analyst must remain at the heart of the intervention. This may be quite different from serving the conscious wishes of the A of C. To my mind, fostering personal development is an act dominated by love that often requires activity and contact with powerful aggressive forces harnessed to constructive projects.

In this vein, I would like to introduce some speculations about the resistance in analysts to serve as good objects in this way. For the analyst who sees in the analyst of concern a future aspect of him or herself that is unbearable, PAC work may be impossible. Identification with the A of C is to be expected. The absence of some degree of conscious identification is quite problematic as it suggests that a threat to the PAC member's own omnipotence and self-integration has elicited a defensive use of splitting and omnipotent denial. 'This could never happen to me' is the impossible wish that creates a barrier to emotional contact between the PAC member and the A of C. In such a situation, the PAC member unconsciously sets up an emotional quarantine to stay separate from the perceived defective and 'bad'. Denial and splitting, unconsciously and defensively employed by the PAC member, interfere with making contact, thinking and thoughtful functioning.

Over-identification is what I call the experience of seeing oneself now or in the future all too clearly in the troubled state of the A of C. This too is problematic as it may result in the PAC member treating the situation as if he or she were the A of C. Unconsciously enacting how the PAC member would treat himself or herself interferes with fully integrated assessment of the situation. Consistent with their own characteristic personality and psychic defence systems, the overly-identified PAC member may demonstrate overly-punitive or overly-dismissive attitudes towards the A of C. Guilt-prone analysts may tend to adopt a highly punitive and controlling attitude towards the A of C as if the A of C were an errant part of the PAC member's self that needs to be reined in. PAC members who are more prone to manic disavowal will tend towards minimizing, making normalizing excuses and even accusing other PAC members of being too severe in their understanding and attitudes.

This aspect of PAC work is crucial and very challenging. PAC members are expected to make emotional contact with the A of C and maintain a thinking mind that is not overtaken by anxiety related to identification with a fellow analyst. If the PAC member cannot maintain close communication with the A of C and maintain autonomy of thinking, the PAC member will have significant difficulty with the PAC function. As with clinical psychoanalysis, the maintenance of these essential internal states and functions will be quite dynamic so PAC members are advised to monitor themselves for interference with this capacity. I believe that we are all to some degree at risk of being overtaken by anxiety and defence in emotionally painful situations and therefore advise that PAC members should not work independently of each other. In my experience, it has been worthwhile to have within the PAC those who have the direct contact with the A of C and other members held in reserve for ongoing consultation throughout the process. These 'reserve consultant' members would not have direct contact with the A of C and provide important support and autonomous perspective to the direct-contact PAC member who is engaged in a very emotionally dynamic experience with the A of C.

The work of a PAC requires the formation of judgment while maintaining a non-moralistic attitude. Some analysts may unconsciously struggle with an experience of themselves as a persecuting object in bringing the analyst of concern in contact with the painful facts and evidence of their condition and the necessity of painful life actions such as retirement. Not all aggression is destructive or punitive, but when it comes to impacting the life path of a fellow analyst, concerns about the capacity to balance and integrate one's own love and hate may reach exquisite proportions. Fears of 'doing harm' to a colleague contribute to the reluctance to serve on a PAC. Similarly, fears that a referral to a PAC may cause harm to the analyst of concern may result in the tolerance of troubled behaviour in a colleague without recourse to the PAC.

It seems evident that PAC work is perceived as dangerous business on many levels. To meet this serious concern, PACs must establish the capacity to contain the individual and community sense of danger and unbearable pain in order to assist the analyst of concern in making contact with knowledge of his or her capacity or incapacity to function as an analyst.

Brief history of PACs in America

The history of PACs in America is a story of thoughtfully filling a vacuum once the vacuum was perceived. It started with a casual conversation in the early 1990s between the Chair of the American Psychoanalytic Association (APsaA) Committee on Psychoanalytic Education, Sander Abend, MD, and Jerome Winer, MD, the newest member of the Committee. Abend had received an inquiry as to what his local institute did about impaired psychoanalyst faculty and members. Winer and Abend each reported that their home institutes did not have any considered way of dealing with impaired analysts.

The vacuum was now perceived, and Winer set to work. He volunteered to form a study group on impaired analysts in 1993 and is to be credited with moving the work forward such that the APsaA today has a formal policy that highly recommends that each component institute, society and centre of APsaA develop and maintain a locally appropriate Psychoanalyst Assistance Committee (PAC).

Winer recalls the enthusiasm and commitment of the study group members arising from the perception that analyst impairment was 'an important problem and little was being done about it.' Over 3–4 years, this group contacted all the institutes of APsaA, researched the psychoanalytic literature and found 'all kinds of anecdotes and no one had a systematic approach' according to Winer.

The study group became the APsaA Committee on Impaired Faculty Analysts (CIFA) in 1996. In 1998, Winer made a proposal to the APsaA Board on Professional Standards (BOPS) to adopt a requirement for all member institutes to establish and maintain a local PAC. The proposal was readily adopted. With this adoption, the organizational will to structurally address the problem of analyst impairment became a constructive force that led to a broadening of the mandate to all societies as well as institutes.[4]

A new committee, the Joint Psychoanalyst Assistance Committee (JPAC), formed to assist local institutes to understand the mandate and to assist in the process of the development of a locally appropriate PAC. Given the variation of size and tenor of individual institutes and societies, no template was drawn up nor any specific requirements developed other than the requirement to establish and maintain a locally appropriate PAC.

JPAC has changed its name to Committee on Psychoanalyst Assistance Committees (CPAC) and continues to function as a national resource for consultation about general matters of Analyst Assistance Committee work. CPAC has accumulated and maintains a collection of the PAC Mission and Guidelines documents of institutes, societies and centres of various sizes. There is considerable diversity in this collection enhancing their usefulness as references.

It has been a mostly steady process such that by 2008, CPAC determined that, nationally, APsaA was approaching complete compliance with the mandate. Winer admits that he was rather 'dispirited' in 2009, when the wording was changed from a mandated requirement to a 'highly recommended' status. This was the outcome of considerable study and legal consultation in response to concern raised by one institute about the potential conflict between state 'duty to report' laws and the necessary confidentiality of PACs. This is an important and complex issue that I will take up further in the chapter sub-section on designing a PAC.

Over the ten years of implementation of the national mandate, CPAC had the opportunity to work with many individual analysts from across the nation who display realism, idealism, commitment and even passion about the development of PACs. They spoke to the committee of both the support and the resistances they were facing locally.

It is clear that the mandate from the national organization was a very effective and possibly essential tool in the face of the resistances. While most local institutes and centres of APsaA now have a PAC on paper, it is not clear to what extent the PACs are being utilized. This remains an area of study and consultation for the CPAC.

Designing a PAC that works for your local community

There is no template for forming a PAC that suits your unique analytic organization, yet it is not necessary to re-invent the wheel as you approach this challenge. There is an accumulation of experience from which I will identify key issues and make recommendations.

The guiding principle must be an emphasis on assistance. As Winer (2002) puts it, the PAC mission is to 'Assist the impaired analyst back to health or transition out of practice with dignity' (p. 15). The recommendations to follow developed during my seven years as a committee member of the APsaA Committee on PACs chaired throughout by Jerome Winer. I gratefully acknowledge the presence of his original and forward thinking in each of these recommendations.

The PAC should not be in the business of diagnosing or providing treatment. The PAC may, and probably will, advise the analyst of concern to seek appropriate diagnosis and treatment of illness, somatic and psychological. With this information, the PAC may assist the analyst of concern in determining their present and future capacity to continue to function competently as a licensed professional.

Thus the PAC may be called upon to make judgments about impairment, but the PAC is not an adjudicating body. This does distinguish it from an ethics committee. Ethics committees may have hearings and may impose corrective or even punitive sanctions. PACs do not have hearings and do not mete out sanctions.

Although each party, the A of C and the PAC, will probably seek legal consultation, it is desirable not to allow attorneys into the PAC process itself. Knowledge of legal ramifications for all involved parties is quite important, but the PAC is not charging or prosecuting the A of C. To maintain a non-litigious, assistance-oriented atmosphere, attorneys need to be excluded from the PAC process.

Many decisions about structure and process of the PAC follow from the basic premise of assistance. For some, the emphasis on assistance evokes an image of friendly and informal interaction with the analyst of concern. Experience indicates that this is well intentioned but often impracticable. As discussed in earlier sections of this chapter, the resistance to PAC work may be quite formidable. Having the analyst's best interests in mind probably involves 'helping' the analyst to face and work out a plan in the face of painful inner emotions and external consequences. This work should be done with compassion, tact and concern, but it is unlikely that it will be perceived throughout as informal and friendly.

Elements that support the function of the PAC:

- Integrity of process: Clear written guidelines of the PAC to include written mission, structure and procedures.
- Transparency and member access to PAC procedures.
- Procedures that address privacy and dignity.

- Autonomy of PAC from other governing structures of the institute, society or centre.
- Development of a track record of maintaining privacy and dignity; this will enhance referrals to the PAC.

Referral sources to include:

- Self, colleagues, candidates, family, friends, patients
- Source may choose to be identified or remain anonymous to the analyst of concern (A of C).

Who to cover:

- Faculty
- Graduates, active members
- Candidates traditionally are not covered by PACs as the various Deans and Training committees are responsible for the professional conduct and development of the candidate. Deans and Training Directors will probably wish to consult the expertise of the PAC members.

Many of the above items are relatively self-explanatory, so for the sake of brevity, I will now shift to some of the thorny issues to be considered.
Thorny issues:

- Mandatory reporting laws
- Autonomy and confidentiality vs. credibility and integrity
- Mandatory participation

In the United States, professionals are licensed by states and regulated by state laws. Within any state, the regulations for each discipline, such as MDs, PhD psychologists, clinical social workers, family therapists, may differ. In some states, there appears to be a conflict between state reporting laws concerning impaired professionals and the confidential conduct of PACs. In some states, the law may be worded and interpreted to mean that *any* knowledge of impaired behaviour on the part of a health care provider must immediately be reported to the state board regulating that individual's professional discipline. It is not sound or appropriate to put an institute, society or centre in the position of violating the laws of their respective states, but many analytic institutes in states with mandatory reporting laws have chosen to form PACs. Interpretation of laws is complicated and requires professional consultation. Such consultation will probably include knowledge of the intent of the law (the 'spirit' of the law) and the enforcement trends in that locale. In several states in which there are mandatory reporting laws, legal counsel have taken the position that a PAC that is engaged in the work of bringing analysts back to health or terminating practice is unlikely to be the object of state prosecution for maintaining confidentiality in the course of its work. If the state regulatory body perceives that PACs are working to maintain competency of its members, it is not likely to interfere with that work in order to take on the burden itself. If the state regulatory body perceives that PACs are shielding its A of Cs from scrutiny and accountability, the state may bring action for non-compliance with mandatory reporting laws. Many PACs proceed with the understanding that the confidentiality of the PAC could be perceived as conflicting with the strictest interpretation of state reporting laws. In any and all cases, should the PAC determine that an analyst is impaired and continuing to practise despite the best efforts of the PAC, mandatory reporting would be invoked with the impaired analyst being notified of this necessity in advance. *Expert legal counsel on the state laws governing the practice of the membership of your organization is essential for the development of the PAC.*

Another thorny issue that relates to confidentiality is that the PAC works almost in secrecy. The existence, mission, procedures and list of PAC members are all transparent, but the PAC actually operates without the knowledge of any but the involved party. I call this the conflict of confidentiality and autonomy vs. credibility and integrity. The blackout of information outside of the committee may result in community concerns that 'nothing is being done' by the analytic organization. This can be very disturbing to those who are aware of a troubled but practising analyst in the community. These individuals may make a referral to the PAC, but due to confidentiality, even the referral source is not automatically privy to the proceedings of the PAC work with any individual. Training directors and other institute leaders have voiced the view that they are entitled to information about a troubled member in order to safeguard the training programme in relation to impaired faculty, training and supervising analysts.

The concerns are valid but the 'costs' of compromising the confidentiality and autonomy of PACs are too high. Any compromise of confidentiality shifts the perception of the PAC from assistance towards 'policing'. It is a shift towards prioritizing the analytic organization over the assistance of the A of C. Who will refer themselves and what spouse or colleague will make a referral to the PAC if the specifics of the painful situation are not to be kept in strict confidence? It is the responsibility of the PAC to communicate a conviction that a well-utilized and well-functioning PAC is one of the best ways for the leadership to safeguard the training and the overall analytic community and its members.

How is a PAC to earn credibility as a well-functioning agency of the analytic organization if it operates behind a blackout curtain?

I have several suggestions to mitigate this difficulty:

1. Build visibility and respect in the community with forums, programmes, newsletter articles, etc.
2. Establish regular liaison activity with the leadership.
3. Work with the A of C to seek permission, when indicated, to notify appropriate parties outside the PAC of the proceedings and action plan. Good outcomes are likely to include encouragement of appropriate dissemination of information by the A of C or by the PAC with permission of the A of C.

In my view, there are two situations in which confidentiality should be breached with or without the permission of the A of C. The first has been alluded to in terms of the compliance with state reporting laws if the PAC concludes that the analyst is impaired but is not taking adequate actions to regain competence or retire from practice.

The second is the situation where the analyst of concern is 'uncooperative' despite the best efforts of the PAC. Ideally, strictly voluntary participation would support the assistance focus. Given all that has been said so far in this chapter, it is easy to imagine that many in need of assistance would not participate voluntarily. Hopefully the PAC will take all opportunities to examine and adjust its own efforts to serve its containment function to enable the A of C. The PAC may also advise the A of C to seek individual psychological treatment for further assistance, but ultimately, there may remain troubled analysts who cannot and will not be amenable to PAC efforts. The procedures of the PAC and of the analytic organization must be prepared for such a situation.

Repeated experiences across the nation with 'uncooperative' analysts of concern have resulted in the local adoption of PAC procedures with some 'teeth'. Many analytic organizations now make it a condition of membership to collaborate with the PAC. An analyst who refuses to participate may jeopardize membership. An analyst who participates to some extent but is judged to be uncooperative either in the study process or in implementation of the action plan may be referred to the organizations' Ethics Committee with advance warning.

Mandated reporting of impairment, expulsion from membership or referral to ethics committee for non-participation with the PAC are serious actions in the face of serious troubles. The inclusion of these procedures may appear to detract from the ideals of analyst assistance. I believe they are consistent with the ideals of analyst assistance as developed in this chapter. Upholding the ideals of providing a containing experience for an A of C may require an enforcement component much like the holding of the terrified child for a necessary medical procedure. We may all wish for an 'ideal' experience in which there is full voluntary cooperation, growth-promoting mutual engagement and an outcome satisfactory to all, but experience suggests that this is often enough not the case. PACs must anticipate and provide for the circumstance of non-cooperation of the A of C.

Conclusions

The chapter sub-title reflects my belief that the practicalities of psychoanalyst assistance must flow from a philosophy of the mission. As analysts, we have an opportunity to utilize the richness of our analytic knowledge in addressing the problem of professional impairment of colleagues. I have called upon the psychoanalytic heritage of Elliott Jaques to present the A of C as a colleague in a crisis of adult development, of Freud and the contemporary Kleinians to understand the resistance to seeing the problem in our midst, and of Wilfred Bion for the container-contained model for formulating the mechanism of function of PACS.

To my mind, the essence of a PAC is the safeguarding of competent, ethical practice for the well-being of the analyst of concern, his or her patients, his or her family and friends, students and supervisees, colleagues and the analytic community itself. An impaired analyst who continues to practise without full accommodation of the impairment is not safe. He or she is at risk in terms of malpractice, ethical misconduct, loss of referrals, premature terminations, loss of income, reputation, legacy and self-respect. Friends and family of the impaired analyst are exposed to these risks by association. Patients, students and supervisees are at risk if left to deal with the effects of an impaired analyst without the support of the analyst or the analytic community. The integrity of the analytic community and the respect in which it is or is not held by the local community are also at risk. Many are vulnerable, and the consequences of impaired practice are potentially serious and broad.

Notes

1 My long-time colleague on the Committee on Psychoanalyst Assistance Committees (CPAC) of the American Psychoanalytic Association (APsaA) Steve Firestein is fond of saying, 'The problem is analysts don't die'. He of course is referring to an unconscious fantasy of immortality, a defensive fantasy in relation to anxieties about the dissolution of self.
2 This question of analyst self-disclosure in relation to analyst illness is a complex topic that is specifically considered in the work of others such as Fajardo (Chapter 8 in this book), and not my point. My point concerns Dr F's rigid idealization of standards and intolerance of any deviation. As it turned out, this rigidity indicated a vulnerability to splitting and idealization in order to manage anxiety.
3 The work of Training and Supervising analysts is rather extensively exposed within the community compared to the solo practitioner graduate analyst. From the perspective of analyst assistance, this means that the troubles of a TA/SA are more likely to come to light. This is a challenging responsibility and opportunity for the analytic community.
4 Historically, APsaA institutes encompassed the educational bodies responsible for training, and societies were membership bodies for graduate analysts.

16

NOW IS THE TIME FOR ACTION

The professional will: An ethical responsibility
of the analyst and the profession

Mary Kay O'Neil

Introduction

All analysts die, some too soon, some suddenly, some before retirement and some
after retirement. Prior to death analysts can become incapacitated and no longer able
to practise optimally. Incapacitation (i.e. physical, affective, cognitive or addictive illness) can occur at any stage of an analytic career but more often as an analyst ages.
Incapacity or death, especially sudden death or unanticipated incapacity, pose particular problems of confidentiality for patients as well as privacy problems for analysts.

Confidentiality is a patient's right and an obligation ingrained in the analytic mind
and enshrined in professional codes. Privacy in this context is defined by the boundary between the professional and personal lives of the analyst. It is the privacy of the
analytic space, of the analytic couple and their dialogue that confidentiality protects.
What is the responsibility of the analyst to protect his/her patients from the experience of sudden loss of their analyst without preparation and without recourse to further confidential assistance? To what extent are analytic organizations responsible for
patients, for their confidentiality and for the privacy of the analyst?

Concern about these issues was stimulated by experience with the sudden deaths of
colleagues,[1] other colleagues' unanticipated and/or denied incapacity to practise, anecdotes of attempts to deal with awareness of incapacitating physical or mental illness
or addiction and recent research. The purpose of this chapter is to propose for individual analysts and psychoanalytic organizations a possible way to take responsibility
for patient care, confidentiality and the analyst's privacy, namely *a professional will*.

The nature of the problem: History and current situation

The need for a professional will suited to analytic practice has been 'in the air' for
several decades. Firestein (1993) published one of the first articles on making a professional will. He introduced it with the following vignette: 15 years previously the
widow of a recently deceased analyst approached his colleagues to report the problems she encountered in dealing with her husband's interrupted practice. Impressed
that her experience was all too typical, a set of guidelines was formulated and circu-

lated to members of their society. Apparently most members either never saw or disregarded the guidelines.

A search of recent literature revealed few articles on analysts' illness, incapacity and retirement, let alone sudden incapacity or death, with virtually no mention of a professional will, except in Firestein's article (2007). There are, however, several insightful papers by analysts who survived life-threatening illness (Abend, 1982; Dewald, 1982; Schwartz and Silver, 1990), and one who faced terminal illness (Feinsilver, 1998). The work of these analysts along with Schwartz and Silver's book *Illness in the Analyst* (1990) shed light on how colleagues maintain their professional lives under great personal stress. For example, Clark (1995), from personal experience with a life-threatening illness, recognized the ethical complexity and asked, 'What would help ill analysts take care of their own needs and regain analytic perspective?' She proposed a consultant for analysts experiencing serious medical problems and recommended someone experienced and objectively straightforward, not a contemporary or friend, who can be consulted in confidence.

Analysts with incapacities besides life-threatening illness (Alzheimer's, other dementias, addictions, accidents) that render them unable to practise are generally not able to discuss or write about their experiences or those of their patients. Nor are they likely to be able to prepare patients for termination or referral. Negative effects of working with serious illness or incapacity can include a mutual collusion of denial, lack of open discussion, role reversal and the impulse on the part of the patient to aid the analyst. Galatzer-Levy (2004)[2] found that analysts' denial of the severity of their illnesses and the patients' collusion can involve significant boundary crossings and violations. Gabbard and Peltz (2001) contended that the analytic community does not handle incapacity effectively, including life-threatening illness and death.

Death, sudden or not, always has a deleterious impact on the patient and on termination. Freedman (1990) interviewed analysands whose analysts had died. He found that the need for ongoing care was dependent on the transference and countertransference at the time that life-threatening illness or death occurred, as well as on the phase of treatment, the ego integration and life circumstances of the patient. The impact is even more devastating when the analyst has made no prior provision for closing a practice.

What are the research findings? A survey (O'Neil, 2005) of all American, British and Canadian psychoanalytic societies and institutes revealed that guidelines for handling confidential material at the time of death, incapacity or retirement were mentioned by only 15 per cent of respondents. The 'professional will' model suggested by the American Psychoanalytic Association had not been widely used. Neither the British nor the Canadian Societies had developed such forms. The British Society, however, required that all analysts provide the society office with a list of their patients or the name of a person designated to care for their practice when necessary. The Canadian Society reported that analysts followed procedures of their other professional organizations or, informally, a colleague or a family member took care of a deceased analyst's records. At the time, no Canadian societies had patient lists or designated persons. Traditionally, planning retirement has been a private matter for individual analysts in the study countries and the society's role has usually been confined to the implicit expectation that an analyst will close a practice with sensitivity to the patients' needs and to confidentiality (Moraitis, 2009).

When analysts are faced with difficult ethical questions, including confidentiality issues, 80 per cent of societies reported that they provide opportunity for consultation: 62 per cent with the chair of the ethics committee, 57 per cent with a member of the society with expertise in ethics, 10 per cent with an ombudsman, 8 per cent with a legal consultant, and 40 per cent provide 'other' unspecified opportunities. Although the principle of confidentiality is enshrined in all ethics codes and opportunity for consultation is available, there is little open discussion within psychoanalytic societies about ethical ways of closing a practice, whether sudden or planned. Only 9 per cent of the respondents reported that their society suggests a process for handling confidential material upon retirement and the same percentage had a policy or guidelines for storing and granting access to archival material. Only a few of the larger American societies, (e.g. New York Psychoanalytic Society has a curator for the Archives and Special Collections of the A.A. Brill Library) and the British Society has official archives. Fewer have policies for preserving and accessing material. The Canadian Society has no official archives.

The above research data is limited to the American, Canadian and British IPA Societies and cannot be generalized beyond these. Would European and South American analysts and those from various cultures view a professional will and archives differently? There is no evidence to suggest that their situation differs.

What about the current situation? The American Psychoanalytic Association, after 25 years of discussion usually ending with 'we should do something about that,' is now considering the possibility of making an analytic will mandatory. Firestein, in a personal communication, said that he has received numerous requests for his 1993 article from societies attempting to develop a professional will suitable for their membership. Clark (personal communication), working with American societies, has suggested that a copy of each member's professional will be deposited with the local society and that a 'fail safe' committee be organized to step in where there is no designated person. The British Society made their somewhat vague procedures more specific by requiring, for the right to practise as an analyst, that all members name a designated person. They are working on a will form. The Canadian Society at the 2009 Annual General Meeting passed a motion that 'All Canadian Psychoanalytic Society members and candidates provide their Branch Society (for candidates, their Institute) with co-ordinates of a Designated Person to be contacted in the event of their inability to practise'. The designated person (or if decided by the analyst, the society) would have access to the analyst's office and current patient list. The following year, the Canadian branches reported about 70 per cent compliance. Some members had not yet submitted a name but had colleagues who would care for their practices. Naming a designated person was seen as the first step towards having a professional will. To date, none of the societies surveyed have made a will mandatory, unlike other professions such as medicine (psychiatry), psychology and social work which may soon do so. Directives from other professions might not be suitable to an analyst's practice.

Psychoanalysts have been aware for at least 35 years'[1] that preparation for a sudden or planned closing of a practice assisted by a will is of utmost importance. The advantages, resistances to and recommendations for a professional will require delineation because 'Now is the Time for Action'.

Advantages of a professional will

The habit of having an analytic will begins with the new graduates.[3] If it is recognized that a time could come when one's primary therapeutic tool (use of the self) is out of order (patients perceive this quite accurately), then both patient and analyst needs can more easily be considered. A professional will raises awareness of human vulnerability; cuts through the defence of denial of death and dilutes reinforcement of a transference wish for the analyst to be the invulnerable deity, the all-giving mother, the strong father, and so on. A professional will specific to analysts and particular jurisdictions facilitates ethical patient care from the beginning of a career and when revised at each phase of one's career, respects concomitant changes in practice practicalities. Such a will helps keep the analytic tool functioning in stressful circumstances as it contributes to a secure practical base. In difficult situations it can facilitate the analytic relationship and therapeutic work, protect patient confidentiality and the privacy of the analyst.

Incapacity or death raise confidentiality issues as analytic boundaries are redefined. Others (family and colleagues, lawyers, the police, etc.) can have valid reason to gain access to patient lists, clinical files and professional papers, thereby opening the possibility of inappropriate inspection of the analytic frame. The analyst may have had no opportunity to prepare patients, organize files, separate what is confidential from what is not, complete insurance forms, do a final billing or organize professional papers. In traumatic situations the family, the society and concerned colleagues are often left to manage the unexpected ending of a practice as best they can. Obvious confidentiality advantages of a will suited to an analytic practice include: only the designated person needs access to an analyst's files; patients can be more appropriately notified and offered consultation; candidates in analysis and supervision can be more sensitively dealt with by the institute; clinical records required legally or for further patient care can be separated and made available as needed; working or process notes containing the analyst's hypotheses, speculations and very personal material can be destroyed without having to be seen by others unnecessarily, and the business aspects of closing a practice can be more efficiently managed. Additionally, analysts can decide in advance what among their personal and professional papers is to be public information and what is to be kept private, and what to contribute to society and institute archives. Certain unpublished papers, presentations and relevant correspondence, and audio or video tapes can be designated to be kept; others can be destroyed ahead of time or marked to be destroyed.

The professional will can relieve pressure on the bereaved family and colleagues to assist traumatized patients and candidates while maintaining confidentiality and protecting privacy. Besides the relief of pressure, a will can protect the reputation of the psychoanalytic community and its organizations as responsible entities, ethically and sensitively caring for those they serve and educate. Methods can be developed to encourage candidates and young analysts to think of unexpected eventualities early in their careers and to encourage mature analysts to make plans for the ethical closing of their practices and for possibly contributing their papers to psychoanalytic archives and history.

Resistances to a professional will

Guided by a professional will, closing an analytic practice is made easier for bereaved survivors, including patients, to manage the practicalities of dealing with the trauma of loss. However, achieving and maintaining such organization presents one of the major hurdles to analysts accepting a professional will as necessary to ethical practice. Although most analysts follow professional guidelines to keep their records confidential, it is likely that most analysts have idiosyncratic ways of keeping files and financial records, not to speak of the complexities introduced by the increasing use of computers and encoded files.

A number of questions come to mind. Should IPA societies require every analyst to have a professional will? What about organizing a society/institute committee to: develop a generic professional will form suitable to the particular jurisdiction; facilitate members completing a will and assist in finding a designated colleague; co-ordinate the implementation of members' wills; include professional wills in the teaching curriculum for candidates and discuss the issues with new graduates? Should this committee be connected to the society's ethics committee, or have separate status as an Analyst Assistance Committee? Misunderstandings about confidentiality and the purpose of taking even the first step of naming a designated person are not uncommon.[4]

There are, of course, other questions that present further hurdles but for which there are not yet clear answers. For example, should professional will instructions include how to access computerized files and what to do with them? How would an analytic will differ from requirements of other professions for closing a practice? How does one find a colleague to agree to be a designated person, and for older analysts, a younger colleague? The task would become easier and be accomplished earlier in a practice if a professional will were required. Some analysts, to protect confidentiality, do not keep any patient files. Would they consider it a breach of confidentiality to make available the whereabouts of a patient list in a professional will? Or, conversely, is it unethical not to make it easier for patients readily to avail themselves to assistance if the treating analyst is no longer able to practise? If, when and how should patients be told that they are named in a practice list available to the designated person and/ or to the society? Do patients have a right to say that they do not want their names included or to specify where they want to be notified? Should they be given a choice? Other analysts had concerns about the legality of a professional will within their jurisdiction and about conflicts with their other professional organizations. There is need for serious discussion of the issues.[5]

Although answers can be found for external hurdles, the internal ones are often based on resistances more difficult to identify and overcome. Denial of the reality that we will one day die is both an adaptive and mal-adaptive defence; it is adaptive in that more emphasis is put on living and working well and mal-adaptive in that professional preparation for that eventuality fails to be made. As Firestein (2007) poignantly stated, 'It is always a catastrophe when an analyst dies. This is true even when death occurs in a termination phase or shortly after, because what has occurred registers not as mutual emancipation following achievement of treatment goals, but as desertion and abandonment.' He noted (1993) that thinking about death and making a professional will is 'thinking the unthinkable'.

Less obvious and yet more delicate is the problem of decline of the analyst through gradual incapacity. Denial of incapacity, including life-threatening illness, contributes to specific transference and countertransference problems. In the transference, a reawakening of reactions to earlier losses, idealization ('you are the only analyst who can understand me'), role reversal with the patient caring for the analyst in the face of the analyst's rapidly diminishing capacities. Analysts have concern about losing their analysing capacities, of being found incompetent by colleagues and of diminished income through loss of patients. Most analysts practise privately, many without secretaries or institutional support and the analytic frame (time, fee, frequency) may be different for each patient. Denial, guilt and shame can cause them to struggle in isolation with the wrenching conflict between their own needs and those of their patients. The analyst's need for reassurance of his/her capacity to function analytically can lead to inappropriate personal revelations or, conversely, excessively rigid secrecy. When patients cannot discuss what is happening within the analysis, curiosity is stimulated and information is sought outside the analysis, at times in ways that can intrude on the analyst's privacy. The resulting impact deprives patients of the opportunity to prepare optimally for the impending loss and its consequences. Secrecy and lack of open, honest discussion of the analyst's reality thus precludes a true analytic process, (Galatzer-Levy, 2004; Morrison, 1997). It is only when factual information is given, titrated to each patient's need, that an efficacious analytic process can proceed towards a constructive termination or, in a favourable circumstance, continuation of treatment when the analyst recovers.

Analysts know that confidentiality is 'constitutive of the analytic process itself' (Lear, 2003). This knowledge does not preclude intrapsychic conflicts about the maintenance of confidentiality throughout one's entire career. Denial can be a defence against the analyst's conscious or unconscious conflict between the ethical obligation of confidentiality and the wish to reveal successes with patients – the satisfactions and accomplishments of one's life work – and/or to confess and receive absolution for failures. Such conflicts become more intense and, as Arlow (1990) noted, confidentiality is less conscientiously managed under life-threatening stress. Often there is a conspiracy of denial in the society due to sensitivity for the privacy of a colleague, or to avoid being intrusive, critical, or accusatory of incompetence, or simply reluctance to confront an unpleasant situation. Sandler (2004) called attention to the massive complacency of the British Psychoanalytic Society in the case of Masud Khan's increasing incompetence due to egregious boundary violations. Referring to Gabbard and Peltz (2001), she notes that particular difficulties are associated with boundary violations by training analysts, because of the profound repercussions in psychoanalytic institutes and the transgenerational transmission of violations and the special problems these present to psychoanalytic organizations at all levels.

Clearly, societies and institutes have a role in avoiding organizational denial. Since archives and archivists who provide guidelines for preserving analytic material are rare, organizational opportunity for preserving analytic papers after death is warranted. The stories of the founders, of the contributions of senior analysts and of analytic organizations are essential to the history of psychoanalysis, which contributes to the continuity and relevance of the profession. Without archives it is difficult to track the origins, development and vagaries of psychoanalytic concepts. Without some record, accurate biographies of analysts and their careers cannot be written. Societies struggle to find space and funds for archival material. Most depend on interested members to maintain the history of their organizations. For the most part analysts are unaware of options for preserving their own material or for contributing to psychoanalytic history. Ethical ways of contributing to archives have become more complicated with increasing use of audio recordings of analytic sessions and computerized files. Even with attention to identity protection and patient consent, serious breaches can occur while the analyst is alive, as well as following the patient's or analyst's death (Middlebrook, 1991). Even consenting patients cannot be fully informed of the potential future use of 'taped archives' for research and historical purposes. Nor can an analyst know what will be made of private/professional material (e.g. letters, notebooks or recorded thoughts). An analytic will at least provides the opportunity for analysts to state how to protect their clinical material and other papers.

Recommendations

A professional will is no substitute for psychoanalytic understanding of clinical experiences as well as of confidentiality and privacy dilemmas. Nor is it a substitute for psychoanalytic organizations taking responsibility for developing policies and guidelines to assist analysts. Nevertheless, in the light of the above advantages and resistances to a professional will the following recommendations are offered.

1   Analysts need ample opportunity for open and frequent discussion of the definition, relevance, advantages, hopes, fears and resistances to a professional will (as distinguished from a personal will).
2   Such discussion needs to begin with candidates in the training programme and encouraged among new graduates as well as seasoned analysts.
3   Local societies and institutes need to take responsibility and facilitate members having a professional will in a step-wise progression.
4   The first step is to require that the name of a designated person be deposited with the society. If the analyst prefers, a list of patients with contact information can be kept with the society in a sealed envelope. It should be explained that confi-

dentiality is maintained in that the list is used by one person only if the analyst is no longer able to practise.

5   Provide a model of a professional will suitable to an analytic practice within a particular jurisdiction. (The appendix at the end of this chapter offers a model of what to include.) Check with requirements of analysts' other professions to include analytic differences and avoid conflict.

6   A distinction needs to be made between an analyst's professional will and a society committee to assist ill or incapacitated analysts and/or colleagues who realize an analyst is in difficulty. A will and such a committee (separate from an ethics committee) can be mutually facilitating.

7   It behoves each society, with guidelines from the National Society or the IPA, to develop ethical ways of preserving relevant material and assisting analysts in preserving or disposing their professional material. Analysts need to be made aware of facilities for depositing papers that contribute to psychoanalytic history. Archival policies for different kinds of material (including audio and video tapes, computer files, e-mail) and increased financial support for archival facilities are required.

8   Each society could provide a consultant or a committee (in smaller societies – the Executive) to clarify and answer analysts' questions about designated persons, wills and archives as well as how best to plan early on for sudden or planned closing a practice.

Conclusion

The professional will appropriate to a psychoanalytic practice is one way of facilitating the ethical closing of a practice and a step towards ensuring patient confidentiality and analyst privacy. Such a document becomes a practical part of a secure frame. Then, with the facilitation of the society and with plans in place for the possibility of a premature unexpected closure and for eventual retirement, including ways of caring for analytic papers after death, analysts can focus more readily on the intense and intimate work of caring for patients. Now is the time for individual analysts and psychoanalytic organizations to take their responsibility in this regard and to act.

Appendix

Model of what can be included in an analytic will

(This model is based on the suggestions of Firestein (2007) and those of other colleagues.)

Instructions

In the event of incapacity to practise or my death I request that a designated colleague (give co-ordinates) and/or the local psychoanalytic society consider the following:

Patient care

1   Note the whereabouts of a list of current patients, and how they can be reached. (A sentence or two about the nature of the treatment can be useful.)
2   Inform patients in a timely and sensitive manner of my incapacity or death.
3   Arrange for colleague(s) and/or the local psychoanalytic society to offer patients the opportunity for consultation pertaining to their continuing therapeutic needs.
4   Note the whereabouts of a list of candidate analysands or supervisees and recommendations to the director of the institute for ongoing analysis or supervision.

Patient records; clinical files and working notes

1   Locate clinical files containing minimal essential information as required by professional licensing or registration bodies. These are to be kept for the requisite number of years. Patients' files required for further treatment can be released in copy form, with patients' written consent.
2   Destroy working/process notes stored separately in filing cabinet or cupboard.

Office arrangements

1   Change the answering machine message to notify patients of cancellation of appointments and provide a contact number of designated person or the society.
2   Place a similar note on the office door for patients who arrive before they can be contacted.
3   Provide instructions to a doorman to give an appropriate message to arriving patients.
4   Note the location of current agenda, appointment and financial records (including current accounts). These records (kept for the duration of the statute of limitations in the analyst's jurisdiction) are needed for collecting outstanding fees, insurance claims and tax purposes.
5   Note the location of patient's prior authorization to release information to third parties or other written agreements between analyst and patient.
6   Obtain information from attached notes for access to computer files pertaining to financial records, patient care or professional papers.
7   Note instructions for dealing with audio or video tapes containing confidential material.

Notice of death to professional organizations and journal subscriptions and obituaries

1   Notify the attached list of professional organizations and journals that member is deceased.

2   Include name and vital statistics for the obituary sections of newsletters or journals.
3   Cancel memberships, journal subscriptions and request refunds.
4   Locate current CV and notes of professional contributions that can be useful for writing formal obituaries, especially for analysts who have made significant contributions to the literature, analytic organizations and teaching.

Professional papers and library

1   Search for professional papers, including correspondence, position papers, published and unpublished articles, presentations, speeches, awards and current CV. These could be organized to tag items which might be useful to analytic archives or the analyst's family as well as those to be destroyed.
2   Donate books, etc., after discussion with the family, to preferred institutions and or to a professional library. Suggestions for books not accepted, e.g. sell or donate to candidates or other professionals.

(The analytic professional will, updated periodically, and a current CV can be stored with a colleague(s) and/or the psychoanalytic society as well as with family.)

Notes

1 M. K. O'Neil (2005 to 2009) 'Confidentiality when Psychoanalysts Are Incapacitated or Die: The Purpose of a Professional Will'. Unpublished paper presented and discussed at psychoanalytic meetings in Montreal, Toronto, Vermont, New York, Israel and at the 2005 IPA Congress in Rio de Janeiro. (The problems of dealing with sudden death stimulated this work. One example: the death of a colleague suddenly during the night, came to my attention when a friend called because at the time of her appointment she found the office door locked. The society administrator was informed and, with family help, some contact information was found. A few patients were offered consultation; others introduced themselves at a funeral reception and consultation was arranged; still others heard of his death in an obituary or from an answering machine message to contact the society.

2 Galatzer-Levy (2004) contends that legally, morally and ethically, all analysts have a professional responsibility to make plans for their own disability and death. It follows that informed consent, an aspect of the obligation to give patients reliable information on which they can make a rational decision, applies to professional wills and is likely to be of increasing interest to psychoanalysts. It can also be argued, however, that informing patients of an analytic will distorts the transference and affects the purity of the analytic process.
    This issue is akin to the technical controversy over whether an analyst should reveal personal information about serious illness or increasing incapacity. Abend (1982) maintains that no information need be offered. Galatzer-Levy maintains that when an analysis is likely to be interrupted by death or disability, the patient should be given the best possible information so as to make reasoned choices. Analytic literature reveals a growing consensus among analysts that offering appropriate information and validating patient observations facilitates the analytic work whereas denial avoids reality and, at worst, stops the analytic process.

3 The increasing average age of the analytic community, the acceptance of older candidates in their 40s and 50s, and the resulting appointment of even older training analysts underlines the need for a professional will beginning from the point of graduation.

4 During discussions, some colleagues expressed discomfort in providing information about a will to the society. This was partially due to confusion between a personal and a professional will. Once this was clarified, the confidentiality/privacy issue still contributed to unease about providing a patient list to the society. There is less discomfort in providing the name of a designated person to be contacted in case of an emergency. However, if this person is unavailable at the time of unforeseen circumstances, the society or other colleagues have to take over and at least knowing the whereabouts of a professional will would be useful.

5 Winer (2002) encouraged the establishment of analyst assistance committees to develop guidelines and procedures for assisting incapacitated colleagues. It is interesting to note that in the research referred to here, almost half of the societies surveyed noted in their comments that they either had or were developing committees that analysts could consult on ethical issues or on helping colleagues with decreasing analytic capacity.

17

THE AGEING CANDIDATE

Will the empty couch become an empty institute?

Maria Teresa Savio Hooke

Candidates now seem to apply for psychoanalytic training in the second half of their lives. This will have consequences for our institutes and for the psychoanalytic community. Why is this happening? Have the motivations to apply for training changed? Are these changes related to internal or to socio-cultural factors? What will be the impact of older candidates and the lack of younger generations on the future of psychoanalysis? How will they contribute to our institutes and how can our institutes contribute to their development? These are some of the topics that I will consider in this chapter.

The crisis of psychoanalysis

From a historical perspective, we can see that awareness of the diminishing number of patients and candidates crystallised around the years of the so called Crisis of Psychoanalysis, a wake-up call in 2001/2002 that gave focus to a long standing malaise. Psychoanalytic societies started looking at themselves and examining the way they were functioning. They also started to take seriously the (mostly legitimate) criticisms directed at them as inward-looking and elitist and the prospect of the decline of psychoanalysis as a profession.

It was during this process of reflection and re-thinking that the first studies emerged and the issue of the lack of candidates and of the ageing candidate began to be researched and debated in psychoanalytic societies and conferences.

In 2002, the British Society debated the consequences of an ageing membership and commissioned a demographic profile of the Society.

In 2004, a Report of the IPA House of Delegates talks about: 'The general decline of candidates and patients in Western Europe compared with growth in the East where new groups were admitted'.

In 2004, a report from the IPA's Developing Psychoanalytic Practice and Training (DPPT) initiative, instigated by the then IPA Secretary General Donald Campbell, gives a clear indication of the concerns in the psychoanalytic community about the diminishing number of candidates in the course of describing the aims of the funded projects. To mention just a few: 'To establish a series of working parties whose overall aim is to shift the climate, to raise morale and to change psychoanalytic culture'; 'To enquire why medical students and clinical psychologists decide for or against psychoanalytic training. And what can be done to strengthen psychoanalysis'; 'The study aims to offer an understanding of the factors that determine current diminished interest in psychoanalytic training and practice'; 'To establish a centre for evaluation and psychoanalytic referrals'; 'The research aims at investigating the main causes of the decreasing demand for psychoanalysis and to develop a plan of action to increase the number of patient and candidates'; 'To provide a compelling case for training in psychoanalysis and for considering psychoanalysis as a valuable treatment'.

In 2007 Erlich-Ginor, Klockars, Junkers and Target published a report of the European Psychoanalytic Federation Working Party on Education, 'Who does What' on psychoanalytic education in Europe, which also dealt with the decline of the number of candidates. It showed that between 1998 and 2005 there had been a decrease of 7.1 per cent of candidates in the European Societies, that the typical admitted candidate was female (76.2 per cent) and that 50.6 per cent were between 40 and 49 years old and qualified as psychologists and social workers (62 per cent).

This study put the issue of the ageing candidate on the map for the first time by investigating a phenomenon that was already being discussed in psychoanalytic societies.

In 2010 Leena Klockars and Maria Teresa Hooke presented the results of a questionnaire sent to all the presidents of the European societies at the EPF conference in Brussels, as part of a project of the IPA Committee of Ageing, which aimed to draw a map of ageing of members and candidates in Europe (Klockars and Hooke, 2010; Hooke, 2009). This last research confirmed the earlier findings and showed that over the last ten years candidates have been getting older in the old and more established societies, while the situation appears to be different in Eastern Europe and in new groups and societies where the candidates are younger and where there is no crisis of psychoanalysis. We were also interested in the candidates' perspective and we asked for the collaboration of IPSO.[1] Luisa Marino and Eva Reichelt presented the results of their investigation in 'What the candidates say', which looks at the reasons behind the present situations. An update of this investigation (2011) 'Turning a blind eye to reality'[2] with data from the candidates in North America (by Drew Tillotson) and Latin America (by Adela Escardó, Sylvia Pupo Netto and Valeria Nader) shows that the typical age for starting psychoanalytic training is between 40 and 60 and that North American candidates start their training considerably later than Latin American candidates: most North American respondents (56 per cent) begin their training when they are over 50 compared with only 19 per cent in Latin America.

The issue of the ageing candidate is now on the map in the psychoanalytic community. It is also a concern for the IPA since, as the number of candidates diminishes and the present membership ages, there will not be enough new members to replace the ones who are retiring and dying. Apart from all the other reasons, this is also a financial concern for the IPA as it will have consequences for revenues.

I will discuss the issue of the ageing candidate with reference to different sources: the questionnaire to the presidents of the European societies, interviews I conducted with chairs and members of the Admissions Committee in the Australian Society and interviews with candidates of the Australian Society.

The ageing candidate: What the research shows

Our research shows that the age distribution of candidates in Europe has changed in the last ten years. As a general trend both potential and accepted candidates are getting older: almost half of them are 40–50 years old and about 30 per cent are older than 50. In new societies and Eastern Europe we again encounter this shift of age: 40 per cent of the candidates are between 30 and 40 years old, roughly ten years younger than in component societies. Although only 3.6 per cent of the candidates are over 60, 43 per cent of societies (mainly older ones) include candidates of this age.[3] In one society almost a quarter of the candidates were over 60. Candidates now tend to apply in the second half of their lives, and the age limit of 40 to begin the training, which used to be the common benchmark, has been removed. Some societies – alarmed about the present trend – are in fact thinking of reinstating it, but in some countries it is illegal to discriminate on the basis of age. Most societies state clearly that they would welcome younger candidates. Some societies report that an applicant over 50 is not readily accepted and would have to make a particularly positive impression. The increasing age of candidates is seen as a problem in about 50 per cent of societies, whose members are having discussions about it and have appointed recruitment committees, set up university liaison groups and plan to increase their presence in psychiatry and psychology training.

Has the motivation to train changed?

Around 60 per cent of societies are sure that the motivation to train has changed and we find a common and recurrent reply: the profession of psychoanalyst is not seen today as a career choice by young graduates, it has become a post-psychotherapy profession. There are many reasons for this: there is no money in it, one cannot make a living out of psychoanalysis as it is very difficult to get patients 4/5 times a week, the title is not recognised nor do our institutes award a degree that has official currency, the title is seldom recognised by health insurance companies.

Alternative psychotherapies, psychoanalytic psychotherapy courses and non-IPA psychoanalytic courses offer less demanding training and more guarantees of building up a practice. Such competition means that young people starting their career in the mental health field may be 'lost' to the possibility of psychoanalytic training. Another reported factor is the length nowadays of post academic education, for example to become a psychologist first and then a psychotherapist, and then to decide to become a psychoanalyst, may take up to ten years. Traditionally psychoanalysis was strongly represented in the medical and psychology faculties of the universities and heavily involved in the training of psychiatrists and clinical psychologists. The fact that our academic influence is globally declining means there are no teachers, mentors and supervisors to introduce psychoanalytic thinking and inspire the young generations; thus, when young people are making their career choices, psychoanalysis is not on their radar, they have had no exposure to it. I quote Howard (2009):

It is difficult to attract applicants to a difficult career if "easier" ways are constantly being offered, especially when there is no real exposure to analytic thinking to counterbalance this atmosphere. Combined with the palpable antagonism towards analytic work within psychiatric professional organizations, this creates a corrosive atmosphere of insecurity about the prospects for an analytic career path as a psychiatrist and it should not be surprising to find that few seriously consider analytic training. I doubt that this situation will change within psychiatry during my lifetime.

Nearly all societies consider this a serious development and advocate an increased presence in psychiatry and psychology training courses. This, combined with social changes and the emphasis on quick cures, the very active promotion of cognitive therapies by their practitioners and the active denigration of psychoanalysis by the media makes it difficult to attract applicants. The fact that our institutes are private organizations, are not part of a public framework and do not award 'official' degrees, discourages young applicants who may be looking for an official 'title', which would also allow their patients to benefit from health insurance rebates. In such a problematic external environment, candidates need strong motivation and dedication: our present culture requires our candidates to go against the current cultural trends, while we – the older generations – went with the current trend (Eizirik, 1997). Whether this is real dedication or an overvaluation or idealization of the psychoanalytic training, remains to be seen.

Psychoanalytic training today

Today training seems to be approached differently: not as a career and life choice, but rather as a finishing school, as a way to complete one's education, to deepen one's self-knowledge and interest in the human mind. Applicants are mostly women and psychologists, who have already done psychotherap1y training and possibly had a career in another organization and now – with the children grown up and some financial freedom – feel free to embark on this project. It could also be seen as a response to mid-life crisis, a way of completing one's healing process or an attempt to turn a blind eye to the fact of getting older. This in the context that psychoanalysis is still prestigious in psychology and social work and perceived as an enhancement of professional status. Candidate A: 'I had completed psychotherapy training and wanted to continue learning. I also wanted to be part of a professional group as I can feel isolated working in private practice'. Candidate B: 'I had gone on into my career and into my mid life; I felt that it would be most satisfying to make a difference through my work by developing the skills to work at a deeper level. This view and the desire to work more deeply with patients were formed by my own struggle in my personal analysis and out of a range of clinical experiences'.

This scenario has to be seen in the context of women today having more choices and perhaps the freedom to take risks, branch out and be creative. It is now also commonplace for people to have multiple careers and variable career paths – three or four in the course of a working life are not unusual. The fact that we have fewer male candidates and very few psychiatrists is a serious drawback: it confirms our exclusion from psychiatry, it reduces the heterogeneity of the candidates' groups and the opportunities for cross fertilisation, but also – as much as we may not like it – the reality is that professions that become predominantly female, lose some of their social status and one wonders how much this may also affect the way psychoanalysis is perceived by the outside world.

On the whole the impression one gets in talking to candidates and reading their replies is that the internal motives for applying to train have not changed: there is always the encounter with the unconscious, with one's internal world, through reading, through a teacher, a supervisor, one's analysis, which lights the flame. Candidate C: 'It was while training as a psychiatrist and getting exposure to a psychodynamic way of thinking that it spoke, I think, to a personal need that I was not entirely conscious of, and it was a now or never fork in the road in view of my age'.

What about the young applicants?

This is a complex question. Some societies report that they have younger applicants who come to psychoanalytic training disillusioned by psychodynamic psychotherapy or cognitive therapy. Significantly this occurs in countries where psychoanalysis is recognized by governments among the psychotherapy professions. Other societies report expressions of interest from young graduates and academics who want to train because of their experience in personal analysis, rather than because of their clinical practice, who nevertheless are not prepared for the length and cost of training. This together with the lack of clinical experience makes the situation problematic.[4] It is in consideration of these facts that many societies have now developed introductory courses, feeder courses, pre-clinical courses, and observation courses in order to foster the interest of such potential applicants and to encourage good candidates. On the other hand, when young graduates do apply, the stumbling blocks are lack of clinical experience, immaturity (whatever that means, one assumes lack of life experience) and lack of financial resources. In the French model, one of the difficulties is that young applicants may not have enough personal analysis.[5]

Is the culture of our institutes discouraging young applicants?

External factors play a major role in deterring young applicants, but public perceptions of our institutes and the subliminal messages they send out may also keep applicants away. Some are well known: we have a reputation for not accepting people, so they don't bother to apply. It is interesting to note that the previously mentioned research 'Who does what?' shows that in 2006 there was a 13 per cent increase in acceptances. It remains to be seen whether this is due to an increased awareness of our reputation, a fear of being left without candidates, or both.

We also have a tendency to choose the 'safe' option, the so-called 'mini-analyst' choice, as there is a great anxiety that candidates may damage psychoanalysis or disrupt the dynamics of existing groups. While it is true that we have a responsibility towards our own institutes and especially towards future patients, one also wonders how much this is a projection on to the applicants of the bad object of institutional groups. Another more subtle way of discouraging applicants is to have admission criteria that are so impossibly high and idealized that nobody is ever going to be good enough. A less often mentioned factor is the strange relationship that analytic societies have with age (and time): an individual of 50 or 55 may be considered 'young' or too young to take up a position in their society or become a training analyst, and at the other end of the spectrum analysts of 73 or 75 are still 'too young' to retire. This has consequences: it means that positions in societies are blocked by the elderly analysts who are reluctant to retire. Only one society in Europe has introduced an age limit for office holders, while in another the issue of age of office holders has been raised and discussed and a very important process has followed in which many young colleagues have asked to have more responsibilities. This process sent a very strong signal to the society as a whole.

We may also be unaware of the image we portray to the outside world. Candidate D: 'The analysts are older, you look around and you feel too young . . . It is a body of people who are older and have a great deal of experience, in response you feel you must wait, you are too young'.

Only one society mentioned that training analysts seem to suffer a diffuse prejudice against the young. It is striking that the issue of the envy of the older generations towards the young went almost unmentioned. A normal dose of envy for the young may be a fact of life, as they – among other things – have time on their side, but it needs to be acknowledged. If denied, there is a risk that it may be enacted towards young applicants and young members occupying positions in their societies.

Betty Joseph, in her paper 'Envy in Everyday Life' (1986), talks specifically about this:

> there are bound to be difficulties at every stage of development and particularly in ageing. To age, with what one may call proper resignation, means to be able to allow the younger generations to have things, knowledge, gifts, and a future that the ageing generation cannot have; and it means making way for the next generations, being able to identify with and even enjoy their success, and to regret what one has not achieved as well as enjoy what one has. Excessive envy can make this particular stage of development very difficult and yet everyone has to reach it.

The effect of the ageing candidate on our institutes and on the future of psychoanalysis

If we consider the length of training and the time needed to establish an analytic identity, older candidates will not be ready to work as analysts until an age when people in other professions begin to retire. How much time is left for clinical work, research, scientific production, to contribute to the development of the discipline and to be training analysts, becomes an issue. Is it an ethical consideration to discuss such matters as part of the initial interviews with the applicant, so that we don't collude with a possible denial of ageing? Some societies also expressed concern about the amount of resources expended on educating candidates given the number of years left for them to practise.

However, there are also wider issues that have to do with group morale, image, and the capacity of psychoanalytic institutions for innovation and change. Being part of a society of older people – which conveys the sense of being part of a dying profession – will have an effect on the morale of the members and their belief in a future worth planning for. The lack of younger members will influence the institutes' capacity to take risks and be innovative. Besides, the image we are projecting on the outside world would reinforce media stereotypes and the public perception that psychoanalysis is old fashioned and passé. Another likely consequence will be a diminishing number of analysts working in the community and in the public sector. We have already seen that we are losing influence in institutions; the ageing factor will make this worse. Elliot Jaques, in his paper 'Death and the Mid-Life Crisis' (1965), talks about two types of creativity: what he calls the hot-from-the-fire creativity of the twenties and early thirties 'which tends to be intense, spontaneous and comes out ready-made' and the creativity of the late thirties and after which he calls sculpted creativity, when 'the inspiration may come more slowly and there is a big step between the first effusion of inspiration and the finished product'. To establish and maintain a living and fertile environment, we need both kinds of creativity and we need them to be in dialogue with each other.

We are facing a changed and changing social context

The figures presented are significant for the future of the professions. While many societies have been and are developing strategies and programmes to deal with the situation, no plan is likely to succeed unless we take into account that we operate in a very different social context than we did 20 or 30 years ago. We live now in a society which is fast changing, drawn to the quick fix, technologically advanced and where the status of psychoanalysis among the mental health professions has declined considerably.

Jorge Ahumada (1997), the Argentinean analyst who has written on the crisis of psychoanalysis in modern culture, says that: 'We live in a period dominated by the media and mass communication, with an emphasis on the optional, the transitory and the contingent, in a congestion of information that disturbs the experience of space that we need in our lives and endangers silence, solitude and privacy, which we need for introspection and reflection'. According to Ahumada the result of this is a crisis of everyday self-reflective thought, which in turn makes the psychoanalytic clinical approach alien to the general public.

Otto Kernberg (2011), in an interview with Chanda Rankin, said there is no doubt that we live in a world hostile to psychoanalysis, and that the strong cultural critique of psychoanalysis is not new but now takes the form that psychoanalysis is lengthy, expensive, has not demonstrated its efficacy and effectiveness and patients can be helped by brief therapies. At the same time, the combination of the important development in biological psychiatry, the financial pressure reducing availability of psychotherapeutic treatment, the cultural critique of subjectivity and wish for quick solutions, adaptation – all that has tended to decrease the participation of psychodynamic psychiatry and psychodynamic psychotherapy in the training for psychiatrists.

In one of her last interviews before her death, Hanna Segal (2010) comments that our society is violently anti-mind and that the analytic ethos is in danger when the values and policies of the rich, mighty and powerful come to dominate.[6]

We are all aware of today's cultural shift away from psychoanalysis, which is seen as old fashioned, too slow, and too expensive, and of the fact that we are competing with other therapies, often derived from psychoanalysis and with other psychoanalytic approaches, in a context in which short-term therapies and cognitive behaviour therapy – the so-called evidence-based therapies – are promoted and financed by health insurance companies and seen as more in line with our fast pace of life. Today there is also much more emphasis on relief from distress and incapacity, rather than on self-knowledge and search for the truth in oneself and others.

Perhaps at times we are far too aware of this cultural shift and we tend to forget that it is because of the revolutionary impact of the discovery of the unconscious and the 'talking cure' in the Western world, that today we have such a number of different therapies and that looking for help for mental suffering has become an accepted fact. So, while it is true that psychoanalysis has lost its unique position and has become 'one therapy among many', it is also true that this is a consequence of its influence and generative capacity.

But to prove how fast our social context is changing, it was just yesterday that cognitive behaviour therapy seemed to be the phenomenon to contend with, while today the latest trend to appear on the scene of the talking cures and spreading like a bonfire in the West and the East is the use of new technologies: internet, telephone and Skype. As the media say, 'the shrink is only a click away'. These methods, which were initially adopted in order to deal with the situation of isolation and geographical distances, have left the psychoanalytic community catching its breath and considering, evaluating, and exploring its relationship to this new modernity. Another small but significant shift comes from the United Kingdom: recent research has been challenging the dominance of evidence-based practice (cognitive behaviour therapy) in the treatment of depression and showing the effectiveness of psychoanalytic approaches and it seems that – at least in this country – the external agencies are showing signs of listening (Lemma *et al.*, 2010).

The rapidity of environmental change demands a new alertness on the part of psychoanalytic institutions, a scenario that has proven difficult to manage.

Modernity does not explain everything

As we have seen there are differences between countries regarding the age of candidates: Europe, Eastern Europe and Latin America all present different scenarios. The changed social context cannot be used to explain everything. Different countries may have a similar social context, but very different histories and psychoanalytic legacies. The Eastern European countries do not register a crisis of psychoanalysis or the phenomenon of the ageing candidate. In these countries, where psychoanalysis went underground during the communist regime and where the population suffered long periods of traumatisation and repression, the re-introduction and opening to psychoanalysis has been embraced with enthusiasm and passion; psychoanalysis is seen not only as a therapeutic method to alleviate personal suffering but also as a way to understand and metabolize historical traumas.

In Latin America the situation is different again: here psychoanalysis is embedded in the culture, psychoanalytic groups are engaged with the community and are creative in their outreach activities; the aliveness of the context must be transmitted to the society at large and attract candidates.

If we think about the Far East: Japan, Korea, Taiwan and China, we again have a different situation, with clear individual differences often reflecting the socio-political history of each country. But there is no doubt that the potential for growth in the region is remarkable, fuelled by a rich cultural texture and by the interest of a new generation of mental health professionals in psychoanalysis as a therapeutic method. In China, it is precisely because the culture is looking for spiritual values and because of the ethos of economic progress at all costs, that there is a growing interest in the mind and in the deeper values that psychoanalysis represents. Here the context is one of pioneers, in which psychoanalysis, psychotherapy and psychology are at the beginning and where psychoanalysis has the status and the prestige of its golden years. The traumas of recent Chinese history play a part in an unconscious need for healing and in a search for the emergence of the individual as a separate self from a repressive collective society. Candidates and mental health professionals are young, because this phenomenon is affecting the younger generations: they are the ones emerging and wanting to have an influence.

We are facing a new reality regarding ageing

Demographic change is part of the changing context in which we operate. As Gabriele Junkers said in her paper 'The Empty Couch': 'Living in the 20th century we are faced with a new situation in respect to ageing. Never before have we had such a high number of people as part of our population, never have we had so many who reach a very advanced age.' People live longer, have more opportunities and choices, and it is now commonplace for people to have multiple careers. Also gone are the days in which mainstream medicine and science believed that brain anatomy was fixed and that old age meant inevitable decline of the brain functions. The discoveries in the late sixties and early seventies of the neuroplasticity of the brain, the idea that 'the brain can change its own structure and function through thoughts and activity' (Doidge, 2007), have changed all that. These factors also have to be taken into account in considering the issue of the ageing candidate.

Conclusion

The scenario I have presented is alarming. As we have seen, many societies have responded to this scenario with various initiatives: by undertaking creative outreach activities, by setting up recruitment committees investigating strategies to attract younger members, by implementing university liaison groups, by increasing our presence in psychiatry and psychology training courses, by setting up pre-clinical courses and feeder courses. I do not believe that this is enough to turn the tide and recapture young candidates. The social context in which we operate today has changed so much and keeps changing so fast that it requires psychoanalytic societies to respond with major changes and with a new alertness. The challenges include the cost of training and of training analysis, the possibility for psychoanalytic institutions to set up their own psychotherapy courses, the establishment of clinics where placement for young candidates is possible, making the training part of a public framework, and the need for psychoanalysis to present itself as a modern profession in a modern world and to find ways of recapturing its reputation as an effective therapeutic method for severe pathologies. At the end of the day, a lot will depend on us.

Acknowledgements

I would like to thank my colleagues and the candidates of the Australian Psychoanalytical Society for their thoughts and ideas on this topic.

Notes

1 IPSO (International Psychoanalytical Studies Organization) is the organization representing the analysts-in-training in the societies of the IPA (International Psychoanalytical Association).
2 Panel at the IPA Conference, 2011, in Mexico.
3 I choose not to name each individual society, but rather to give a general picture of what the research shows.
4 By clinical experience we mean experience acquired in working therapeutically with patients.
5 The IPA recognizes three educational models: the Eitingon, the French and the Uruguayan. The issue of personal analysis is handled differently in each model. In the French model it takes place entirely or mostly before admission to training and the quality and depth of the undergone analytical process will be assessed when the applicant applies to training. The emphasis is on the study of the complete works of Freud, considered as the basis of the theoretical training, and supervisions are regarded as an essential part of the training process.
6 *Encounters through Generations*, video produced by the British Psychoanalytical Society.

BIBLIOGRAPHY FOR PART III

Abend, S. (1982) 'Serious Illness in the Analyst: Countertransference Considerations', *Journal of the American Psychoanalytic Association* 30: 365–375.

Ahumada, J. (1997) 'Crise da cultura e crise da psicanálise', *Revista de Psicanálisis de Porto Alegre* 4: 51–96.

Arditi, B. (1988) '*La postmodernidad como coreografia de la complejidad*', XVIII Congreso Latinoamericano de Sociologia, Montevideo.

Arlow, J. A. (1990) 'The Analytic Attitude in the Service of Denial', in H. J. Schwartz and A.-L. Silver (eds), *Illness in the Analyst: Implications for the Treatment Relationship*. Madison, CT: International Universities Press, 1990, pp. 9–45.

Baladier, G. (1995) 'Le présent de la surmodernité', *Sciences Humaines* 5: 22–24.

Baranger, M. and Baranger, C. (1961) 'La situación analítica como campo dinâmico', in *Problemas del Campo Psicoanalítico*. Buenos Aires: Ed. Kargieman, 1969.

Barbanel, L. (1989) 'The Death of the Psychoanalyst (Panel Presentation)—Introduction', *Contemporary psychoanalysis* 25: 412–419.

Bauman, Z. (1989) *Modernity and the Holocaust*. New York: Cornell University Press.

Bauman, Z. (1991) 'Modernity and Ambivalence', *The American Journal of Sociology* 97(5) (March, 1992), pp. 1519–1521.

Bauman, Z. (2000) *Liquid Modernity*. Cambridge: Polity Press.

Bauman, Z. (2005) *Liquid Fear*. Cambridge: Polity Press.

Bion, W. R. (1961) *Experiences in Groups*, London: Tavistock Publications.

Bion, W. R. (1962) *Learning from Experience*. London: Heinemann.

Campbell, D. (2005) DPPT, Questionnaire Working Group presented at the IPA Board Meeting in Rio.

Carlisky, N. and Eskenazi, C. (2000) *Resignación o Desafio: un enfoque transdisciplinario cobre la Sociedad actual*. Buenos Aires: Grupo Editorial Lumen.

Cartwright, D. (2010) *Containing States of Mind*. New York: Routledge.

Castoriadis, C. (1996) 'La crisis actual del processo identificatório', *Zona Erogena* 31: 37–41.

Clark, R. W. (1995) 'The Pope's Confessor: A Metaphor Relating to Illness in the Analyst', *Journal of the American Psychoanalytic Association* 43: 137–149.

Clark, R. W. and Winer, J. A. (2007) 'Help for the Impaired Psychoanalyst', *The American Psychoanalyst* 41(1): 21.

Danon-Boileau, L. (2011) *The Silent Child: Exploring the World of Children Who Do Not Speak*. Oxford: Oxford University Press.

Dattner, R. (1989) 'On the Death of the Analyst: A Review', *Contemporary Psychoanalysis* 25: 419–426.

Deutsch, R. A. (2011) 'A Voice Lost, A Voice Found: After the Death of the Analyst', *Psychoanalytic Inquiry* 31: 526–535.

Dewald, P. (1982) 'Serious Illness in the Analyst: Transference, Countertransference, and Reality Response', *Journal of the American Psychoanalytic Association* 30: 347–363.

Doidge, N. (2007) *The Brain that Changes Itself.* Carlton, Victoria, Australia: Scribe Publications.

Eissler, K. R. (1993) 'On Possible Effects of Ageing on the Practice of Psychoanalysis: An Essay', *Psychoanalytic Inquiry* 13: 316–332.

Eizirik, C. (1997) 'Psychoanalysis and Culture: Some Contemporary Challenges', *International Journal of Psychoanalysis* 78: 789–800.

Eizirik, C. L. (2008) 'Psychoanalysis in a Changing World', *International Journal of Psychoanalysis* 89: 11–14.

Eizirik, C. L. (2010) 'The IPA Administration from 2005 to 2009', in P. Loewenberg and N. L. Thompson, *100 Years of the IPA: The Centenary History of the International Psychoanalytical Association 1910–2010. Evolution and Change.* International Psychoanalytical Association.

Erikson, E. (1956) 'The Problem of Ego Identity', *Journal of the American Psychoanalytic Association* 4: 56–121.

Erlich-Ginor, M., Junkers, G., Klockars, L. and Target, M. (2007) 'Cosi fan tutti. Factual Aspects of Training Institutes in the EPF', *EPF Bulletin* 61: 167–180.

Faimberg, H. (2005) *The Telescoping of Generations: Listening to the Narcissistic Links Between Generations.* London: Routledge.

Fajardo, B. (2001) 'Life-Threatening Illness in the Analyst,' *Journal of the American Psychoanalytic Association* 49: 569–586. (Reprinted in this book.)

Feinsilver, D. B. (1998) 'The Therapist as a Person Facing Death: The Hardest of External Realities and Therapeutic Action', *International Journal of Psychoanalysis* 79: 1131–1150.

Firestein, S. K. (1993) 'On Thinking the Unthinkable: Making a Professional Will', *The American Psychoanalyst* 27: 16.

Firestein, S. K. (2007) 'The Patient or the Analyst Dies: Ethical Considerations', *The American Psychoanalyst* 41: 30–31.

Freedman, A. (1990) 'Death of the Psychoanalyst as a Form of Termination of Psychoanalysis', in H. J. Schwartz and A.-L. Silver (eds), *Illness in the Analyst: Implications for the Treatment Relationship.* Madison, CT: International Universities Press, 1990, pp. 299–331

Freud, S. (1923) 'The Infantile Genital Organization: An Interpolation into the Theory of Sexuality', *S. E.* 1.

Freud, S. (1936) 'A Disturbance of Memory on the Acropolis', *S. E.* 22.

Freud, S. (1941/1926) 'Address in the Society of B´nai B´rith', *S. E.* 20.

Gabbard, G. O., Peltz, M. and The COPE Study Group on Boundary Violations (2001) 'Speaking the Unspeakable: Institutional Reactions to Boundary Violations by Training Analysts', *Journal of the American Psychoanalytic Association* 49: 659–673; 52: 999–1024.

Galatzer-Levy, R. M. (2004) 'The Death of the Analyst: Patients Whose Previous Analyst Died while They Were in Treatment', *Journal of the American Psychoanalytic Association* 52: 1000–1024.

Green, A. (1997) 'Interview', in L. W. Raymond and S. Rosbrow-Reich, *The Inward Eye.* London: The Analytic Press.

Grinberg, L. and Grinberg, R. (1971) *Identidad y cambio.* Buenos Aires: Kargieman; Barcelona: Paidos-Ibérica, 3rd edn.

Grinberg, L. and Grinberg, R. (1989) *Psychoanalytic Perspectives on Migration and Exile.* New Haven, CT: Yale University Press.

Hartmann, H., Kris, E. and Loewenstein, R. M. (1946) 'Comments on the Formation of Psychic Structure', *Psychoanalytic Study of the Child* 2: 11–38.

Hooke, M. T. (2009) 'Ageing of the Candidates in the European Psychoanalytic Societies'. Unpublished Paper given at the EPF Conference, Brussels.

Howard, M. (2009) Interview of M. T. Hooke with Dr. M. Howard as Chair of the Admission Committee of the Sydney Institute for Psychoanalysis.

Hurwitz, M. H. (1992) 'A Psychoanalyst Retires', in *How Psychiatrists Look at Aging*. Madison, CT: International Universities Press.

Huxley, A. (1932) *Brave New World*. London: Chatto and Windus.

IPA Minutes of the Meeting of the House of Delegates, New Orleans, March 2004.

Jaques, E. (1955) 'Social Systems as a Defence against Persecutory and Depressive Anxiety', in M. Klein, P. Heinemann and R. E. Money-Kyrle (eds), *New Directions in Psycho-Analysis: The Significance of Infant Conflict in the Pattern of Adult Behaviour*. London: Tavistock, pp. 478–498.

Jaques, E. (1965) 'Death and the Mid-Life Crisis', *International Journal of Psychoanalysis* 46: 502–514.

Jeffery, E. H. (2001) 'The Mortality of Psychoanalysts', *Journal of the American Psychoanalytic Association* 49: 103–111.

Joffe, W. G. and Sandler, J. (1965) 'Notes on Pain, Depression, and Individuation', *Psychoanalytic Study of the Child* 20: 394–424.

Joseph, B. (1986) 'Envy in Everyday Life', *Psychoanalytic Psychotherapy* 2: 13–22.

Joseph, E. and Widlöcher, D. (1983) *The Identity of the Psychoanalyst*. New York: International Universities Press.

Junkers, G. (2006) *Is It Too Late? Key Papers on Ageing*. London: Karnac.

Junkers, G. (2007) 'Saying Good Bye to the Work as an Analyst'. Paper given at the Finnish Psychoanalytical Society on 27 September 2008, Helsinki. (Published in German in Sylvia Zwettler-Otte (ed.), *Entgleisungen in der Psychoanalyse. Berufsethische Probleme*. Göttingen: Vandenhoeck & Ruprecht.

Junkers, G. (2011) 'Turning a Blind Eye to Reality'. Panel presented by the IPA Committee on Psychoanalytic Perspectives on Ageing.

Junkers, G. (2013) 'Later, Perhaps… Transience and Its Meaning for the Analyst'. (This volume).

Junkers, G. and Klockars, L. (2007) 'Who Does What', *EPF Bulletin* 61.

Junkers, G., Tuckett, D. and Zachrisson, A. (2008) 'To Be or Not to Be a Psychoanalyst: How Do We Know a Candidate Is Ready to Qualify? Difficulties and Controversies in Evaluating Psychoanalytic Competence', *Psychoanalytic Inquiry* 28: 288–308.

Kernberg, O. (1989) 'The Temptations of Conventionality', *International Journal of Psychoanalysis* 16: 191–205.

Kernberg, O. (1998) *Ideology, Conflict and Leadership in Groups and Organizations*. New Haven, CT, and London: Yale University Press.

Kernberg, O. (2000) 'A Concerned Critique of Psychoanalytic Education', *International Journal of Psychoanalysis* 81: 97–120.

Kernberg, O. (2011) 'An Interview with Otto Kernberg by Chanda Rankin', *International Psychoanalysis Blog*, 2011.

King, P. (1983) 'Identity Crises: Splits or Compromises – Adaptive or Maladaptive', in E. Joseph and D. Widlöcher (eds), *The Identity of the Psychoanalyst*. New York: International Universities Press, 1983.

Klockars, L. and Hooke, M. T. (2010) 'Ageing of Members in the European Psychoanalytic Societies', *EPF Bulletin* 64: 265–272.

Kristeva, J. (1993) *Les Nouvelles Maladies de L´ame*. Paris: Libraire Artheme Fayard.

Lasch, C. (1978) *The Culture of Narcissism*. New York: Norton.

Lear, J. (2003) 'Confidentiality as a Virtue', in C. Levin, A. Furlong and M. K. O'Neil (eds), *Confidentiality, Ethical Perspectives and Clinical Dilemmas*. Northvale, NJ: Analytic Press, pp. 3–17.

Lemma, A., Target, M. and Fonagy P. (2010) *The Development of a Brief Psychodynamic Protocol for Depression: Dynamic Interpersonal Therapy*. London: Routledge.

Leonoff, A. (2012) 'On the Matter of an Aging Membership and Its Implications for the IPA'. Paper given at an IPA Board Meeting, January 2012.

Levey, M. (1985) 'The Concept of Structure in Psychoanalysis', *Annual of Psychoanalysis* 12–13: 137–154.

Loewenberg, P. and Thompson, N. L. (2010) *100 Years of the IPA: The Centenary History of the International Psychoanalytical Association 1910–2010. Evolution and Change*. International Psychoanalytical Association.

Lyotard, J. F. (1979) *La Condición Posmoderna*. Barcelona: Anagrama.

Menzies, I. (1961) 'The Functioning of Social Systems as a Defence against Anxiety', in I. Menzies Lyth, *Containing Anxiety in Institutions: Selected Essays, Vol. 1*. London: Free Association Books, 1988.

Michaels, J. J. and Schoenberg, M. L. (1966) 'Some Considerations of a Retirement Policy for Training Analysts', *Psychoanalytic Quarterly* 35: 199–216.

Middlebrook, D. W. (1991) *Anne Sexton: A Biography*. Boston, MA: Houghton Mifflin Company.

Moraitis G (2009) 'Till Death Do Us Part', *Psychoanalytic Inquiry* 29: 157–166.

Morrisson, A. L. (1997) 'Ten Years of Doing Psychotherapy while Living with a Life-Threatening Illness: Self-Disclosure and Other Ramifications', *Psychoanalytic Dialogues* 7: 225–241.

Nist, J. A. and Leite, Y. (trs and eds) (1962) *Modern Brazilian Poetry: An Anthology*. Bloomington, IN: Indiana University Press.

O'Neil, M. K. (2005) 'Confidentiality, Privacy and the Facilitating Role of Psychoanalytic Organizations', *International Journal of Psychoanalysis* 88: 1–20.

O'Neil, M. K. and Zack, D. (Guest editors, 2009) 'In Memory of Eva Lester', *Canadian Journal of Psychoanalysis* 17: 205–218.

Perdigo, G. (2010) 'Fantacism in Psychoanalysis'. Introduction to the Book Launch of M. Utrilla's book *Upheavals in Psychoanalysis*. IPA Conference, New Orleans.

Quinodoz, D. (2009) *Growing Old: A Journey of Self-Discovery*. London: Taylor and Francis.

Quinodoz, D. (2013) 'Does an Older Analyst Have a Role to Fill?' (This volume).

Rendely, J. (1999) 'The Death of an Analyst: The Loss of a Real Relationship', *Contemporary Psychoanalysis* 35: 131–152.

Ricoeur, P. (1970) *Freud and Philosophy: An Essay on Interpretation*. New Haven: Yale University Press.

Robutti, A. (2010) 'When the Patient Loses His/Her Analyst', *The Italian Psychoanalytic Annual* 4: 129–145.

Sandler, A.-M. and Godley, W. (2004) 'Institutional Responses to Boundary Violations: The Case of Masud Khan', *International Journal of Psychoanalysis* 85: 27–44.

Savitz, C. (1990) 'The Double Death: The Loss of the Analyst in the Analytic Hour', *Journal of Analytical Psychology* 35: 241–260.

Schirrmacher, F. (2004) *Das Methusalem-Komplott*. München: Karl Blessing Verlag.

Schur, M. (1972) *Freud. Living and Dying*. London: The Hogarth Press.

Schwartz, H. J. and Silver, A.-L. (eds) (1990) *Illness in the Analyst: Implications for the Treatment Relationship*. Madison, CT: International Universities Press.

Segal, H. (2010) *Encounters through Generations*. Audio-Visual project of the British Psychoanalytical Society.

Steiner, J. (2011) *Seeing and Being Seen: Emerging from a Psychic Retreat*. London & New York: Routledge.

Tallmer, M. (1989) 'The Death of an Analyst', *Psychoanalytic Review* 76: 529–542.

Tallmer, M. (1992) 'The Ageing Analyst', *Psychoanalytic Review* 79: 381–404.

Tausk, V. (1919) 'On the Origin of the "Influencing Machine" in Schizophrenia', *Psychoanalytic Quarterly* 2: 519–556.

Tuckett, D. (2005) 'Does Anything Go? Towards a Framework for the More Transparent Assessment of Psychoanalytic Competence', *International Journal of Psychoanalysis* 86: 31–49.

Van der Leeuw, P. J. (1980) '"Modern Times" and the Psychoanalyst Today', *International Review of Psychoanalysis* 7: 137–145.

Winer, J. (2002) 'BOPS Studies the Functionally Impaired Faculty Analyst', *The American Psychoanalyst* 33(2): 9, 15.

Zwettler Otte, S. (2006) 'The Double-Faced Work of the Propagation and of the Reception of Psychoanalysis', *EPF Bulletin* 60: 170–175.

EPILOGUE

Gabriele Junkers

Why do many of us find it so difficult to plan for retirement from our profession well in advance? How can the unthinkable be made thinkable? How do we experience ageing as psychoanalysts? How can we accept our own transience and deal heedfully with it?

These questions arise with all the more urgency given the increasingly manifest reality of demographic change in general and of the age of our professional group in particular. Indications that psychoanalysts have above-average life expectancy (Jeffery, 2001) are yet another reason why more than half of all analysts today are already over the age of 60.

The authors of this book attempt from various perspectives to examine transience and ageing as facts of life in terms of their significance for the end of an analyst's professional activity. They all share the desire to put the 'inexpressible' into words and approach it in the common conviction that ageing in a psychoanalyst and bidding farewell to work behind the couch can give rise to both individual and institutional problems the frank discussion of which is taboo in our groups.

Avoidance of important questions always indicates that we suspect that answers to them will not be forthcoming. But if we have recognised that many of us need to disavow the fact that we are growing older and ill in order to defend against unbearable mental pain, is it not time to make use of the detour represented by support from the institution? So should we not begin to reflect in our various groups about the realities of personal experience and the consequences for our groups and institutions, with a view to drawing up recommendations, offering help and establishing rituals that can subsequently be implemented in practice?

This book cannot supply ready-made solutions to the complex, serious and weighty issue of how, as a psychoanalyst, one should shape one's ageing. Instead, it casts light on the challenges inherent in this phase of life, and examines them in order to initiate a debate on the shaping of a good end to one's professional career. In this connection, the fact that, as Freud pointed out, the tendency to disavow is something fundamentally human is repeatedly emphasised. We must nevertheless insist on particular care and heedfulness in relation to this part of our lives, in order:

- to protect our patients and candidates from analyses that are collusive, go seriously awry, are prematurely terminated or are even broken off;
- to protect sick analysts from harming their hard-won reputations; and
- to preserve the entire group from harm to the psychoanalysis that unites it.

Even if a universally valid solution cannot be found to the problems addressed here, I advocate the adoption of measures that may help to reduce the risk of wounds and retraumatisation in *both* candidates *and* patients. For this reason, I should like to initiate not only a debate within the institutional context of psychoanalysis but also comprehensive deliberations on ways of including provision for assistance in the statutes of our institutes and societies. This would be consistent with the experience that rituals and custom help us, as they do within society as a whole, to cope with situations that are not readily endurable for the individual.

To sum up, I will select some of the many problems outlined and for discussion among psychoanalysts: recommended

A   Concerning psychoanalysts working in clinical practice:

- Retiring procedures in general require thorough discussion. An age limit for doing training analysis as well as clinical psychoanalytic work behind the couch should be discussed and introduced in spite of the major individual age-related differences described. Most studies and surveys suggest that the limit could be about 70 years.

- How might such a provision be implemented in practice? Gabbard proposes the application of the age limit recommended for the former Topeka Institute for Psychoanalysis, where a dedicated committee of analysts held a confidential meeting at two-year intervals to confirm that a colleague over the age of 68 was capable of treating patients. In the event of doubt, a neuropsychological test was recommended in accordance with the conditions laid down by the training committee (Gabbard, 2011, personal communication).

- The making of a 'professional will' (or directive), as proposed by O'Neil, should be obligatory for every member as a matter of professional ethics. Ongoing awareness of the relevant issues should be ensured by constantly rekindled debate within the group (including the candidates).

- A specific aspect to be addressed in the professional will should be the handling of confidential patient and candidate records – for instance, who should be responsible for their destruction.

B   Concerning the institution:

- The issues described in this book give rise to structural, administrative, financial and ethical problems for the psychoanalytic organisations. Possible solutions must be not only comprehensively discussed, but also, when finalised, provided for in the structure of the organisation and actively implemented.

- Demographic change compels us to consider how institutions are to manage with the expected decline in financial resources due to the larger number of older members with low incomes or none at all. Policies of reduced or skipped fees in advanced age should be discussed and readjusted.
- The tasks to be performed within an institute or society, most of which are carried out on a voluntary basis, should be shared among members in different age groups. This reorganisation should be matched to the changing external conditions of our professional activity and to the inner resources at the disposal of the individual members.
- Invited to act as an external moderator in various psychoanalytic groups, I have repeatedly encountered a tendency to put off current issues in the psychoanalytic community until 'later, perhaps . . .' There is a widespread disinclination to reflect in concrete terms not only on one's personal future, but also on the future of the analytic group. For this reason I suggest that each institute or society should at regular intervals draw up a *plan* for its future work covering a period of some ten years. In this process, both optimists and pessimists should be able to voice their opinions on the future of psychoanalysis.
- The conspicuous age difference between 'old' and 'young' psychoanalytic societies to which Klockars (Chapter 12) draws attention arouses one's curiosity: what happens at the beginning when we are still working as pioneers in our respective countries? Are we in the established societies with predominantly older members perhaps clinging rigidly to a system that no longer seems able to kindle the interest and passion of potential candidates for training? Might we ourselves, by our familiar form of 'lived' psychoanalysis in the old-established societies with their venerable histories, actually be contributing to their ossification?
- Analysts who find themselves in difficulty should be able to access help within their societies as recommended by the American Psychoanalytic Association (along the lines of the Psychoanalyst Assistance Committee). I personally would not favour the delegation of age- or sickness-related issues to the ethics committee, because, after all, these are predominantly human rather than strictly ethical problems. In my view, a better solution would be the formation of a support committee composed of a small number (say, three) members of different ages and sexes. The handling of confidentiality and abstinence could be facilitated by supraregional membership.
- Peer culture/improvement of collaboration among analysts: How can we successfully address the confusion of abstinence with a posture of passive silence in the psychoanalytic group? Can the institution help if I become aware of age-related problems but cannot act for reasons of abstinence?

C   Concerning candidates:

- Do we need a compulsory age limit for training candidates? According to Hooke, a candidate admitted at the age of 60 will not be able to commence his or her first fully autonomous analytic treatments before about the age of 66. The 70-year age limit mentioned earlier, due to the risk of illness, will be reached before the first generation of analysands have terminated. Is it ethically acceptable to train a candidate over the age of 60 with little prospect of a future in the profession? In my view, training candidates should be admitted only if they are not significantly older than 50 years of age.

—   I would recommend drawing up a special professional code of conduct, including concrete examples, presented to candidates and discussed in seminars as soon as they embark on treatments of their own. The points addressed should include age-related matters, health care and financial arrangements, dealing with illness, insurance issues and what should happen in the event of restricted professional competence.

This book began by asking what form one's departure from professional life should take. In the course of the discussion this led on to the question of the future of psychoanalysis: is the psychoanalytic idea sustainable? What is the outlook if fewer and fewer young analysts are trained and 'our psychoanalysis', which has impressed its stamp on the professional lives of our generation, faces an uncertain future? The sombre prospect of fewer and fewer candidates and a diminishing number of psychoanalysts in large areas of the world, ultimately resulting in a 'world without psychoanalysis', is one we find hard to bear. For this reason, we cannot avoid mourning for an object within in ourselves which we call 'our psychoanalysis' and which seems at risk of evacuation. But we are reassured by the thought that there is – and always will be – an unconscious that is imperishable.

Yet what form will be assumed by the analysis about which our children and grandchildren will one day be able to say: 'That is *our* psychoanalysis'?

It is unlikely that we shall be able to bequeath 'our psychoanalysis' – as seen from our present-day perspective – to posterity as a 'landscape in bloom'. But perhaps this book can trigger a debate whereby we can acquire the strength and new inner spaces not only to mourn for what we believe to be lost, but also creatively to discover new paths that are as yet inconceivable to us. Both in psychoanalysis and in our globalised society, we must try to accustom ourselves to diversity and to arrive at a kind of coexistence within which we can combine ideas in new forms while at the same time interacting with alternative conceptions in such a way as to allow the islands of our respective cultures the space they need for their continued existence. Perhaps we shall then be able to pass on to our children and grandchildren the fruits of the analytic work we have done in and on ourselves.

INDEX

abandonment 78, 135
Abend, Sander M. 35–7, 62, 64, 68, 69, 143, 159n2
abstinence 27–8, 37, 38, 64, 97, 173
acting out 63
Adorno, Theodor 121
age limits: Norway 42; retirement 14, 30–1, 97, 103–4, 110, 166; training analysts 13, 99, 103, 172; training candidates 163, 173–4
ageing 3–4, 8, 129; 'ageing usefully' 12; analyst's awareness of ageing process 10–11; characteristic illnesses 49–50; Eissler on 34–5; IPA/IPSO candidates' perspectives on 111–18; mid-life crisis 132–3; psychoanalytic societies 96–100, 101–10; training candidates 161–70; transience 21–5
aggression 13
Ahumada, Jorge 167
alexithymia 89
Altmeyer, M. 47
American Psychoanalytic Association (APsA) 62–3, 149n4, 173; professional wills 151, 152; Psychoanalyst Assistance Committees 131, 143–5, 149n1
'analytic affiliations' 33
analytic capacity, changes in 99, 130–1, 132, 135, 136–7, 139, 150, 155
analytic dyad, disrupted by death of analyst 87–8, 89
'analytic third' 67, 71
analytic toolkit 26
annihilation anxiety 22
anxiety: analyst's illness 62–3, 74, 76–7; crisis of impairment 133; of failure 116; identification of problem with analyst 137; mid-life crisis 132–3; PAC members 143; separation 20, 21, 86

archives 156, 157
Arendt, Hannah 121
Arlow, J. A. 63, 155
artists 4, 10
Australian Psychoanalytical Society 111, 162

Baudelaire, C. 39
Bauman, Zygmunt 121–2
Bayley, J. 29
Bion, Wilfred xix, xxii, 20, 96, 98, 125, 137, 138, 148
Bleger, J. 25
bodies 23, 26, 48–9
Bonaparte, Marie 107
Borges, J.-L. 38–9
Boston Institute 97
boundary violations 100, 151, 155–6
Bouvet, Maurice 32
brain neuroplasticity 169–70
Brazil 110n1, 126, 127
the breast 51
bridging analysts 88, 89–90
British Psychoanalytical Society 97, 151–2, 155–6, 161, 170n6
burn out xvii

'calendar' termination 43
Campbell, Donald 161
Canadian Psychoanalytic Society 110n1, 151–2
cancer 33, 61, 65, 70, 72–5, 78n1, 82, 83, 106
care, dependence on 50
Carlisle, Evelyn 65–6, 79–81, 99
Cartwright, D. 138
child patients 77
China 169
Cicero, Marcus Tullius 22

180